Green Project
Management

Richard Maltzman • David Shirley

CRC Press
Taylor & Francis Group
Boca Raton London New York

CRC Press is an imprint of the
Taylor & Francis Group, an **Informa** business
AN AUERBACH BOOK

CRC Press
Taylor & Francis Group
6000 Broken Sound Parkway NW, Suite 300
Boca Raton, FL 33487-2742

© 2011 by Taylor and Francis Group, LLC
CRC Press is an imprint of Taylor & Francis Group, an Informa business

No claim to original U.S. Government works

Printed in the United States of America on acid-free paper
10 9 8 7 6 5 4 3 2 1

International Standard Book Number: 978-1-4398-3001-7 (Hardback)

Library of Congress Cataloging-in-Publication Data

Maltzman, Richard.
 Green project management / Richard Maltzman, David Shirley.
  p. cm.
 Summary: "Offering the latest in green techniques and methods, this book is designed to help project managers maximize limited project resources and get the most out of a finite budget. It provides proven techniques and best practices in green project management, including risk and advantage assessments and the procurement of incentives such as grants, rebates, and tax credits. With illustrative case studies and insights from acknowledged leaders in green project management, this book is a crucial addition to any project manager's library in this age of ecological awareness."-- Provided by publisher.
 Includes bibliographical references and index.
 ISBN 978-1-4398-3001-7 (hbk. : alk. paper)
 1. Project management--Environmental aspects. 2. Management--Environmental aspects. 3. Business enterprises--Environmental aspects. 4. Environmentalism. 5. Sustainability. 6. Social responsibility of business. I. Shirley, David. II. Title.

 HD69.P75M357 2010
 658.4'083--dc22   2010028306

Visit the Taylor & Francis Web site at
http://www.taylorandfrancis.com

and the CRC Press Web site at
http://www.crcpress.com

Contents

Foreword xi
Acknowledgments xv
The Authors xvii
Introduction..xxi

SECTION I   Surfing the Green Wave

Chapter 1   Problem Drivers and Indicators.. 3

    Climate Change 3
    Population Increase..6
    Rapidly Developing Nations and Resource Depletion...........7
    Environmental Degradation and Loss of Biodiversity...........8
    Government Agencies, Mandates, and Guidelines 8
        Global Agencies, Mandates, and Guidelines......................9
            ISO 14000...9
            Kyoto Protocol...10
            European Environment Agency (EEA) 11
        U.S. Agencies, Mandates, and Guidelines...........................11
            Environmental Protection Agency (EPA) 11
            California's AB32 12
            Western Climate Initiative (WCI)...............................13
            The Eastern States Standard...13
            U.S. Conference of Mayors...14
        Bottom-up Demand from Project Stakeholders,
        Sponsors, and Customers...14
    Endnotes...16

Chapter 2   Green Project Terminology: The Language of the
              Green Wave.. 17

    Carbon Footprint and Sustainability 17
        The Environmental Lens 20
        The Cycle of Sustainability.. 20

Cradle to Cradle...21
The Natural Step...22
Corporate Social Responsibility and the Green Project
Manager...23
Biodegradable...25
Greenwashing...26
Triple Bottom Line 28
Eco Audit.. 28
Reduce, Redesign, Reuse, Recycle.................................29
Renewable Energy 30
    Wind... 30
    Solar... 30
    Geothermal..31
    Sustainable Biomass...32
    Wave Motion and Tides...35
SMARTER Objectives..35
Endnotes...37

Chapter 3   Understanding Green Project Fundamentals 39

Green, Quality, and Greenality......................................39
Reducing Nonproduct Output....................................... 43
The Project Management Institute and Greenality.............45
Cost of Greenality 47
Project Life Cycle Thinking 48
Project Cycle of Sustainability......................................49
Environmental Scope..50
Environmental Risks 50
Stakeholders 51
Endnotes 51

Chapter 4   Types of Projects: A Rainbow of Green 53

Green by Definition... 54
Green by Project Impact (or the Lack Thereof) 60
    On the Sea... 60
    Going Underground...61
Green by Product Impact...62
Green—General..65

A Rainbow of Green... 66
Endnotes 66

SECTION II   Hiking the Project

Chapter 5   Project Ideation 71

Why Are Projects Initiated?...72
How Are Projects Chosen?..74
Decision-Making Tools and the Green Component 75
Creating the "Green"-Friendly Decision-Making
Environment 75
Changing the Way People Think about Green......................76
Decision-Making Tools 77
    Brainstorming...77
    Reverse Brainstorming 78
    Force Field Analysis..79
    Cost-Benefit Analysis...79
Validation of the Decision..81
Creating a Green Charter..82
The Initial Project Kickoff Meeting 83
Acting on the Idea 84
Tools and Techniques.. 84
Greenality of Project Communications 85
The Spirit of the Communication 85
Jeopardy and Escalation Processes 86
Greenality of Suppliers 87
Endnotes.. 88

Chapter 6   Developing the Project... 89

Project Planning 89
Sustainability and the WBS 95
Who and What Are Required for the Project 96
Greening the People... 96
Greening the Schedule...97
Greening the Project Purchasing (Procurement)
Process 100

Greening Project Costs 102
Greening Project Quality 103
    Transcendent Greenality 104
    Product-Based Greenality 106
    User-Based Greenality 106
    Manufacturing-Based Greenality 106
    Value-Based Greenality 107
Risk and Greenality 107
Greenality Outputs 109
    Environmental Management Plan 109
Endnotes 110

Chapter 7 Executing the Project 111

The Project Team 111
The Kickoff Meeting (Implementation) 113
Greenality Assurance 115
Tracking Project Process 116
    Status and Progress Reporting 117
Using Social Media to Green Communications 118
Execution of Greenality Efforts 120
Warning Signs of Greenality Problems 122
Greenality of Suppliers 123
Capturing Greenality Lessons Learned 124
Endnote 124

Chapter 8 Taking the Watch (Monitoring and Controlling) 125

Greenality Data Collection and Analysis 127
Measuring the Performance of Greenality 130
Controlling the Issues 131
Keeping on an Even Keel 132
Change Control and Greenality 133
Effective Actions to Abate Greenality Issues 136
    Corrective 136
    Preventative 136
    Band-Aid 139
Endnotes 141

SECTION III   Approaching the Finish Line

Chapter 9   The Beginning and the End? 145

Heaven on Earth 145
Life Cycle Thinking Basics 146
Life Cycle Assessment 149
A Brief History 151
Standards for LCA 153
Carbon Footprinting Based on LCA 154
Performing an LCA 155
How to Promote the Use of an LCA 155
The Life Cycle of the Product of Your Project 156
   LCA Fundamentals 157
      ISO 14040 158
   Goal Definition and Scoping 158
   Inventory Analysis 160
   A "Bar Chart" 161
   Impact Assessment 163
   Interpretation 167
   Reporting the Results 170
   LCA Software Tools 171
   Limitations to Conducting an LCA 172
   Maintaining Transparency 172
Endnotes 173

Chapter 10 Lean Thinking, Muda, and the Four Ls 175

Lean Thinking and Your Project 175
Lean Methods 177
   What Is Lean? 178
   Wastes 179
   A New Waste? 180
   The Basic Principles of Lean Development 181
   The Seven Wastes of Software Development 181
   5S 186
   Summary—The 4L Approach 188
Endnotes 188

Chapter 11 At the Top of Their Game 189

    Patagonia 190

    Timberland 192

    Interface 194

    Google 196

    Office Depot 199

        Buying Green 199

        Being Green 200

        Selling Green 201

        Corporate Social Responsibility 201

    Microsoft 202

        What They Do for Us 202

        What They Are Doing for Themselves (and Us) 203

    General Electric 204

        Ecomagination 206

    Steward Advanced Materials—Home of "The Toxin
Terminator" 206

    Sun Chips 207

        Solar Collector Technology 207

    Summary 208

    Endnotes 208

Chapter 12 Enabling Green to Earn You "Green" 211

    Green Government Purchasing—EPA 211

        History of the U.S. EPA's EPP 212

            Principle 1. Environment + Price + Performance
= Environmentally Preferable Purchasing 212

            Principle 2. Pollution Prevention 213

            Principle 3. Life Cycle Perspective/Multiple
Attributes 214

            Principle 4. Comparison of Environmental
Impacts 214

            Principle 5. Environmental Performance
Information 215

    Grants and Rebates 216

        What Is Available? 216

The American Recovery and Reinvestment Act
(ARRA) and Green 216
U.S. Department of Energy 218
Solar Rebates and More from the State of
Florida 220
Energy Providers..221
Energy Audits... 222
Actions Undertaken 223
Bank of America 224
Apple Corporation.. 224
Schneider National 224
Lockheed Martin 225
Raytheon... 226
University of Michigan 226
Quickies 227
DuPont 228
Portsmouth Brewery 228
The Kohler Company... 228
Endnotes 229

SECTION IV   Crossing the Finish Line

Chapter 13 Tips, Tools, and Techniques to Green (A Green
Project Manager's Toolbox) 233

Endnote.. 242

Chapter 14 Resource Information 243

Books We Think You Should Read or Reference 243
Suggested Reading on Life Cycle Assessment 243
Collaboration Tools and Resources 244
Resource for Improving Team Collaboration Using
Web-Based Media.. 245
Green Efforts by Companies and Other
Organizations—A Sampler 245
Web Sites Worth a Visit and a Stay 247

Additional Tools and Resources for Green Project
Managers 253
Endnote...253

Index.. 255

Foreword

It is my distinct pleasure to provide the Foreword to *Green Project Management*. Having worked in the field of environmental sustainability for most of my government career, I am happy to see publications such as this one that provide useful guidance to assist project managers in advancing the sustainability agenda within their companies as well as across society.

Project management has been a formally recognized profession since the 1950s. Successful project management has traditionally meant delivering a product or service on time and within budget constraints, using resources (people and materials) in an optimal way, and satisfying the needs of the customer (and of the boss!). With the increasing attention being given to sustainable development and the overall growing awareness of environmental concerns, especially global climate change, the allure of becoming green is inspiring project managers to include environmental goals in their activities. Nowadays, suggestions for how companies and individuals can "go green" can be found almost everywhere.

With the Pollution Prevention Act of 1990, the U.S. Congress established pollution prevention as a "national objective" and the most important component of the environmental management hierarchy. The U.S. Environmental Protection Agency (EPA) defines pollution prevention (P2) as "reducing or eliminating waste at the source by modifying production processes, promoting the use of nontoxic or less-toxic substances, implementing conservation techniques, and reusing materials rather than putting them into the waste stream." As national policy declares that the creation of potential pollutants should be prevented or reduced during the production cycle whenever feasible, the EPA has been a leader in advancing the adoption of green manufacturing. The United States set about establishing a network of successful efforts to help promote and implement P2 (cleaner production in Europe and elsewhere) opportunities. After years of controlling pollution at the end of a pipe, or by treating its effects after the fact, the EPA is now operating under the principle that preventing pollution is cleaner, cheaper, and smarter than simply moving contaminants around, from air, to water, to land.

The term *green project management* (GPM) is not used frequently in the guidance that EPA has developed over the years to help show industry (aiming mainly at small and medium-size enterprises) how they can identify P2 opportunities and take action. However, the many efforts under the P2 program, such as green chemistry, green engineering, green products, greening the supply chain, etc., are directly related to GPM. Information on these and other efforts can be found at EPA's P2 Web site (http://www.epa.gov/p2/).

Successful pollution prevention programs often depend on a single person taking on the green challenge and carrying the message of P2 forward. Such "champions" are necessary for successful implementation within companies. Project managers, in general, are *perfectly positioned* to act as change agents since projects are indeed all about change. GPM is not only about "what" we do; it also requires a change in "who" does it. *Project managers are the essential change agents.*

Everyone is talking about going green. On the surface, it seems like an easy thing to do, but what does it mean to "green" our traditional approach to project management? Mainly it involves changing the way we think about projects. GPM is a model where we think green throughout our project and make decisions that take into account the impact on the environment. Including environmental goals in project planning and management encompasses diverse activity, comprised of multiple approaches and based on a range of options for action. The resurgence of the green movement in recent years gave birth to GPM, which combines environmentally friendly standards with project management methodologies and processes. Typically, GPM is guided by an organization's environmental management system (EMS) and considers various operational elements, such as responsibilities, authorities, procedures, and resources.

Because GPM is still in its relative infancy, there are many opportunities for learning and growth. There are also many opportunities for misuse. *Greenwashing* is a term that was coined in the 1980s to describe a misleading or deceptive practice of putting a "spin" on activities to make them appear environmentally beneficial when they are not and are usually motivated solely by the potential to increase profit. We are slowly making progress in recognizing superficial green activities and going beyond greenwashing. This book will further that improved understanding. *Green Project Management* is aimed at helping project managers:

- Understand what it means to truly think green
- Discover the ethical basis for GPM
- See how environmental choices and profit can have compatible goals

- Learn the steps to move toward GPM
- Identify useful tools and techniques

Case studies are compelling ways to shift people's thinking (humans are hard-wired for storytelling). *Green Project Management* contains numerous case studies and illustrations to demonstrate how successful companies and organizations have effectively approached GPM. Mixed in is very practical step-by-step guidance on how to proceed.

An effective sustainable product index must go beyond the facility walls. Project managers must learn how to simultaneously consider a broad spectrum of potential impacts (energy and climate, nature and resources, material efficiency, people and communities) throughout the life cycle of their products and services. Take for example Apple's new iPad (http://www.earthpm.com/2010/01/apple-ipads-greenality/). Apple's environmental program considers select life cycle impacts across the cradle-to-grave stages of their products. The environmental goals that they have established include decreasing contributions to climate change, reduced use of toxic substances, energy and material efficiency, and end-of-life recycling. So then, how green is the iPad? According to Apple CEO Steve Jobs, the iPad is arsenic-free, brominated flame retardants (BFR)-free, mercury-free, and polyvinyl chloride (PVC)-free, and is highly recyclable.

Progress in the next generation of GPM will depend on dealing successfully with several upcoming future challenges. Looking ahead, biotechnology and nanotechnology offer multiple benefits as they make major shifts in many of the products we make and sell. But they also promise new sources of environmental problems that will require new thinking and new solutions. GPM will be an essential element as these fields evolve.

GPM is a key component in the sustainability agenda. In the end, it's the choices that we make on a daily basis that affect our environment now and for generations to come. Remember, it's about the *planet, projects, profits, and people.*

Mary Ann Curran, PhD
Life Cycle Assessment Research Program Manager
U.S. Environmental Protection Agency
Cincinnati, Ohio

Acknowledgments

I would like to thank my dog Murphy for making me get out of the house no matter what the weather. I do some of my best thinking during our long walks along the beaches of Cape Neddick, Maine. I'd like to thank Dr. Rick Keating, formerly of New England College, now with Western New England College, and Diane Zold-Eisenberg from Northern Essex Community College, for allowing me to bring my project management experience into the classroom. I'd like to thank my coauthor Rich Maltzman for his creativity and his suggestion that we "do something together," which got this snowball rolling downhill and turned into an avalanche. To my mother, father, and sister who always believed in my abilities more than I did. Not a day goes by that I don't think about them and know they are watching over me. And to my wife, Judi, I wouldn't know what to do without your love and support.

Dave Shirley

My sincere thanks go out to my family—my best friend and devoted wife, Ellen, and wonderful children, Sarah and Daniel, for their support, encouragement, kidding, prodding, faith, curiosity, and patience. To my mom, dad, sister, extended family, and friends—my thanks as well. This would have been impossible without you. There are also innumerable project management peers, students, and colleagues, as well as bosses and employees, from whom I've learned, and continue to learn, so, *so* much. I'd like to thank my coauthor Dave Shirley, who brought order to my sometimes (OK, *often*) outlandish ideas and kept this effort flowing. And, like Dave, I also need to thank my dog Buddy for periodic consultations and advice, and for getting me out of the house for a nice walk or to see if, hopefully, the mail carrier was coming by to deliver him a treat.

Rich Maltzman

Both authors would also like to acknowledge Mary Ann Curran, PhD, of the U.S. Environmental Protection Agency, for her deep technical knowledge and invaluable assistance in expanding and completing our section on life cycle assessment. To the many other people who helped make this book possible, we also salute not only the time you gave us, but more important, the good work you are doing. We would like to thank John Wyzalek, senior acquisitions editor, for giving us a chance to write about this very important topic, and Amy Blalock, project coordinator, for her help with our manuscript, as well as other individuals from our publisher, CRC Press, a Taylor & Francis Company, who helped us along the way.

The Authors

 **Rich Maltzman, PMP*,** has been an engineer since 1978 and a project management supervisor since 1988, including a recent two-year assignment in the Netherlands in which he built a team of PMs overseeing deployments of telecom networks in Europe and the Middle East. His project work has been diverse, including projects such as the successful deployment of the entire video and telecom infrastructure for the 1996 Summer Olympic Games in Atlanta, and the 2006 integration of the program management offices (PMOs) of two large merging corporations. As a second, but intertwined career, Rich has also focused on consulting and teaching, having developed curricula and/or taught at

- Boston University's Corporate Education Center
- Merrimack College
- Northern Essex Community College
- University of Massachusetts–Lowell

Rich has also developed project management professional (PMP) exam prep courseware, including exams and books. He even edited and was "the voice" for a set of eight audio CDs—a major part of a PMP prep course for an international company, for whom he has also facilitated PMP exam study groups. Rich was selected for the modeling team for the fourth edition of the *PMBOK Guide* published by the Project Management Institute (PMI) in 2008, and contributed to the chapters on quality and risk.

Recently, Rich presented at two international conferences—the PMO Symposium in San Antonio, Texas, and the PMO Summit in Coconut Grove, Florida, the subject being the development framework for project managers.

Currently, Rich is senior manager, learning and professional advancement, at the Global Program Management Office of a major telecom concern.

---

* PMP is a certification mark of the Project Management Institute, Inc., which is registered in the United States and other nations.

Rich's educational background includes a BSEE from the University of Massachusetts–Amherst, and an MSIE from Purdue University. In addition, Rich has a mini-MBA from the University of Pennsylvania's Wharton School and a master's certificate in international business management granted jointly from Indiana University's Kelley School of Business and INSEAD of France. From a project management standpoint, Rich received his PMP in 2000 after earning the Stevens Institute's master's certificate in 1999. He has presented papers on project management at conferences in Huizen, the Netherlands, Mexico City, and Long Beach, California.

Rich is currently coauthoring a book with Ranjit Biswas, PMP, titled *The Fiddler on the Project,* a portion of which is being collaboratively written on the Web via a wiki, http://fiddlerontheproject.wikidot.com, and posts regularly on his blog, Scope Crêpe, http://scopecrepe.blogspot.com.

 **Dave Shirley** has been an instructor and consultant, and has more than 30 years' experience in management and project management, in the corporate, public, and small-business arenas.

As a member of the graduate faculty at New England College, he developed and teaches Managing Projects in Healthcare. As part of the Master's of Management (MoM) in Healthcare Administration and the MoM in Project Management and Organizational Leadership, he has taught project management at hospitals and businesses as well as online and on campus for the past seven years. He also developed, directed, and taught a project management certification program at Northern Essex Community College in Haverhill, Massachusetts. Dave is a senior instructor and consultant for Action For Results, and a senior instructor for ESI International, both leading project management education and training companies. He is also an adjunct professor for Southern New Hampshire University, teaching corporate social responsibility.

As a distinguished member of the technical staff with AT&T and Lucent Technologies Bell Laboratories, Dave was responsible for managing the first light-wave transmission products as well as several quality efforts. He was also AT&T's project manager for the first fiber-to-the-home effort in Connecticut, and was the Lucent Technologies' program management director, managing several large telecommunications' companies' equipment deployment. Dave has many years of experience in developing, leading, and managing teams.

Dave's educational background includes a BA degree in geology from Windham College, Putney, Vermont, and an honors MBA degree from Monmouth University in Long Branch, New Jersey. He also holds master's certificates in project management from Stevens Institute of Technology, Hoboken, New Jersey, and American University in Washington, DC, and is certified as a Project Management Professional (PMP) by the Project Management Institute (PMI).*

---

* PMI is a service and trademark of the Project Management Institute, Inc., which is registered in the United States and other nations.

Introduction

In recent years, business seems to understand the message that green is important—or at least that it will help sell products and services. Recently, the authors were booking an online airline ticket on JetBlue. At the close of the purchase, a choice came up. Did we want to offset the carbon we'd be using on our trip by purchasing carbon credits? It would cost only a few dollars. So, even an airline branded *Blue* is showing it's *Green*.

We know, firsthand, then, that business is beginning to appreciate the value of green. That's of course in harmony with an increasing "green wave" of awareness among the general population. In fact, there has been much discussion surrounding the topic of green business but very little about green projects, green project management, and green project managers, and this is interesting to us because we see projects as the "business end" of business. Projects are where *business ideas* become *reality*, after all. Projects, by *definition*, use *resources*. Shouldn't projects, therefore, be a key area of any focus on green business?

We decided to try to fill what we see as a lack of attention to green project management and focus the energy (excuse the pun), research, and recommendations regarding *green business* as a *microcosm of business that is project management,* consolidating it into this book about green project management.

On our journey to do that, we felt we were literally one word short. We needed a word that would communicate a project's green-ness, or eco-friendliness, or enviro-efficiency, or earth-awareness, without using those clumsy-sounding hyphenated words. With our background in project management training and quality, we decided to coin our own word, *greenality*. It's no coincidence that this word ends the same way as *quality*. Greenality, like quality or granularity, is something that can be measured along a scale. In the book we will make several parallels between greenality and quality. They have some striking similarities. We've chosen to define greenality this way: "the degree to which an organization has considered environmental (green) factors that affect its projects during the *entire project life cycle and beyond.*" It contains two project management processes: (1) creating a plan to minimize the environmental impacts of projects (this includes efforts to simply run the project more efficiently and effectively), and (2) the monitoring and controlling of the environmental impacts of the *product* of the project.

In the book we will use the term to define a scale of greenality that can apply to the various project process groups (initiating, planning, executing, monitoring and controlling, and closing) as well as different project-defined phases.

In our research for the book, as well as in our many decades of project experience, we also realized that "greening a project" is much more than saving the environment (not that that isn't a noble effort). We know from running hundreds of projects that a project with a high score in greenality is going to be an effective and efficient project—saving resources, which translates to saving money. A project with a high greenality score *is good for the bottom line.*

As green business author Gil Friend says, "You don't have to choose between making money and making sense."[1] In this book we will explore the processes necessary to move your organization and its projects much higher on the scale of greenality, and show how that high score will positively affect the bottom line. We will look at a "rainbow of green," defining projects that are aimed at conservation or generating energy, those projects that have an immediate impact on the environment, those projects that have a product that will impact the environment, and others, because every project has a green element. We'll talk about "cycles of sustainability," and provide a template for defining different cycles.

We'll also look at different industries' best practices and benchmarks for achieving high greenality scores, including use of metrics and benchmarks for your journey up the scale. We will define the green project management process to help guide you through the inputs, tools, techniques, and outputs as well as how those processes can be applied. We'll provide facts, trends, and interviews with industries' "greenality leaders" to help you gain higher greenality scores. We will help your organization view your projects (as stated by Esty and Winston in *Green to Gold*) "through an environmental lens."[2] This will naturally (again, excuse the pun) involve ways to improve individual project managers' greenality.

Finally, we will define some of the ways to earn green (cash), through grants, rebates, and tax credits, to take advantage of the "green wave," as well as find sources for earth-friendly products, and provide a road map for individual credentialing of project managers who have demonstrated knowledge and skills in this area.

1. A project run with green intent is the right thing to do, but it will also help the project team do the right thing.
2. Project managers must first understand the green aspects of their projects, knowing that this will better equip them to identify, manage, and respond to project risks.
3. An environmental strategy for a project provides added opportunity for success of both the project and the product of the project.
4. Project managers must view their projects through an environmental lens. This increases the project manager's (and the project team's) long-term thinking and avails the project of the rising "green wave" of environmentalism.
5. Project managers must think of the environment in the same way they think of quality. It must be planned in, and the cost of "greenality," like the cost of quality, is more than offset by the savings and opportunities it provides.

FIGURE I.1
EarthPM assertions.

As we begin this book, we cannot help but state our assertions. We call them assertions, but they could be called guiding principles, and they comprise the vision and mission for this book. They are listed in Figure I.1.

Project managers have *always* been green—perhaps without knowing it. By definition, we are constantly trying to reduce costs, increase value, and protect scarce resources, and *that* is being green. In our eyes, all of the processes to accomplish these noble project management goals have been fragmented and just happen to be missing the environmental label. In fact, as in our assertions, sometimes we just need an environmental lens through which to view the saving of resources (for example) as a green effort as well as a project management (PM) effort.

There was a time when project management was called "the accidental profession" because one didn't start out being what is now called a "project manager." This didn't mean that we didn't manage projects, because that is exactly what we did. However, with the help of organizations like the Project Management Institute, the field and the discipline—and career—of project management have been legitimized. PM has evolved, gained recognition by organizations, and continues to grow exponentially into a validated, stimulating profession. Using a set of disciplined and integrated processes, we think that we as PMs can turn the "accidental green project manager" into a professional green project manager who always understands the green aspects of their projects and views their projects through an environmental lens. Please join us on this transformation.

ENDNOTES

1. Gil Friend, with Nicholas Kordesch and Benjamin Privitt, *The Truth About Green Business*. (Upper Saddle River, NJ: FT Press, 2009), on the cover.
2. Daniel C. Esty, and Andrew S, Winston, *Green to Gold*, (Hoboken, NJ: John Wiley & Sons, 2009), pg. 3.

Section I

Surfing the Green Wave

You're not a wave, you're a part of the ocean.

Mitch Albom

1

Problem Drivers and Indicators

CLIMATE CHANGE

The IPCC was formed jointly in 1988 by the United Nations Environment Programme and the United Nations World Meteorological Organization. The IPCC brings together the world's top scientists, economists, and other experts, synthesizes peer-reviewed scientific literature on climate change studies, and produces authoritative assessments of the current state of knowledge of climate change.

There is a flood of information available on climate change. It's in the news, it's on talk radio, and among the problem drivers we'll discuss, it's the one that is most likely to be pushing organizations toward "green," or at least green messaging. Project managers, for the most part, are a pragmatic lot. We have to be. Although project management is both an art and a science, we rely on the "science part"—and our left brains—for the bigger part of our management of projects. Take earned value management as an example. This is founded on mathematical principles and uses ratios to calculate whether a project is ahead, behind, or right on schedule and budget. As project managers, we crave these methods, which bring order to the chaotic world of projects. Despite this, or perhaps because of it, even the most skeptical left-brain thinker should be able to appreciate the facts about global warming. There may be quite a bit of debate around what the true *causes* are, but one only has to look at the Intergovernmental Panel on Climate Change's (IPCC) Fourth Assessment Report (2007)[1] first to answer the question on whether or not there is a significant change in the world's climate, and second to answer the question, "why is the climate changing?" We use the words *climate change* because the National

Academy of Sciences prefers that term over *global warming*. The term *climate change* has a much broader implication than just a simple warming effect for the planet. It refers to "any distinct change in measures of climate lasting for a long period of time."[2] In other words, climate change means "major changes in temperature, rainfall, snow, or wind patterns lasting for decades or longer."[3]

The global temperature record shows an average warming of about 1.3°F over the past century. According to the National Oceanic and Atmospheric Administration (NOAA), seven of the eight warmest years on record have occurred since 2001. Within the past 30 years, the rate of warming across the globe has been approximately three times greater than the rate over the last 100 years. Past climate information suggests the warmth of the last half century is unusual in at least the previous 1,300 years in the Northern Hemisphere.

There *is* the nagging question as to whether the climate changes and warming of our planet are part of a much larger cycle, a warming trend, so to speak, after a period of cooling, or are something much more dramatic, more lethal—and something for which we humans can take the brunt of the blame. Well, IPCC scientists believe that there is a greater than 90% chance that most of the warming we have experienced since the 1950s is due to the increase in greenhouse gas emissions from human activities. With the panel, a scientific body made up of thousands of scientists from all over the world, believing so strongly that it is not a natural cycle, but rather that the climate changes are human-made, and will continue to happen unless something is done, we, as pragmatic project managers, might just need to listen. Even if (and we are not advocating this position), but *even if* there is an underlying natural warming trend, humankind's contributions are aggravating the situation. And even if we choose to disregard this input from subject matter experts (SMEs) and disavow any belief in climate changes, regardless of their cause, guess what? Even then, we *still* have to pay attention because huge numbers of people (the Green Wave) do believe this and do believe that individuals and organizations need to be more responsible. Furthermore, these huge numbers of people, dear cynical project managers, are your customers, your subcontractors, your suppliers, your sponsors—and they (like it or not) are changing their spending and vendor selection habits based on those beliefs. You can see that it doesn't really matter if you agree with them (or the thousands of scientists) or not.

What *are* the statistics showing? And what *are* the scientists saying? The National Academies of Sciences in their 2008 brochure "Understanding and Responding to Climate Change, Highlights of National Academies Reports" tell us that "temperatures have already risen 1.4°F since the start of the 20th century—with much of this warming occurring in just the last 30 years—and temperatures will likely rise at least another 2°F, and possibly more than 11°F, over the next 100 years. This warming will cause significant changes in sea level, ecosystems, and ice cover, among other impacts. In the Arctic, where temperatures have increased almost twice as much as the global average, the landscape and ecosystems are already changing rapidly."[4]

The National Academies are nongovernment, nonprofit organizations that were set up to provide independent scientific and technological advice to the U.S. government and nation. The National Academies include three honorary societies that elect new members to their ranks each year—the National Academy of Sciences, National Academy of Engineering, and Institute of Medicine—and the National Research Council, the operating arm that conducts the bulk of the institution's science policy and technical work. The Academies enlist committees of the nation's top scientists, engineers, and other experts, all of whom volunteer their time to study specific issues and concerns.

Further, the U.S. Congress has not passed one bill to cut global warming pollution, which may be a good thing. The best type of movement is the grassroots movement, not one that is legislated. As project managers, those of us who are turning ideas into reality, we're sitting right here at the grass roots.

There is an interesting article in a recent issue of *Fly Fisherman Magazine*[5] that could be viewed as good news, bad news. The good news is that there is a possibility that new fisheries are opening up in the Arctic Circle. The bad news is that the new fisheries may be caused by certain species of fish, like sockeye and pink Pacific salmon, searching for cooler waters to spawn in because their usual waters are warming.

POPULATION INCREASE

As of July 2009, the world population was approximately 6.8 billion people, an increase of 313 million since 2005. That is 78 million people added to the world roll every year! Assuming that this trend will continue, expect *9.1 billion* people in 2050. As Tom Friedman says in *Hot, Flat, and Crowded*, the *increase* in population in the next 40 years is equal to *the earth's population itself in the year 1950!* So in many of our lifetimes, we will add *another Earth's worth* of population to our planet. And where is this population being added? In the countries that can most easily sustain the growth? No. The population of a majority of *underdeveloped* countries—those *least able to sustain the population increase*—is growing at the fastest rate, 2.3% per year (see Figure 1.1). With an increase of about 3 billion people in the next 40 years, significant projects will need to be undertaken to provide even the basic necessities, like food, water, and housing. Innovation will be the rule in our shrinking environment, and it will be green innovation needed to protect an already fragile environment. Project managers will need to be skilled in identifying those green innovations and implementing them in their projects.

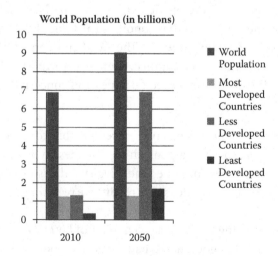

FIGURE 1.1
World population. Data from United Nations, *World Population Prospects: The 2008 Revision Population Database,* United Nations, New York, 2009.

In 1900, only 13% of the world's population lived in cities. By 2050, that number will have risen to 70%. We are adding the equivalent of seven New Yorks to the planet every year.

RAPIDLY DEVELOPING NATIONS AND RESOURCE DEPLETION

With population growth comes the need to provide those basic needs mentioned previously, and it also places a major strain on the resources available. In the Netherlands, even more so than in other nations, *land,* as a resource, is at a premium. This is a country that is 55% below sea level. The sea and, water in general, are ever present. In some countries, filling in wetlands is considered a less than ideal approach to development. The Netherlands has started to take a different approach, which is also being used in other parts of the world. Instead of working against the water, this approach works with the water. According to the J. K. (Koen) Olthuis, architect for Waterstudios, NL, "The New Water" (Het Nieuwe Water) is a benchmark project in Dutch water management development. The artificially maintained water level of this former polder, (a low-lying tract of land enclosed by embankments known as dikes) which measures approximately 2.5 km by 500 m (70 ha), will be raised to chest level, creating a site that not only will act as a regional contingency water storage area, but also will host a multitude of water-related developments including 1,200 dwellings. The first project of the New Water will be the apartment complex called Citadel. Ecological, recreational, and residential demands are integrated into a landscape that is organized into different thematic compartments, each offering a specific experience of the water, specific building typologies, and a range of different ecological habitats. In the ecological zone there will be the stilthouses, which are free from the water's floor so they don't affect the zone. Construction started in 2009. For futher information about this project and other innovative projects, go to http://waterstudio.nl/. This type of green project is being adopted for use in other areas of the world to help with rapidly developing nations and the associated issues of resource depletion. This is an example of a project born from an environmentally focused portfolio. See

Chapter 4, "Types of Projects: A Rainbow of Green," to understand that a project does not have to be born this way or provide a green end product to be responsible and green.

Every year, over 40 million acres of tropical rain forest are destroyed through *burning* and *logging*.

ENVIRONMENTAL DEGRADATION AND LOSS OF BIODIVERSITY

Environmental degradation and loss of biodiversity go hand in hand. When people decide that the environment takes a backseat to something else, like greed, environmental degradation occurs. Take the rain forest of Brazil for instance. Every year, there is deforestation of approximately 77,000 square miles. That's in the Amazon basin alone, but there are other South American, African, and Indonesian forests being cut as well. Continuing with that example, consider how many species are being lost because of that deforestation and the resulting loss of flora and fauna habitat.

Pollution is another cause of environmental degradation. It includes air pollution, smog and ozone depletion, and water pollution, including improper or lack of sanitation facilities and industrial-waste dumping. It also includes the by-product of natural disasters. An example of a natural environmental disaster is Hurricane Katrina and its aftermath of flooded sewage treatment plants and the destruction of oil storage facilities. There are also disasters caused directly by the human hand. An example of that is the Chernobyl nuclear power plant failure in 1986. Both of these (natural or human-made) have the potential to adversely and temporarily or permanently negatively affect the biodiversity of an area.

GOVERNMENT AGENCIES, MANDATES, AND GUIDELINES

The following information is intended to be a sample of the mandates and guidelines available for review by project managers. In no way is it intended to be exhaustive.

Global Agencies, Mandates, and Guidelines

ISO 14000

ISO (International Organization for Standardization) is the world's largest developer and publisher of international standards.

ISO is a network of the national standards institutes of 162 countries, one member per country, with a Central Secretariat in Geneva, Switzerland, that coordinates the system.

ISO is a nongovernmental organization that forms a bridge between the public and private sectors.

ISO 14000, also known as the Global Green Standards, is a set of standards developed by the International Organization for Standardization. It is essentially a family of standards including 14001:2004 and 14004:2004 that address the various aspects of environmental management. As standards or guidelines, they provide a framework for companies to work with to validate that either their processes are green or they are in a concerted effort to make them green. According to the International Organization of Standardization, "ISO 14001:2004 gives the *generic requirements* for an environmental management system." Most environmental management systems (EMSs) are built on the age-old plan-do-check-act cycle (see Figure 1.2). Built into that philosophy is the principle that companies will continually improve their processes with regard to environmental impacts. It doesn't necessarily "certify" that a company is green, only that the company is continually working toward improving its greenality. The EMS includes all of the things we talk about in this book—reduce/redesign, reuse, and recycle—to minimize your environmentally impacting footprint, and, just as important, to improve the efficiency of your project. In other words, as project managers, we are continually trying to improve the efficiency of the resources we are utilizing. ISO provides a formidable set of standards that a company needs to meet, similar in rigor to the ISO 9000 standards, which are focused on quality. This link between quality and environmental efficiency is a theme of our book. The ability to prove adherence to the standards can qualify an organization for ISO 14000 certification after an audit of their processes is conducted by an official certification body. For further information and certification bodies by economy (county), see http://www.iaf.nu/.

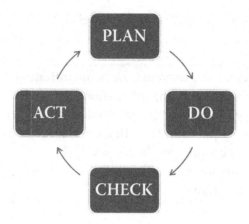

FIGURE 1.2
PDCA cycle.

ISO 14004:2004 takes the guidelines a step further and "provides guidance on the establishment, implementation, maintenance and improvement of an environmental management system and its coordination with other management systems." The guidelines have recently been revised in the hopes that they will be more easily understood, making them more "user friendly" and further promoting the use of environmental management systems.

Kyoto Protocol

The Kyoto Protocol is an international agreement linked to the United Nations Framework Convention on Climate Change. The major feature of the Kyoto Protocol is that it sets binding targets for 37 industrialized countries and the European community for reducing greenhouse gas (GHG) emissions. These amount to an average of five per cent against 1990 levels over the five-year period 2008–2012.

The major distinction between the Protocol and the Convention is that while the Convention **encouraged** industrialized countries to stabilize GHG (greenhouse gas) emissions, the Protocol **commits** them to do so.[6]

It was adopted in Kyoto, Japan, on December 11, 1997, and went into force on February 16, 2005. In total, 184 "parties of the convention"[7] have ratified the agreement. While the United States has signed the agreement, it has yet to ratify it and therefore is not bound by the agreement. For complete information on the Kyoto Protocol and how nations can participate, go to http://unfccc.int/2860.php.

European Environment Agency (EEA)

The European Environment Agency (EEA, http://www.eea.europa. eu/) is a collection of the European Union countries (27) and Iceland, Liechtenstein, Norway, Switzerland, and Turkey. The six West Balkan countries are cooperating countries: Albania, Bosnia and Herzegovina, Croatia, the former Yugoslav Republic of Macedonia, Montenegro, and Serbia. "The European environment information and observation network (Eionet) is a partnership network of the EEA and the countries. The EEA is responsible for developing the network and coordinating its activities. To do so, the EEA works closely together with national focal points, typically national environment agencies or environment ministries. They are responsible for coordinating national networks involving many institutions (about 300 in all)."[8]

U.S. Agencies, Mandates, and Guidelines

Environmental Protection Agency (EPA)

The Environmental Protection Agency (EPA) was established in 1970, under then president Richard Nixon, in response to a growing concern about the need for cleaner water, land, and air in the United States. Prior to that there was no coordinated approach to stemming the tide of environmental damage. Wetlands were being filled at an alarming rate; air quality in some cities had deteriorated to the point that the air was unhealthy. Many rivers were contaminated with heavy metals, polyvinyl chloride, and sewage wastes, endangering not only the rivers, streams, estuaries, and oceans, but the drinking water supplies as well. Groundwater contamination was a significant problem, rendering private as well as public water supplies deadly, an issue brought to the forefront in the 2000 movie *Erin Brockovich*, about the title character's epic fight with Pacific Gas and Electric over hexavalent chromium contamination of the groundwater in Hinkley, California, between 1952 and 1956.

The EPA's mission is "is to protect human health and the environment. Since 1970, EPA has been working for a cleaner, healthier environment for the American people."[9] In that effort, the EPA develops and has enforcement powers over legislation designed to protect the environment. These are not guidelines but rather mandates, and the project manager should be familiar with the particulars of any legislation that can affect their project, including some of the more far-reaching regulations such as:

- The Clean Air Act (1970, amended 1977 and 1990)
- The Clean Water Act (1972, amended 1977)
- Energy Policy Act (2005)
- Pollution Protection Act (1990)

For further and extensive information about the EPA and its regulations, go to http://www.epa.gov/.

California's AB32

Because this 2006 legislation is the first of its kind, we have included the details here. AB32 is a comprehensive program that uses market and regulatory mechanisms to "achieve real, quantifiable, cost-effective reductions of greenhouse gases (GHG)." It makes the Air Resources Board (ARB) responsible for monitoring and reducing GHG emissions and continues the existing Climate Action Team to coordinate statewide efforts. It authorizes the governor to invoke a safety valve in the event of extraordinary circumstances, catastrophic events, or the threat of significant economic harm, for up to 12 months at a time. This requires the ARB to:

- Establish a statewide GHG emissions cap for 2020, based on 1990 emissions by January 1, 2008.
- Adopt mandatory reporting rules for significant sources of greenhouse gases by January 1, 2008.
- Adopt a plan by January 1, 2009, indicating how emission reductions will be achieved from significant GHG sources via regulations, market mechanisms, and other actions.
- Adopt regulations by January 1, 2011, to achieve the maximum technologically feasible and cost-effective reductions in GHGs, including provisions for using both market mechanisms and alternative compliance mechanisms.
- Convene an Environmental Justice Advisory Committee and an Economic and Technology Advancement Advisory Committee to advise ARB.
- Ensure public notice for and opportunity for comment on all ARB actions.
- Prior to imposing any mandates or authorizing market mechanisms, ARB is required to evaluate several factors, including but not limited to impacts on California's economy, the environment, and public

health; equity between regulated entities; electricity reliability; conformance with other environmental laws; and ensuring that the rules do not disproportionately impact low-income communities.

• Put together a list of discrete, early-action measures by July 1, 2007, that can be implemented before January 1, 2010, and adopt such measures.[10]

Western Climate Initiative (WCI)

The Western Climate Initiative is a partnership, a commitment between several western U.S. states and Canadian provinces, including Washington, Oregon, California, Montana, New Mexico, Utah, and Arizona, along with British Columbia, Manitoba, Ontario, and Quebec. Observers include Idaho, Colorado, Alaska, Kansas, Nevada, and Wyoming, as well as Saskatchewan and Nova Scotia, and the Mexican states of Baja California, Sonora, Chihuahua, Coahuila, Nuevo Leon, and Tamaulipas. It is a "cooperative effort to address climate change and implement a joint strategy to reduce greenhouse gas emissions."[11]

The Eastern States Standard

Eleven eastern states—Pennsylvania, Connecticut, Delaware, Maine, Maryland, Massachusetts, New Hampshire, New Jersey, New York, Rhode Island, and Vermont—have signed a letter of intent "to reduce greenhouse emissions by developing a regional low fuel standard."[12] As stated, this agreement commits the states to seek alternative-fueled vehicles using hydrogen fuel cells, electricity, and biodiesel, for instance. These states are already members of the Regional Greenhouse Gas Initiative, Inc. (RGGI, Inc.), "a non-profit corporation created to support development and implementation of the 10 participating states' CO_2 Budget Trading Programs."[13] It is an interesting program in that it is a market-based "cap-and-trade" approach. There will be an established multistate emissions budget (cap). According to RGGI, Inc., that cap will gradually decrease until it is 10% less than at the start. It will require electric power generators to hold allowance covering their CO_2 emissions. There will be a market-based auction to support "low-carbon-intensity" solutions (like solar and wind power) and employ offsets to help companies meet their compliance obligations.

A gallon of gas burned by our cars contributes 19 pounds of **carbon dioxide** to the atmosphere. That's 150 tons a year for a car driving just 15,000 miles.

U.S. Conference of Mayors

Douglas H. Palmer, mayor of Trenton, New Jersey, and president of the U.S. Conference of Mayors, and Conference Executive Director Tom Cochran officially launched the U.S. Conference of Mayors Climate Protection Center on February 20, 2007, in recognition of an increasingly urgent need to provide mayors with the guidance and assistance they need to lead their cities' efforts to reduce the greenhouse gas emissions that are linked to climate change. Of course the mayors have always been active in promoting policies on a variety of issues, but this center specifically addresses the need for global climate protection. According to their Web site, this initiative is a "giant step beyond advocacy of a stronger federal role in reducing emissions." It drives it down to the local level, **just as we are advocating that the best way to accomplish greenality is to drive the effort down to the project management level**. For further information on the U.S. mayors' efforts, go to http://www.usmayors.org/climateprotection.

Bottom-up Demand from Project Stakeholders, Sponsors, and Customers

As important as any mandate or guideline is the demand from the stakeholders, including sponsors and customers. Sometimes it may not be as clear as a mandate or even a guideline, and is further complicated by conflicting goals and objectives. It is an area of primary concentration for the project manager because, after all, project management is all about properly setting project expectations and then meeting or exceeding those expectations. We'll discuss expectations at length in Section II of the book. For now, it is important to understand some of the latest demands from stakeholders, and what influence they have on prospective projects.

Of the many stakeholders in a project, of prime concern is the sponsor or funding entity, and to a great extent financial institutions are looking for organizations to be environmentally conscientious. It may be that their stakeholders, the people like you and me who supply the money that the banks lend, are being more vigilant about where we want to invest our money. If we see money going to green companies, we may be more likely to use that financial institution.

Climate change in particular is in the forefront of people's minds. *Your* project stakeholders see it in Al Gore's *An Inconvenient Truth*,[14] in the wildfires of number and scope at a level above historical records in the increasingly dry (U.S.) West, in the unusually heavy and persistent rains in the East, or an inordinate number of tornados in the Midwest.

> The physical conditions causing drought in the United States are increasingly understood to be linked to sea surface temperatures (SSTs) in the tropical Pacific Ocean. Studies indicate that cooler-than-average SSTs have been connected to the recent severe western drought, severe droughts of the late 19th century, and pre-colonial North American mega-droughts. Some climate model projections suggest that warming temperatures resulting from increased greenhouse gases in the atmosphere could return the western United States within decades to more arid baseline conditions similar to those during earlier times.[15]

More and more people are becoming aware of and concerned about climate change. Given the choice between a company that is trying to reduce its greenhouse effect (GHE) and a company that is not demonstrating a desire to reduce its GHE, and given the "temperature" of consumers, the choice is easy. Consumers are voting with their pocketbooks. "Green" companies like Timberland, Patagonia, and Stoneyfield Farms continue to prosper, even in a down economy. In July 2009, when other companies were closing stores, Timberland opened an eco-friendly store in New York City. In a May 8, 2007, article in the *Financial Times,* David Wighton reported that Citigroup, the world's largest financial services group, would commit $50 billion to environmental projects during the next decade and commit to increase 10-fold to $10 billion its planned investment to reduce its own greenhouse emissions. He also reported that Citigroup has begun to advise borrowers to make their projects more environmentally sustainable to reduce their risks amid concerns about future environmental regulations. Other financial institutions like Bank of America are also committing to greater emphasis on the environment.

Everywhere you look are ads and more ads touting green. There are green landscaping companies using organic-based fertilizer; there are green cleaning companies advertising the use of products safe for children, pets, and the environment. With all the attention on green advertising of manufacturers and service providers, it is hard to imagine that it isn't influencing the buying habits of the consumer.

Consider that, as reported in the column "The Buzz" in the September 2009 edition of *PM Network,* the monthly magazine of the Project Management Institute, "Nearly two-thirds of U.S. consumers said they'd be willing to pay a 10 percent premium for a home with green features." (That's not a paltry sum on a home worth $300,000–$500,000 and more.) Keeping all that in mind, the project manager has to ensure that the product for the project will have a high greenality score, to differentiate the product from the competition (or just to stay in competition). Also, the process to *get to* the end product must have a high greenality score to differentiate the organization from another. Green is not going away. The project manager needs to be able to take the initiative to do the right thing, and the benefits of a high greenality score will follow.

ENDNOTES

1. International Panel on Climate Change, Core Writing Team, *Contribution of Working Groups I, II and III to the Fourth Assessment Report of the Intergovernmental Panel on Climate Change,* ed. R. K. Pachauri and A. Reisinger (Geneva, Switzerland: IPCC, 2007).
2. Ibid.
3. Ibid.
4. The National Academies, *Understanding and Responding to Climate Change: Highlights of National Academies Reports* (Washington, DC: National Academies Press, 2008), 2.
5. Mark Hume, "High Arctic Strays, Salmon in Strange Places," *Fly Fisherman,* December 2009, 12–14.
6. United Nations Framework Convention on Climate Control (UNFCCC), *Introduction,* http://unfccc.int/kyoto_protocol.
7. Ibid.
8. The European Environment Agency, *General Brochure,* http://www.eea.europa.eu/ publications.
9. U.S. Environmental Protection Agency, mission statement, http://www.epa.gov.
10. Office of the Governor (California), press release, September 27, 2006, http:// gov.ca.gov.
11. Western Climate Initiative, *About The WCI,* http://www.westernclimateinitiative.org.
12. Environmental News Service, *11 Eastern States Commit to Regional Low Carbon Fuel Standard,* January 6, 2009.
13. Regional Greenhouse Gas Initiative, *About RGGI,* http://www.rggi.org.
14. *An Inconvenient Truth,* documentary, directed by Davis Guggenheim (Paramount Classics, 2006).
15. Peter Folger, Betsy A. Cody, and Nicole T. Carter, *Drought in the United States: Causes and Issues for Congress,* Congressional Research Service Report, RL34580, March 2, 2009.

2

Green Project Terminology: The Language of the Green Wave

As with every discipline, there are some key terms and fundamental concepts to learn so let's start with those. Project managers know that being conversant in a practice area is critical, not only to truly perform well, but to increase our personal credibility and to get good results. One cannot succeed in a technical firm dealing, for example, with sophisticated pharmaceutical drug introductions and refer to the products or the process components as "whatchamacallits" and "thingamajiggies." You may not need to be a full-fledged expert in the technology, but you'd better know how to talk to and understand your subject matter experts and customers. The green wave context is no different. The bad news is that the green wave has a large vocabulary and a set of new concepts to understand. The good news is that most of the concepts center around an important few (it's that Pareto principle at work again), and we can filter that large vocabulary down to a relatively few terms that you'll need for "green wave" conversancy. For the project manager, the remainder can be acquired as you go through the various processes of green project management.

CARBON FOOTPRINT AND SUSTAINABILITY

Carbon footprint and *sustainability* are two important terms in the green wave. *Carbon footprint* is important for several reasons. It is the residue left behind when using carbon-based fuels, analogous to the footprint you leave behind when walking across a sandy beach. The problem with the carbon footprint is that, unlike your footprint in the sand, it is not easily erased by the tide. Your carbon footprint is made up of two components, a direct

17

component and an indirect component. Let's look at your own home's carbon footprint as an example. The direct component includes such things as the output of your home heating, ventilation, and air conditioning (HVAC) system, or the gas mileage of your car, for instance. The indirect component includes items like the energy it takes to deliver the things you buy, the transportation for your groceries, or the energy it takes to manufacture your television set. It is also important because it can be somewhat mitigated—or at least reduced—by actively reducing energy consumption, by specifying products whose makers have reduced their carbon footprint or, when that isn't enough, by purchasing or trading carbon offsets, which is something of a controversial subject: "Buying offsets for an energy-wasteful home or business and calling it environmentally responsible is akin to buying a Diet Coke to go with your double bacon cheeseburger—and calling it a weight-loss program. Efficiency (and calorie reduction!) comes first" (Joel Makower).[1]

Purchasing carbon offsets is a personal decision. Here are a few companies that offer the service: terrapass (http://www.terrapass.com), NativeEnergy (http://www.native energy.com), Carbonfund (http://www.carbonfund.org), among others.

You may not think you have much control over the indirect component of your carbon footprint, but you do. For example, you can mitigate the transportation of your groceries by buying local products when you can, utilizing farmers markets during the summer, or purchasing at an area farm stand. Carbon offsets are another way to mitigate both direct and indirect components of your carbon footprint. But, as mentioned earlier, they are controversial in the fact that they can be perceived as being an excuse to pollute. "I don't have to reduce my carbon emissions. All I have to do is buy carbon offsets to mitigate those emissions." As a project manager, your personal code of ethics, even if you are not a member of the Project Management Institute and don't necessarily adhere to their Code of Ethics and Professional Conduct, would not allow such an argument. Carbon offsets are effective when used as intended. It is the responsible thing to do in situations where an organization or individual has a plan for zero emissions, and is working toward that plan. Until they get to zero emissions, the organization or individual can buy carbon offsets to fund equivalent savings, or momentum toward those savings, elsewhere. Once zero emission is achieved, there is no need to continue to purchase offsets. When choosing a company from which to purchase offsets, look for one with longevity and a good track record from investors.

The Project Management Institute is the leading global association for the project management profession. Since its founding in 1969, it has been at the forefront of working with business to create project management standards and techniques that work in all project environments.

PMI defines sustainability. We wanted to know how PMI defines sustainability, so we went to the latest (2009) edition of the *Combined Standards Glossary* (4th ed.)[2] and found this definition: "sustainability: a characteristic of a process or state that can be maintained indefinitely." We think that definition does not carry with it the more balanced, more earthly view. It's accurate, perhaps only because it's so bland and flat. So what else is there in the way of defining sustainability?

It is all about balance. We agree with the definition but there is much more to it. Sustainability is a balance that allows for our continued existence. The most widely quoted definition internationally is the "Brundtland definition" of the 1987 Report of the World Commission on Environment and Development—that sustainability means "meeting the needs of the present without compromising the ability of future generations to meet their own needs."

We spoke at length about a **project management definition of sustainability** with educator Gilbert Silvius, professor at Utrecht University of Applied Sciences. Gilbert is the initiator of that school's Master of Project Management program—the first accredited Master of Project Management in the Netherlands (see Figure 2.1).

"Although some aspects of sustainability are found in the various standards of project management," he said, "it has to be concluded that the impact of sustainability is not really recognized yet. The way projects are managed, measured, and reported doesn't reflect the different aspects of sustainability that can be derived from the concepts of sustainable development." Gilbert went on to say, "It is clear that a lot of work still has to be done on the implications of sustainable project management and that there is a growing need for expertise, criteria, and concepts to practically implement the concept in the management of projects."

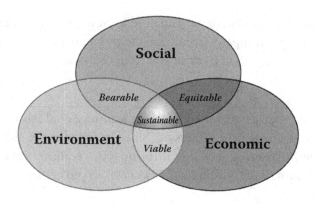

FIGURE 2.1

Interrelating life cycles. Adapted from A. J. G. Silvius, J. van der Brink, and A. Köhler, "Views on Sustainable Project Management," In *Human Side of Projects in Modern Business,* IPMA Scientific Research Paper Series, ed. Kalle Kähköhnen, Abdul Samad Kazi, and Mirkka Rekola, 2009, p. 26 (Helsinki, Finland: IPMA). With permission.

If we agree that sustainability does have the aspect of "the ability of future generations to meet their own needs," it begs the question: have we even begun to accomplish—or even properly *consider*—that? Politics aside, looking at sustainability in projects, the project manager needs to evaluate the project through the concept of an "environmental lens."

The Environmental Lens

An assertion from EarthPM is that "project managers must view their projects through an **environmental lens**. This increases the project manager's (and the project team's) long-term thinking and avails the project of the rising green wave of environmentalism."[3] It is through that lens that the project manager will view the various aspects of the product of the project and the project's processes as well, to ensure that what *can be done* to increase greenality *will be done*. The higher the greenality of the project, the lower the impact of the project itself on the environment, and the greater the sustainability of the project's product.

THE CYCLE OF SUSTAINABILITY

While we are talking sustainability, there is another concept, called the *cycle of sustainability*. A perfect cycle of sustainability utilizes everything it produces and in effect has zero emissions, zero waste. This may be impossible to achieve to perfection, but nature comes very close. Consider the earthworm for instance. Its sole purpose or *raison d'être* (unless you are a fisherman or a bird, that is) is to process dirt. Dirt goes in one end and comes out the other, improved from its entry point. The worm's unique anatomy allows for mixing of organic material (dirt) with its own secretions, creating a much richer soil after it passes out of the worm. So the cycle would be dirt, through worm, better dirt, and nothing is wasted.

And of course, not all trash even makes it to the landfill. The Great Pacific Garbage Patch, which is a swirling vortex of waste and debris in the Pacific Ocean, covers an area twice the size of the continental U.S. and is believed to hold almost 100 million tons of garbage.

—treehugger.com

There are many examples in nature of cycles of sustainability, some simple, some more complex. The real challenge for the project manager comes when he or she has to determine the cycle of sustainability for a project. How are they going to show that there will be little or no waste, that everything that can be utilized will be utilized? Further, how will they show that the project (including the product and the process) considered all the possibilities when constructing the cycle of sustainability? They will do it with a new thinking paradigm. That paradigm includes viewing the project through the environmental lens, being aware of the project's impacts as well as how to mitigate those impacts, whether by design, or when necessary through offsets. It is "green thinking," and it becomes easier as you gain experience with the new paradigm.

CRADLE TO CRADLE

Part of green thinking is the cradle-to-cradle (C2C) concept. It used to be that we thought of projects as cradle to grave. William McDonough and Michael Braungart[4] argue that the conflict between industry and the environment is not an indictment of commerce but an outgrowth

TABLE 2.1

Take, Make, Waste

Cradle to Grave	Cradle to Cradle
Take	Closed Looks
Make	Technical "Nutrients"
Waste	Eco-effectiveness

of purely opportunistic design. The design of products and manufacturing systems growing out of the Industrial Revolution reflected the spirit of the day—and yielded a host of unintended yet tragic consequences. They make the case that an industrial system that "takes, makes, and wastes" can become a creator of goods and services that generate ecological, social, and economic value (see Table 2.1). Mr. McDonough sent us this quote: "Our goal is a delightfully diverse, safe, healthy and just world, with clean water, air, soil, and power, economically, equitably, ecologically, and elegantly enjoyed."[5]

THE NATURAL STEP

The Natural Step[6] is one of the founding concepts in green thinking. According to those fundamentals, there are four system conditions and each must be addressed by a principle of sustainability. It includes four *conditions* of sustainability and then answers each one with a *principle* of sustainability (see Table 2.2).

What it boils down to is that almost all green efforts are centered on these four principles. At first glance, the four conditions and principles may seem overly altruistic and impossible to achieve. However, look more closely at what is being advocated. The conditions and principles point to the fact that something needs to be done to stop our contributions to the buildup of the most toxic by-products of our society, not that we can't stop using natural resources. We just need to use them in a more responsible way.

Couple these conditions and principles with the five assertions from EarthPM (see Introduction) and one can easily see the intersection between green and project management. In order to serve the four principles, future projects will need to be coordinated in a disciplined manner. Who has the better capabilities to support the principles than the project manager? Recall the definition of project management: "it is the

TABLE 2.2

The Natural Step

Conditions	Principles
In a sustainable society, nature is not subject to systematically increasing the following conditions:	To become a sustainable society we must answer with the following principles:
1. Concentrations of substances extracted from the earth's crust	1. Eliminate our contribution to the progressive buildup of substances extracted from the earth's crust (for example, heavy metals and fossil fuels).
2. Concentrations of substances produced by society	2. Eliminate our contribution to the progressive buildup of chemical compounds produced by society (for example, dioxins, PCBs, and DDT).
3. Degradation by physical means	3. Eliminate our contribution to the progressive destruction of nature and natural processes (for example, overharvesting forests and paving over critical wildlife habitat).
4. In that society, people are not subject to conditions that systemically undermine their capacity to meet their needs.	4. Eliminate our contribution to conditions that undermine people's capacity to meet their basic human needs (for example, unsafe working conditions and not enough pay to live on).

Note: Adapted from The Natural Step, http://www.naturalstep.org.

application of knowledge, skills, tools, and techniques to project activities to meet or exceed stakeholders' needs and expectations from a project."[7] We take it one step further and add, "to make any decision necessary to be environmentally responsible."

CORPORATE SOCIAL RESPONSIBILITY AND THE GREEN PROJECT MANAGER

How can a project manager influence corporate behavior? Can the project manager help a corporation attain social responsibility? Corporate social responsibility (CSR) is directly related to green project management by definition. To define CSR, once again one only has to look to Natural Step's four conditions/principles for a sustainable society. The authors have always asserted that project management is a microcosm of general business. We just see project management as being a core sample and special case of general business. That special case includes a certain ethical and moral consideration that may not necessarily be a driving force behind general business decisions. Driving forces behind general business decisions are usually bottom line driven. In a lot of cases, leadership does balance the need to make a profit with the need to demonstrate CSR. But business is project driven. No matter how you think about it, business is providing something to a stakeholder or group of stakeholders, whether it is sustainable energy, legal services, or any number of other things. Everything that is not steady-state operation is a project, and the project is managed by someone, whether or not the person has the specific title of "project manager." Because everything is a project and every project is managed "somehow" (well or badly), those people (and for the sake of argument we will call them project managers) are the leading edge of the change. So, who better to emphasize CSR, particularly if it isn't in the corporation's DNA? Every corporation should be accountable to lead in a way that models responsible behavior.

What does CSR look like? It comes in many forms. It could be Timberland Corporation's support of City Year. It is not enough to adopt the "do no harm" mentality. So, CSR may look like Starbucks' commitment to ethical coffee sourcing.[8] According to the Howard Schultz, chairman, president, and CEO of Starbucks, "In fiscal 2007, 65 percent of our coffee was purchased from C.A.F.E. (Coffee and Farmer Equity) Practices–approved suppliers who are integrating our rigorous standards for sustainability throughout the coffee supply chain. Our goal is to be purchasing 80 percent of our coffee through C.A.F.E. practices by 2013, and extending the program's reach to areas in Africa and Asia." In addition, CSR could come in the form of DESERTEC as detailed in Chapter 4, or any number of corporations supporting their own energy-reducing efforts. Of course some of those projects may be self-serving, but they are conserving not only their energy, but ours as well, which makes them CSR. The key to remember is that each and every effort undertaken is a project, and each and every project will need someone to manage it. Wouldn't it be better to have a person (project manager) who is the most familiar with CSR and the greenality effort?

City Year was founded in 1988 on the belief that young people can change the world.

At City Year's locations across the United States and in South Africa, young people—called "corps members"—serve full-time for 10 months.

City Year's vision is that one day the most commonly asked question of a young person will be, "Where are you going to do your service year?"

City Year leverages the talent, energy, and idealism of corps members who serve as tutors, mentors, and role models to help students stay on track—and get back on track—to graduate.

BIODEGRADABLE

Biodegradability of products used by project managers and by the products of their projects is another one of the key issues with which PMs must deal. *Biodegradable* has a variety of definitions depending on the point of view. The foci of the definition differences have to do with rate of biodegradability and if the product is really biodegradable. One of the products that is getting a lot of interest is biodegradable diapers. We use this example because it illustrates the definition, not because Green PM is at its infancy. Still, it's a reminder that, indeed, Green PM is at a very tender age! Disposable diapers have always been a problem in landfills. Their tendency to hang around forever has caused a surge in the manufacture of "biodegradable diapers." While diapers make up only about 3% of the landfill space, they lag behind only newspapers and food/beverage containers, and amount to 10 billion diapers annually in the United States. The energy costs to wash cloth diapers far outweigh the benefits of using cloth diapers. Parker Mathusa, program director of the New York State Energy Research and Development Authority, explained that cloth diapers changed six times a day use 142 gallons of water a week to launder. Cloth diapers generate 50% more processed solid waste than disposables and consume three times more nonrenewable energy sources, such as oil and natural gas, for heating and pumping water to wash them than do disposables. The controversy now arises with biodegradable diapers in that if they are put into plastic bags and put out for trash collection, they will not be exposed to the elements they need to biodegrade. Some manufacturers, Procter and Gamble being one of them, are recommending that biodegradable diapers be composed to allow the same organisms that are present in compost piles to "eat" the diapers. Additionally, it has been found that biodegradable diapers may contain more plastic than disposable diapers, to make up for their lack of strength. As you can see, the biodegradable controversy continues. One of the best Web sites we have found to help the project manager with biodegradable solutions is that of Biodegradable Products Institute, Inc., out of New York City (http://www.bpiworld.org/).

GREENWASHING

Greenwashing is a derogatory term for a variety of practices that appear green but in actuality give only lip service to being green. "More than 98% of supposedly natural and environmentally friendly products on U.S. supermarket shelves are making potentially false or misleading claims."[9] The word has been around since 1999, when it was defined as "disinformation disseminated by an organization so as to present an environmentally responsible public image" by the *Oxford English Dictionary*.[10] While we've read definition after definition (with some being rather complex), various "deadly sins of greenwashing," and much more, for simplicity's sake we will put it this way—you will know it when you see it. It is deception, making people believe that a company, a product, or a process is green when in actuality it is not. It also has the caveat that it is intentional. There will be some instances when there is an honest belief that what is being portrayed is green, when in fact it may not be. That is more of an uninformed disclosure rather than greenwashing. Using the old "duck analogy" backward, "if it doesn't walk like a duck, quack like a duck, or swim like a duck, it probably isn't a duck." So, if it doesn't feel "green," it probably isn't.

The term *greenwashing* was coined by suburban New York environmentalist Jay Westerveld in 1986. He used the word in an essay in regard to the hotel industry's practice of placing placards in each room promoting reuse of guest towels to "save the environment." He argued that the hotel industry was doing little or nothing else to help the environment and that playing on guests' environmental consciences to reuse towels was merely a ploy to save money.

Every year, The Green Life (http://www.thegreenlifeonline.org) has a campaign called "Take Green Wash to the Cleaners" in which they highlight some of the year's biggest deceivers. In 2005, they featured Ford Motor Company and its "blue oval" as symbols of environmental commitment. However, when you compare the overall fleetwide fuel economy, Ford at the time was the worst of all the major automobile manufacturers. And, to top it off, the company allocated $8 million for lobbying at the state and federal level against mandates to reduce carbon dioxide emissions.[11] In 2006, The Green Life featured Nestlé Company when it introduced its "Partner's Blend" instant coffee, which bears the fair-trade label. However, this coffee represents about only 0.01% of Nestlé's coffee imports "and with the remaining 99.9 percent, Nestlé continues to use their large market share to keep small coffee farmers in poverty, while reaping huge profits."[12]

Here are some "green tests" you can do to help make the decision between green and greenwashing:

- Labeling is one of the easiest ways to "greenwash." There are labeling words that are supported by strict independent certification, like *organic,* backed by the U.S. Food and Drug Administration's (USFDA) National Organic Program, or *green seal,* a certification founded in science-based standards (http://www.greenseal.org).
- If it seems too good to be true, it probably is. Be skeptical of claims made by notoriously nongreen sources, like oil companies and automobile manufacturers. We are not saying that boycotting these companies is the answer, just that if you are buying because of a "green claim," you may want to rethink the reasoning.
- Don't just accept, check it out. There are a number of sites that provide information about green or not green. We have included some of those in Chapter 12.

From the UK's Department of Environmental and Rural Food Affairs comes their "Green Claims Code."[13] A green claim should be:

- Truthful, accurate, and able to be substantiated
- Relevant to the product and the environmental issues associated with it
- Clear about what issue or aspect of the product is in question
- Explicit about the meaning of any symbol used in the claim
- In plain language and in line with standard definitions

TRIPLE BOTTOM LINE

Triple bottom line can be simply defined as the business connection between *people, planet,* and *profit.* Not so simple is the balance between those three elements. However, the project manager is no stranger to balance. For a long time it was *cost, time,* and *quality.* Most recently it has become balancing all of the project "risks." If we think about the past, wasn't it all about profit? What makes you think that it still isn't about profit? People, planet, and profit are not necessarily mutually exclusive. As a matter of fact, the opposite is true. By using the techniques of greening a project's processes and product, there should be a positive effect on the planet. By saving energy, for instance, fewer resources are consumed, meaning a cost savings—increased profit. Saving resources can translate into saving "human resources," making people more efficient. Managing that *triple bottom line* makes sense going forward, and it is not any different from what the project manager has been doing. That's why we believe that project managers should and will lead future green efforts. (See Figure 2.2 for a representation of the triple bottom line called "the triple-P.")

ECO AUDIT

The term *eco audit* is particularly interesting in that it is very ambiguous. The way we see it is that it is application based. The industry you are in will dictate the standards against which you are judged during an eco audit. At this point those standards seem to be moving targets, and there certainly isn't one standard that we can point to that is everything to everybody. What we've been able to ascertain is that most eco audit offerings are really about carbon dioxide usage analysis. The carbon footprint calculator can be defined as a personal eco audit, at least at the carbon footprint level. However, to take a personal eco audit, extensive survey information must be collected relative to your reduce, reuse, and redesign efforts. We believe that just as a personal eco audit is more than just calculating a carbon footprint, industry-wide eco audits will have to include more than carbon dioxide usage.

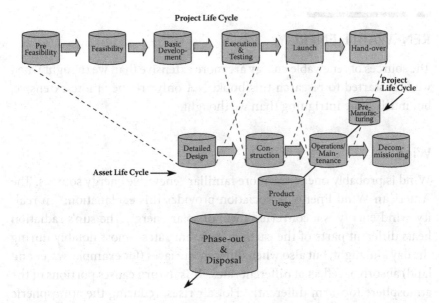

FIGURE 2.2
The triple-P concept of sustainability. From California Academy of Sciences, San Francisco.

REDUCE, REDESIGN, REUSE, RECYCLE

It is not by accident that the words are listed in this order. The best solution to save valuable resources is to reduce their usage. The project manager, in the forefront of resource usage, has the largest impact. Finding more innovative, efficient, and smarter ways to spend the limited resources is a way to reduce their usage. When all possibilities to reduce resource usage are exhausted, redesign is another possibility. The project manager can ask the following questions:

- Is there a way to change the project management process so that it is more efficient and use fewer resources?
- Is there a way to redesign the product of the project to use less of whatever resources are needed to manufacture, implement, or control the product?
- What can I do to help the process and product?
- What can the team do to help the process of product—the whole process, from inception to disposal?

RENEWABLE ENERGY

The sources of renewable energy are more extensive than we thought when we first started to research this book. Not only are they more extensive, but much more intriguing than we thought.

Wind

Wind is probably one of the more familiar renewable energy sources. The American Wind Energy Association provides this explanation: "In reality, wind energy is a converted form of solar energy. The sun's radiation heats different parts of the earth at different rates—most notably during the day and night, but also when different surfaces (for example, water and land) absorb or reflect at different rates. This in turn causes portions of the atmosphere to warm differently. Hot air rises, reducing the atmospheric pressure at the earth's surface, and cooler air is drawn in to replace it. The result is wind. Air has mass, and when it is in motion, it contains the energy of that motion ('kinetic energy'). Some portion of that energy can convert into other forms—mechanical force or electricity—that we can use to perform work."[14]

Within 10 years, wind power could provide 20% of America's power. And, offshore wind turbines have the potential to produce as much power as all of the power plants in the United States.

—treehugger.com

Solar

Speaking of solar, solar energy has been used as long as man has been around. In ancient Egypt, people worshipped the sun god Ra, and they derived both physical and metaphysical energy from the sun. Solar energy continues to be used for things as simple as line drying clothes. Interestingly, a California government Web site (http://www.energyquest.ca.gov) points out that "decaying plants hundreds of millions of years ago produced the coal, oil and natural gas that we use today. So, fossil fuels are technically a form of solar energy stored millions and millions of years ago. Indirectly, the sun or other stars are responsible for ALL our energy. Even nuclear energy comes from a star because the uranium atoms used in nuclear energy were created in the fury of a nova—a star exploding." Solar water heating has been utilized in the United States since the 1890s. "In 1897, 30 percent of the homes in Pasadena, just east of Los Angeles, were equipped with solar water heaters. As mechanical improvements were made, solar systems were used in Arizona, Florida and many other sunny parts of the United States."[15] We are most interested in the application of the generation of solar thermal electricity. Huge solar panels collect sunlight to heat water, producing steam to run electricity-generating turbines. One of the downsides is that electricity cannot be generated during cloudy days, thus triggering larger projects like DESERTEC, featured in Chapter 4.

Geothermal

Geothermal is using heat from within the earth. Geothermal energy is one of what we consider the more interesting renewable energy sources because one of the authors has a background in geology. There are a couple of ways to utilize earth to produce geothermal energy. One is using deep wells to tap into superheated water or steam and pumping that to the surface for heating purposes or to run turbines to generate power. The second is to use stable temperatures closer to the surface. During the 1950s, we used to "drive" wells to use for watering lawns, rather than using the more expensive town water. What we found was that the water was a consistent 52° in temperature, a nice refreshing temperature in the summer. So how does 52° water help save energy? The water is already "heated" or "cooled" to 52°, therefore requiring less energy to heat it or cool it to the desired temperature than the winter water, which may be close to 32°, or the summer water, which may be at 80° or more. The method used to heat and cool the water is through a geothermal heat exchanger, in most cases a ground source heat pump that exchanges warmth or cooling from the earth. We will not take up your time detailing how heat exchangers work; just suffice it to say it is a more efficient method than air-sourced heat pumps or electricity. One caution, however, is that the initial start-up costs including the equipment are greater than the more conventional methods. However, it is possible to justify the added cost with a longer payback period and overall energy savings. And remember that geothermal energy does not have only to do with water. By building underground and taking advantage of the constant temperature of about 56°F and the thermal lag of the earth, structures can be made much more energy efficient. An example is the library at Purdue University, in which the ground level is the roof and the library continues downward for five stories. See the article at http://www.homes-eco.com/underground-homes/ for more about underground-energy savings.

Sustainable Biomass

Sustainable biomass is probably one of the more interesting of the renewable-energy sources. According to the Biomass Centre (http://www.biomassenergycentre.org.uk) out of the UK, there are five basic categories of materials used as sustainable biomass fuels: virgin wood, energy crops, agricultural residues, food wastes, and industrial wastes and coproducts. Virgin wood includes products from forestry operations. There is a wide swath of land covering the northern parts of Vermont, New Hampshire, and Maine that has been traditionally "logged" for the purposes of paper production and building products. Those lands are also owned by various lumber companies. These operations, while focused on the paper and lumber production, do yield a large amount of by-product from debarking and branch trimming, as well as trees that cannot be used in the actual product production due to poor quality of one sort or another. Additionally, virgin wood can also come from the production process, waste from the lumber mills as an example. The third source of virgin wood is from tree-trimming operations from large Christmas tree farms or other large operations providing ornamental products.

Energy crops are those crops that are grown specifically for use in the generation of energy. The best known of these crops are corn and soy beans, used in the production of ethanol, the additive in gasoline. The Texas State Energy Conservation Office (http://www.seco.cpa.state.tx.us) is looking at the possibility of other energy crops grown in their area like sugarcane, switchgrass, and sorghum. Agricultural residue differs from energy crops in that it is the by-product of agricultural processes—even the by-product of energy crop production, like corn stalks or straw from grains such as wheat and rice.

According to the National Science Foundation, "Green gasoline technologies recycle carbon instead of adding net carbon to the atmosphere. The same carbon that comes out of a tailpipe when green gasoline is

burned is taken out of the atmosphere by the next crop of green gasoline plants. With non-renewable sources of fuel, the source carbon had
been isolated within the Earth, but adds to total atmospheric carbon
when it burns."

Green gasoline is another product derived from sustainable biomass. The
National Science Foundation (NSF) tells us the following.

There are three main catalytic mechanisms to convert plants into
gasoline:

1. *Gasification* is one of the oldest mechanisms to make gasoline from
   non-petroleum sources, but since it had primarily been used to
   convert coal or natural gas into gasoline, but it is only now finding
   applications as a green gasoline process. In gasification, extreme heat
   breaks the plants down to the fundamental components of carbon
   monoxide (CO) and hydrogen (H_2). The gasses are passed over catalysts which grab the CO and H_2, and depending on which catalysts
   are used, recombines them into gasoline. The process is well-established but is currently only feasible at large scales. It is expensive and
   not efficient when plants are the feedstock.
2. *Pyrolysis* is also a mechanism that uses heat, but it uses less than gasification, and like all of the catalytic approaches (including the method
   used in George Huber's laboratory at the University of Massachusetts–
   Amherst) it is so efficient that it does not require any external energy
   source. Researchers even hope to eventually use the heat produced
   by the pyrolysis process to generate electricity. While new for green
   gasoline applications, the process has a number of advantages in that
   it can use any plant starting material, including waste paper and grass
   clippings, and is efficient. So far, the process can produce components
   of gasoline, but not yet the full suite of components found in transportation fuels.
3. *Aqueous phase processing* starts with sugar, but sugar is somewhat
   easily derived from plants. At room temperature, the sugar is mixed
   with water and passed over specialized catalysts. If the catalysts are
   properly selected, the end result can be a wide range of substances,
   from gasoline (all 300-plus chemical components) to diesel to jet
   fuel to the precursors for pharmaceuticals and plastics. The process, under development at Virent Energy Systems, Inc. in Madison,

Wisconsin, and initially at the University of Wisconsin–Madison, in James Dumesic's laboratory, is currently being scaled up for commercial applications. With buy-in from a number of major industry partners, Virent is hoping to bring this green gasoline process to market within the next 5 to 10 years.

- The sugar source for aqueous phase processing can come from such plants as sugar beets and sugarcane, and many researchers are devising ingenious ways to create sugars from all the parts of a plant. Some researchers are also working on growing new plants that are easier to convert into sugars.
- Source plants, such as switchgrass, can be grown on marginal lands, so neither food sources nor pristine forests need to be impacted.[16]

Food waste, from a variety of sources, is also being considered and in some cases is already being used as an alternative energy source. One source is from fast-food and other restaurants that generate grease from the food preparation process, like cooking burgers. The UK seems to be leading this effort, using food wastes from the supermarket. According PDM, a UK recycling and processing company, "The collected products go through an innovative process which separates the food material from any packaging. The food products are either then re-processed to recover valuable materials that are used in the manufacture of bio-fuels, or are used as a 'neat' biofuel for direct biomass combustion." Another source is household garbage. There is a project in the Virgin Islands called Wāstaway. The goal of the project is take household garbage and create a product that can be used as an alternative fuel source. They have developed a "process that takes unsorted household garbage and converts it into a product called Fluff®, which can then be easily used in a variety of other ways. Fluff is similar in consistency to wood pulp, and can be processed for use as a growing medium for plants and turf, can be gasified to generate steam, can be converted to synthetic fuels such as ethanol, diesel, and gasoline, or can be compressed and extruded to make products such as construction materials."[17]

The final alternative biomass fuel source is that derived from industrial waste and nonproduct output of manufacturing and other industrial processes. One of the sources of this alternative fuel is municipal wastes. However, all of the literature so far points out that while burning municipal waste at high temperature to produce some energy recovery is preferable to burning it and not recovering any energy, according to the EPA, nothing says that this can be done with any cost efficiency. So garbage as an alternative fuel source seems to be many years away. However, tire-derived fuel (TDF) has proven to be an interesting alternative. According to the EPA (http://www.epa.gov/waste/conserve/materials/tires), tires produce about the same amount of energy as oil and 25% more energy than coal, and the ash residue may contain lower heavy-metal content than some coals. Industries that are particularly suited for TDF are paper and pulp, cement, industrial boilers, and electric utilities. The Rubber Manufacturers Association (http://www.rma.org), as of their 2006 report, shows that there are 188 million tires stockpiled in the United States. This number is continuing to decline, but still presents a significant problem, or a source of fuel depending on how you look at it.

Wave Motion and Tides

Wave motion and tides are probably two of the more controversial and least defined of the alternative energy sources. There has been some study of both of these alternative energy sources. Ocean Power Technologies (http://www.oceanpowertechnologies.com) among others have designed a buoy that is capable of generating power from wave action. There have been rumors of an attempt to harness the tidal power in northern New England and into Canada where tidal differences can be 9–12 feet and more, generating huge volumes of water moving in and out of estuaries and rivers. There is a plant operating in La Rance, France, generating approximately 240 megawatts of power, but issues of impacts on the area fisheries may be insurmountable.

SMARTER OBJECTIVES

One way to get smarter about green project management is to get SMARTER about green project management. What does that mean? Some of the "more seasoned" of us may recall the old TV series, *Get Smart*, and the more youthful readers will certainly know the *Get Smart* movie that came out a few years ago (based on that original TV show). The title, and most of the writing, was very clever, and "played with words." This would figure, since the writers included comics Mel Brooks and Buck Henry, and starred funnyman Don Adams. Smart (played by Adams) was the name of the protagonist agent, and the bad guys were always trying to "get" (as in capture) Smart. But it was of course also a reference to getting smarter—as in "gaining intelligence or wisdom." And most of us in the wonderful world of management will recognize the acronym SMART for dealing with goals and objectives. Remember?

S—specific, significant, stretching
M—measurable, meaningful, motivational
A—agreed upon, attainable, achievable, acceptable, action oriented
R—realistic, relevant, reasonable, rewarding, results oriented
T—time based, tangible, trackable

The time for getting SMART has passed. It's gone. It's fizzled. It's deceased. Would you believe that it is at least getting old? Instead of getting SMART these days, we think we need to be SMARTER. How, you ask, can we be SMARTER? Glad you asked.

We can be SMARTER by adding two more letters to SMART. Of course, those two letters are E and R.

E—Environmentally
R—Responsible

In other words, it's not just enough to set our project goals and objectives as we said earlier; we also have to consider the effectiveness of the processes of the project itself, its own waste and inefficiencies, and the end product and its disposal or reuse.

Remember, it is not only the project manager who should be asking these questions, but the entire set of human resources available *throughout* the project should be asking these questions.

When the reduce/redesign possibilities have been explored, the next step is to ascertain whether or not there is anything in the process or product that could benefit from reuse. Is there anything from an existing project process or product that can be utilized in the new project process or product? The entire focus here is to avoid recycling as much as possible. Recycling, although a nice thought, poses its own set of problems. One only has to look to China and their increasing, and illegal, "recycling" stockpile of electronic devices such as CRT screens, old televisions, and computers. Attempts to remove precious metals and other valuable components are causing untold damage to the physical environment and thus to the local population. From the method of burning electronic components, there is toxic air, and from the acid baths to remove precious metals, there is water pollution. According to the EPA, more than 2 million tons of electronics are discarded in the United States annually. All of that has to go somewhere. Even when companies like Sony, Dell, Apple, and others have the best intentions by offering recycling programs for their products, the best recycling effort is no recycling. But as we know, that solution is impossible, so utilizing recycling as the least preferred method is the right choice.

We'd like to close this chapter with an inspirational word from Storm Cunningham. Storm is an always-in-demand keynote speaker and author of the recent books *The Restoration Economy* (2002) and *reWealth* (2008). Storm is founder of the Revitalization Institute, whose mission is "to advance integrated renewal of communities and natural resources worldwide," and the CEO of the Resolution Fund, which is focused primarily on training the public and private sectors to be better partners in revitalization, and connecting the right private resources to the right public projects at the right time. He's also apparently quite a fan of our profession. In his chapter "Global Trends in Project Management" in *Project Management Circa 2025*,[18] Storm says: "Turning our damaged natural, built, and socioeconomic assets into revitalization is now the world's most complex and urgent challenge. The case can be made ... that project and program managers can and should be the lead profession for the revitalization of our communities and the restoration of our natural resources." Storm actually closes the chapter with a direct invitation to PMI members, encouraging project managers by saying that they are best positioned to facilitate the renewal of the planet. "Grand words," he says, "but true nonetheless."

ENDNOTES

1. Joel Makower, *Energy's 'Three Rs': A Primer*, June 2006, http://www.worldchanging.com/archives/004522.html, pg. 1.
2. Project Management Institute, *Combined Standards Glossary* (Newtown Square, PA: Project Management Institute, 2009).
3. EarthPM, *EarthPM's Five Assertions of Green Project Management*, part of mission statement, 2007 © http://www.earthpm.com.
4. William McDonough and Michael Braungart, *Cradle to Cradle: Remaking the Way We Make Things* (San Francisco: North Point Press, 2002).

5. Quote provided by William McDonough, FAIA, used with permission.
6. The Natural Step, "4 Sustainability Principles," http://www.naturalstep.org/.
7. J. LeRoy Ward, *Dictionary of Project Management Terms* (Arlington, VA: ESI International, 2008).
8. Starbucks Corporation, *Fiscal 2007 Corporate Social Responsibility Annual Report*, http://www.starbucks.com/aboutus/csrreport/Starbucks_CSR_FY2007.pdf.
9. Scott Case (TerraChoice to U.S. Congress), quoted in "Eco-design or Greenwash? Steering a Path through the Misinformation," presentation by Christopher Kadamus, CambridgeConsultants,Cambridge,England,http://www.cambridgeconsultants.com, October 20, 2009, used with permission.
10. *Oxford English Dictionary* (2nd ed.), 2009.
11. The Green Life, *Featured Greenwasher*, http://www.thegreenlifeonline.org/green-washerfebruary2006.html.
12. Ibid.
13. "Eco-design or Greenwash?," presentation by Christopher Kadamus, Cambridge Consultants, Cambridge, England, http://www.cambridgeconsultants.com, October 20, 2009, used with permission.
14. American Wind Energy Association, *Wind Energy Basics: What Is Wind Energy?*, http://www.awea.org/faq/wwt_basics.html.
15. The California Energy Commission, Energy Story, Chapter 15: Solar Energy, http://www.energyquest.ca.gov/story/chapter15.html.
16. National Science Foundation, *Fact Sheet: What Is Green Gasoline?*, http://www.nsf.gov/news/newsmedia/greengasoline/index.jsp.
17. WästAway, welcome message on home page, http://www.wastaway.com/.
18. Storm Cunningham, "Global Trends in Project Management," in *Project Management Circa 2025*, ed. David Cleland and Bopaya Bidanda (Newtown Square, PA: Project Management Institute, 2009).

3

Understanding Green Project Fundamentals

GREEN, QUALITY, AND GREENALITY

There is an equation and a new word we like to use to show the relationship between green and quality. It's a simple equation:

$$Green + Quality = Greenality$$

Greenality is the new measurement for a project's green quality. Greenality does not have a long history, nor does it have a set of distinguished people standing behind it, gurus like Philip Crosby, W. Edwards Deming, and Joseph Juran, but those people, whether they realized it or not, laid the foundation for greenality. There are many parallels between greenality and quality. When a company relies 100% on inspection to ensure quality, a certain attitude permeates the working environment, that any "mistakes" will be caught by the inspectors. Moreover, inspection is both tedious and monotonous and leads to its own set of issues, such as missed defective product because of boredom. It requires vigilance. So, like quality, greenality must be *designed in*—not inspected in. The processes of the project and its outcome should serve sustainability and not require workers to be vigilant at all times. Greenality becomes an up-front and integrated activity for both the product of the project and the process of managing a project.

TABLE 3.1

Contrast of Quality Masters and Greenality

Philip Crosby	W. Edwards Deming	Joseph Juran	EarthPM (Greenality)
Conformance to requirements	Constancy of purpose (don't change policies in midstream)	Specific standards and specifications for specific processes	Conformance to requirements
Prevention is preferable to inspection.	Cease dependency on inspection		Must be planned in
Zero defects	Don't accept "that's good enough."		Don't accept "that's good enough."
Quality is free.	Break down barriers between functions.	There is a cost to poor quality.	Greenality is free.
	Don't award business based solely on price.	Stability and consistency in processes.	Check your supply chain for green ingredients.
	Constant improvement	"Breakthrough" results in achieving higher targets.[a]	Constant improvement

[a] Juran Institute.

What else can we learn about greenality from the quality masters? Take a look at Table 3.1.

Philip Crosby, sometimes known as the "father" of quality management, asserted one of the most influential statements about quality management—that "quality is free." While his 1979 book is titled *Quality Is Free*, it is the subtitle that has more meaning to greenality: *How to Manage Quality—So That It Becomes a Source of Profit for Your Business*. Greenality must be managed the same way, and we say that its project manager leads the management of greenality. In Section II, we'll discuss in detail what the project manager can do during each project phase to ensure that quality is an innate factor for a project. As an example, in the initiation phase management must proactively insist on quality. To paraphrase Crosby, "management has to get right in there and be active when it comes to greenality." Two of the other relevant messages from Philip Crosby are: "It less expensive to prevent greenality issues than to have to rework, scrap, or service them"; and "It is always cheaper to do the job right the first time." When you think in terms of greenality or quality, think of the short- and long-term ramifications if things are not done right. Quality issues in the form of "cost of noncompliance" are obvious: increased expenses due to having to do that rework of scrapping, added warranty work, legal challenges, and degradation of an organization's reputation. Greenality issues—though not as obvious—are just as detrimental to an organization. If greenality is not considered in this day and age, will consumers continue to buy those products? If greenality is not considered, in light of newer regulations and standards will the project ever see the light of day, or will it be mired in legal proceeding? And if greenality is not considered, and you buy into the claims of the thousands of scientists regarding climate change, on top of these product and enterprise issues there are the overriding environmental problems you are leaving our children and their children. Even small delays in implementation can cost companies millions in revenues and loss of market share. Two other thoughts that directly relate to greenality from Philip Crosby are: "It is always cheaper to do the job right the first time"; and "Quality is free, but it is not a gift."[1]

We also see a definite parallel between W. Edwards Deming's quality initiatives and greenality. The first example of this was demonstrated in the initial resistance he received when he first proposed his 14-point business philosophy. For a full definition of that philosophy, go to http://www.lii.net/deming.html. During the early 1950s, Deming proposed his philosophy, whose 14 points can be distilled down to three areas: constancy of purpose, continuous improvement, and removing functional barriers. However, there was a marked resistance by American businesses to Deming's ideas. The businesses' attitude was that the United States was making the most superior products on the market, there would not be any competitors, and the businesses knew best for their customer. Deming tried to tell them that it wasn't the case. U.S. businesses, he said, were relying too much on the past, competition was on the horizon, and the *consumer* would drive the market. The superior product position, he said, was temporary.

Finding no place in the United States that would embrace his message, Deming turned to Japan, which became a willing and eager student. While it took some time, we all know what happened to the market for U.S.-produced goods like consumer electronics and automobiles. It is a different world than when Deming was trying to "sell" his quality message. We now know how the world is inextricably tied together environmentally. An explosion in population in the Pacific Rim affects Europe and the United States, by taxing already limited worldwide resources like

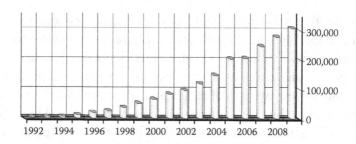

FIGURE 3.1

PMI membership growth: 1992 through November 2009.

energy and food. Isolationism is not an option. However, greenality faces similar adoption issues to those that were faced by the early gurus of quality management such as Deming: misunderstanding of the costs versus the benefits, strong leadership, and the "we've been doing it this way for years" attitude among others. One thing we do have going for us is the relatively new field of project management. Certainly, project management has been around a while, as a discipline since the 1950s. The seminal event for the discipline was the formation of the Project Management Institute in 1969. Since that time the field has been growing in both popularity and influence. Today, PMI has hundreds of thousands of members worldwide (see Figure 3.1).

The critical mass of project managers can provide the strong leadership in greenality efforts. What's the connection? Project managers are the ones who direct the consumption of resources in a project, and the ones who can instill a life cycle mentality into the project from its inception (see Table 3.2).

Joseph Juran spent more than 70 years in the quality field. His major contribution is the *Quality Control Handbook,* still in use today after 48 years. He applied statistical methods like the Pareto principle (80% of the problems are caused by 20% of the issues) to help companies understand and improve the way that quality was managed. We feel, however, that his most important parallel to greenality is his view that isolating the human issues is the key to solving quality (greenality) problems. Specifically, human beings are prone to resist change. Greenality thinking, like quality thinking, is a change in culture. Once the resistance to change is understood and addressed, greenality, like quality, becomes second nature. It is designed in, not inspected in. Again, project managers are the logical choice to lead the cultural change, because, by definition, leading projects is leading change (see Table 3.3).

TABLE 3.2

Quality/Greenality Trilogy[a]

Quality Planning	Greenality Planning
Identify who are the customers.	Identify who are the customers.
Determine the needs of those customers.	Determine objectives.
Translate those needs into our language.	Translate those objectives (SMARTER).[b]
Develop a product that can respond to those needs.	Develop a plan to address those objectives (SMART**ER**).
Optimize the product features so as to meet our needs and customers' needs.	Optimize the green objectives so as to meet our needs and customers' needs.
Quality Improvement	**Greenality Improvement**
Develop a process that is able to produce the product.	Develop a process that addresses the greenality issues.
Optimize the process.	Optimize the process.
Quality Control	**Greenality Control**
Prove that the process can produce the product under operating conditions with minimal inspection.	Prove that the process can produce a product with high greenality with a minimal inspection.
Transfer the process to Operations.	Ensure product is environmentally responsible in the future.

[a] Based on the quality management ideas of Joseph Juran in his book, *Quality Control Handbook*, ed. Frank M. Gryna (New York: McGraw-Hill, 1988).
[b] For further information on SMARTER, see Chapter 2.

REDUCING NONPRODUCT OUTPUT

Nonproduct output (NPO) is an interesting phrase used by many to describe production-related wastes that are not part of the final product. It is essentially what is left prior to reuse or recycling, yet after all efforts for redesign and reduction have been exhausted. The first step in reducing NPO is to try to redesign the product or process so that all of the raw materials necessary (including human resources) are utilized to their maximum extent, ultimately producing zero wastes. As an example, if the product you are producing requires the use of disposable batteries, perhaps it can be redesigned to use rechargeable batteries. However, driving out all NPO in a product or process is a feat that is nearly impossible. There seems to always be some sort of by-product. After all, we humans expel CO_2 as a by-product of breathing.

The second step in reducing NPO is to reduce the usage of the type of raw materials that produce waste. Keeping with the previous example,

TABLE 3.3

Issues or Problems Solved by Green Efforts

Author or Source	Natural Step	EPA	Esty/Winston	European Environmental Agency
Friedman				
Issues or Problems to be Solved by Green Efforts				
Global demand for scarce energy	Concentrations of substances extracted from earth's crust	Water	Water scarcity	Climate change
Transfer of wealth to oil-rich countries and petro-dictators	Concentration of substances produced by society	Air	Resource constraints	Stratospheric ozone depletion
Disruptive climate change	Degradation by physical means	Climate	Global warming	Loss of biodiversity
Energy poverty	People subjected to conditions that systematically undermine their capacity to meet their needs	Waste/pollution		Major accidents
		Green living	Extinction of species	Acidification
Rapidly accelerating biodiversity loss		Human health	Growing signs of toxic chemicals in humans and animals	Troposphere ozone
		Ecosystems		Management of freshwater

with new technologies available the product that you are designing to use four AAA batteries may be able to be designed using two AAA batteries instead. This reduction of what appears to be only two batteries is of course multiplied by the number of products you sell—so this could be a reduction of thousands of batteries. And it makes your product more attractive because it is less costly to maintain.

The third step then is to reuse. There is a distinct difference between reuse and recycle. Reuse indicates that the component to be reused does not have to have anything done to it. Recycling denotes that the component needs to have something done to it before it can be reused. A good example of reuse is in the computer industry. There are times when components, like a motherboard, become useless. Rather than fix the motherboard, it is sometimes more prudent to purchase a new computer. The memory chips and in some cases the removable or hard disk drives remain usable and can be ported to the new computer. The old computer is then recycled, and some components are reused.

Within every product and process, there are ways to reduce NPO. It becomes obvious that the more we redesign and reuse, the less NPO there will be, thus the less we need to recycle. Project managers can lead the reduction of NPO by including the planning for reducing NPO in their up-front project management processes.

New-home construction consumes two-fifths of all the lumber and plywood used in the United States each year. Two million tons of straw are burned or buried each year by farmers, enough straw to build 5 million 2,000-square-foot homes.

THE PROJECT MANAGEMENT INSTITUTE AND GREENALITY

To further the previous discussion, the authors are proposing some changes to the fifth edition of *A Guide to the Project Management Book of Knowledge* (*PMBOK Guide*). The fourth edition was released on December 31, 2008, and it likely will be several years before the fifth edition is released. This is the ideal time to get changes in. Those changes include a new subsidiary

plan to the project management plan called the **environmental management plan (EMP)**.[2] This plan will be specifically focused on the environmental and sustainability aspects of projects. The inputs to the plan will
include the environmental objectives, the environmental policy, and the
environmental risks of the project. A template will be provided. Like the
quality management plan template, the EMP contains considerations for
scope, stakeholders, organizational policies, and risk register, and will use
tools similar to those in quality management like benchmarking, cost-benefit analysis, the cost of greenality, etc. Additionally, a new measurement,
earned environmental value management (EEVM), is being proposed as a
tool for monitoring and evaluating environmental performance variance
for the project.

Along with the addition of a new plan, there are other major areas in
project management relevant to greenality. There should be considerations for the environment and sustainability during the creation of the
project charter. Inputs to the statement of work should include environmental considerations as a business need, in the project scope description,
and in the strategic plan. While *ecological impacts* and *social needs* are
listed in the *PMBOK Guide*,[3] they are listed only in the aspects of projects
undertaken for those purposes. We believe that environmental impacts
and social needs are relevant additions to any project. The project manager, as the lead in the green effort, should have a broader application of
those project aspects.

Taking it one step further, and working to build greenality into the
DNA of project managers, we believe that there should be more consideration for the environmental aspects of projects in the Code of Ethics
and Professional Conduct.[4] Natural and environmental resources are
mentioned briefly in the Code of Ethics and Professional Conduct, but the
commitment should be stronger due to the seriousness of the global situation and our own assertions.[5] The PMI has put wording in their updated
core values (for the first value—project management impact) that states:
"Project Management is a critical competence that has a positive influence
on organization results and society." It's vague, but we believe it refers to
sustainability and environmental aspects of a project and its product.

We are proposing that the following be included:

- Our commitment to sustainability means that we will take efforts on
  our projects (considering both the project itself and its product) to
  help eliminate or reduce:

- the buildup of compounds and chemicals in the earth's biosphere
- the progressive physical degradation and destruction of nature and natural processes
- conditions that undermine people's capacity to meet their basic human needs (for example, unsafe working conditions and not enough pay to live on)

Apple's greenhouse gas emissions are approximately 10.2 million metric tons. According to the Web site, "By reducing our packaging over 40 percent between 2006 and 2009, we ship 50 percent more boxes in each airline shipping container. That saves one 747 flight for every 32,000 units we ship." Apple also increased the percentage of weight of products recycled per year from 18.4% in 2007 to 41.9% in 2008, and has an estimated goal of 50% for 2010. Finally, Apple reduces the energy use in the facilities by installing specific sensors for saving million of kilowatts.

—http://www.apple.com

COST OF GREENALITY

Earlier, we discussed the *cost of greenality*. It is similar to the cost of quality in both the construction and, as stated earlier, its sources of opposition. In order to drive greenality into a project, it is pertinent to discuss the impacts if one *doesn't* drive greenality into a project. So what is *greenality*? Greenality could be defined as the conformance to a set of environmental and sustainability objectives set for the project. We would rather think of greenality in terms of stakeholder needs and expectations. Greenality is focused on continually improving the environmental and sustainability of all of the resources consumed on a project. With greenality built into the project from the start (in the earliest planning stages), all of the participants have matching goals and expectations, including the project team. Therefore, greenality is driven internally as well as externally (see the "Stakeholders" section later in the chapter). When we talk internally, we also mean that the executive teams are focused on greenality and will work closely with the project team to continually improve project greenality. Earned environmental value management is part of a common set of objectives tools used to monitor and control project greenality. The "costs" of greenality, therefore, are the same as the costs of quality: prevention costs, appraisal costs, and failure costs. There will be up-front costs to educate individuals, executives, and project managers alike in the methods of setting environmental and sustainability objectives, as well as the development of tools to help with that process. Additionally, there will probably be greenality reviews, which take time and effort to prepare and participate in. There will be costs associated with monitoring and controlling the aspects of environmental and sustainability objectives. Data collection and analysis to help evaluate both the product of the project and the project management process are included as some of those costs. And finally, failure costs are the reason you are investing in all of these aspects of greenality. Some are tangible and immediate; some are harder to enumerate and/or take generations to accrue. With disciplined prevention and appraisal, the cost of what would have been failures, both internal (recycling, reuse, rework) and external (loss of credibility, warranty), will, in most cases, far outweigh the prevention and appraisal costs, and the long-term effect will be addition to the bottom line. So whereas Philip Crosby said quality is free, we say not only is greenality free, but it likely will make money for the organization, a definite positive for the green project manager trying to get this message across to stakeholders.

PROJECT LIFE CYCLE THINKING

Effective project managers are very good at looking at the "global" view. Their thinking is *life cycle thinking,* from project initiation through closure and beyond. The application of green to life cycle thinking is most important because during every phase of the project the environmental impacts are different. In order to understand project life cycle thinking, it is important to define the project's life cycle in this context. There are many ways to portray a project life cycle:

- Plan, organize, control
- Plan, execute, control
- Initiate, plan, execute, monitor and control, close[6]

- Concept, requirements, architectural design, detailed design, coding and development, testing and implementation (classic software systems design)

Whatever the set of phases or process groups you use, there is one more piece to the life cycle that significantly affects the environmental impact, and that is the sustainability of the project, the long-term effect beyond traditional project thinking, and certainly past that date at which the product of the project is handed over to the sponsor.

PROJECT CYCLE OF SUSTAINABILITY

We are all familiar with a project's life cycle, whether it is defined as:

- Plan, organize, control
- Plan, execute, control
- Initiate, plan, execute, close
- Plan, design, implement, deploy

We may not be as familiar with what we'll call the project's cycle of sustainability. It can be defined as the complete cycle of a project that includes not only the beginning of the project through implementation, but also beyond the defined parameters of a project. Specifically, the true end of the project (or sustainability) is the point where the project no longer exists in any form. As an example, take a polystyrene cup that is relegated to a landfill. Think of that polystyrene cup as the product of a project, which it was. It went through an ideation phase, planning phase, manufacturing phase, and deployment phase, and then the project manager(s) went on to another project. The project to put that cup into production may have reached the end of its project life cycle, but not its cycle of sustainability. The end of the cycle of sustainability may be as long as, well, forever. According to a December 1989 article by William Rathie in *The Atlantic*, "Nothing, not paper, plastic or even food, readily degrades in a landfill—and it's not supposed to. Because degradation creates harmful liquid and gaseous by-products that could contaminate groundwater and air, modern landfills are designed to reduce the air, water and sunlight needed for degradation, thereby practically eliminating degradation of waste." That may be an extreme example, and it is necessary for the project manager to consider the cycle of sustainability as part of "understanding the green aspects of their projects."[7] This aspect of the ideation phase will be covered in more depth in Section II of this book.

ENVIRONMENTAL SCOPE

Understanding and controlling the scope of the project is a well-known core of project management responsibility, and PMs who do this well are the ones that succeed. Is there such a thing as "environmental scope"? Really this equates to the life cycle thinking we discussed earlier. In thinking about the environmental scope of a project, it is important for the project manager (and the team) to use the environmental lens—and the life cycle view—to which we've referred before. Thinking about both the project itself and its processes (especially the resources it consumes), and the product of the project in operation and the resources it will consume during operation, the environmental scope can be determined. Well, not really. We also assert that the PM must expand their view (see Chapters 9 and 10) even to the time at which the product of the project will be disposed of. What environmental considerations from that time in the perhaps distant future (from a PM's viewpoint, anyway) may work their way back to the present and affect project scope now? For example, even if the project is a wind farm or other green endeavor, has the team thought through to what happens when that wind farm is decommissioned? Considerations such as this may "feed back" into project scope because it could change what materials are used in the construction of the turbine towers and blades.

ENVIRONMENTAL RISKS

Recall first and foremost that risks are defined as both *threats* and *opportunities*—negative risks being considered threats and positive risks being considered opportunities. With that in mind, the project manager can see that many environmental aspects and their impacts on the project are really project risks (threats and opportunities).

It is important, however, not to lose sight of the environmental risks during the project phases. Full definition and the tools and techniques to manage project environmental impacts (risks) will be provided in Section II. It is also important to note at this stage that there is one other "phase," sustainability, which, though traditionally outside the PM's thinking (see Chapter 9), must be considered in project life cycle thinking.

Cape Wind is proposing America's first offshore wind farm on Horseshoe Shoal in Nantucket Sound. Miles from the nearest shore, 130 wind turbines will gracefully harness the wind to produce up to 420 megawatts of clean, renewable energy.

Save Our Sound is a nonprofit environmental organization dedicated to the long-term preservation of Nantucket Sound. It was formed in 2001 in response to Cape Wind's proposal to build a wind farm in the Sound.

STAKEHOLDERS

When looking at a project through an environmental lens, could that expand the list of project stakeholders? You bet. Might it change the way you view the interests, power, and influence of the stakeholders you've already identified? Yes, we think so. And could it affect the interactions between stakeholders that you've identified? Absolutely! Since PMI defines a stakeholder as anyone who is affected in any way by a project, we could now say that "future generations" are a stakeholder to all projects. Some may find that a bit "fluffy," but it's actually a good way to keep the green aspects of your projects in focus when you identify stakeholders.

ENDNOTES

1. Philip B. Crosby, *Quality Is Free* (New York: Penguin Putnam, 1980).
2. PMI proposal by Rich Maltzman and Dave Shirley, http://www.earthpm.com/community/communitypmi-proposal.
3. *A Guide to the Project Management Book of Knowledge*, 4th ed. (Newtown Square, PA: Project Management Institute, 2008).

4. The Project Management Institute, Code of Ethics and Professional Conduct, http://www.pmi.org/PDF/ap_pmicodeofethics.pdf.
5. The Five Assertions of EarthPM, http://www.earthpm.com/mission/.
6. *A Guide to the Project Management Book of Knowledge,* 39.
7. The Five Assertions of EarthPM, http://www.earthpm.com/mission/.

4

Types of Projects: A Rainbow of Green

All projects have some element of "green." However, projects differ in the amount of environmental or sustainability aspects they contain—and how those aspects manifest themselves. The five assertions of EarthPM apply to all projects (see Figure 4.1), but an especially significant assertion here is "An environmental strategy for a project provides added opportunity for success of both the project and the product of the project." After all, isn't project success what we are after? And, shouldn't our vision—or even our common sense—compel us to extend our definition of success to include the product of the project? We're so focused on the end game being equal to the handoff of the project's product to the project's customer that we sometimes lose sight of the fact that true success means that the customer is made successful by that project's product—in the steady state.

The Green Project

Recycles 15,000 gallons of donated excess paint and 1.8 million pounds of surplus building materials from individuals, businesses, and local governments each year.

Serves over 15,000 loyal and committed customers annually through their retail store, workshops, and outreach events.

Prevents approximately three tons of reusable materials from reaching the dump each day, which equals 1.8 million pounds of trash put back into reuse each year.

Recycles paper, newsprint, aluminum cans, soup cans, household electronics, and corrugated cardboard.

Operates Recycle for the Arts, providing recycled art supplies

---

1. A project run with green intent is the **right thing to do**, but it will also help the project team **do things right**.
2. Project managers must first understand the green aspects of their projects, knowing that this will **better equip them to identify, manage, and respond to project risks**.
3. An environmental strategy for a project provides added opportunity for success of both the project and the **product of the project**.
4. Project managers must view their projects through an **environmental lens**. This increases the project manager's (and the project team's) long-term thinking and avails the project of the rising "green wave" of environmentalism.
5. Project managers must think of the environment **in the same way that they think of quality**. It must be planned in, and the cost of "greenality," like the cost of quality, is more than offset by the savings and opportunities.

FIGURE 4.1
The five assertions of EarthPM.

To understand how the project manager manages the greenality of a project, we must first understand the types of projects we manage in terms of their greenality.

We discovered a *spectrum of green* among projects (see Figure 4.2). That spectrum goes from "green by definition" on one side to "green in general" projects on the other. Let's look at these one by one.

GREEN BY DEFINITION

Green by definition (GBD) projects include those projects whose products or outcomes are "all about" sustainability or the environment. Here we are talking about those projects devoted to saving energy, generating clean energy, protecting natural resources, or preventing loss of species and other outcomes along these lines. Generally, we can say that these projects' main focus is on the Natural Step[1] issues.

One of the greenest of projects in this GBD category is the Green Project, "a nonprofit organization dedicated to creatively promoting and encouraging environmental sustainability in New Orleans."[2] The organization operates a building materials recycling store, with their supplies coming from their own deconstruction and salvage operations, as well as contributions from others in the community. The Green Project, originally the Mid-City Green Project, was conceived as a multipurpose creative recycling center,

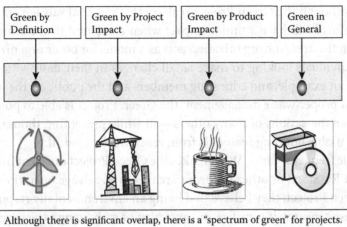

Green by Definition	Green by Project Impact	Green by Product Impact	Green in General

Although there is significant overlap, there is a "spectrum of green" for projects. See the text for examples.

FIGURE 4.2
The "green" spectrum.

based on models from Canada and the United States. It was a fully functioning nonprofit with the appropriate tax status, board of directors, and a rented warehouse (the former Gold Seal Creamery) before a drop of paint was ever accepted, in 1994. The reason the Paint Exchange was started is that no one else was doing it and it needed to be done. It was determined that it would also be a likely candidate to receive one of Entergy's Environmental Matching Grants of $1,000. They did receive the grant, did the research, and, before opening their first Saturday paint collection, they sent press releases tied to miniature paint brushes out to the media. They immediately got a huge response, including all of the neighborhood children showing up. So the first Saturday also turned out to be the beginning of the Children's Art Program—volunteers from Ben Franklin High School's Green Society found flower pots and old chairs out behind the creamery, and got the children painting. After this, every Saturday that they were open they organized art, and later gardening, projects of some type for neighborhood and customers' children. A short time later, the owners of the creamery gave them the use of the empty land in the middle of the block, and the Green Project started both a community garden and a Green Project garden, and sold herbs and vegetables from the latter at the Crescent City Farmers Market until the organization found a new home in the Marigny.

The Building Materials Exchange was also started at the creamery after receiving the first of EPA's sustainability grants, and it soon became the largest component of the Green Project, necessitating the move a few years later. Although the Green Project realizes that material salvage and recycling efforts will have a minor impact when compared to the amount of waste in the area, the organization acts as a model for other organizations and individuals looking to make small changes in their daily actions. By setting an example, and educating members and the public on the importance of proper waste management, the Green Project is able to positively influence the actions of many others—all while preventing thousands of tons of usable building materials from reaching the landfill.

People frequently ask, "What makes the Green Project different from the Habitat Re-Store, or other for-profit architectural salvage operations?" At the Green Project, they believe that living an environmentally responsible life doesn't mean self-sacrifice and austerity, or embracing expensive modern technologies; on the contrary, it should bring you a richer, more interesting, longer and healthier life. Toward that end, they offer multiple ways to promote creative, hands-on recycling. Their educational workshops, Recycle for the Arts program, e-waste recycling, deconstruction fieldwork, latex paint recycling, and community and school outreach events are just as important as the recycled building materials retail store.

One of the best things about the project is that there was little opposition to it, and they have the support of the community, although financial support from the city of New Orleans has been difficult to come by.

Another example of a fascinating GBD project, on a small scale, is the collection of the miniature wind farm projects on the rooftops in New York City. It's not really a new idea. In the mid-1970s, a group installed a serviceable miniature turbine on an East Village rooftop, but it's now been taken to new heights (excuse the pun). Fast-forward to the present day, and developers are now designing buildings with the *intention* of using wind power to supply part of the energy. With high fuel costs and the "green wave," people are considering alternative energy more and more. Wind farms are constructed in open areas. How to best design rooftop wind farms in vertical, urban environments is a continuing challenge to be met by architects and the wind energy industry.

The mini-wind farm is actually a part of a bigger green effort, The Eltona, a 63-unit, five-story, low-income residential rental building located in the Bronx. It is constructed entirely of precast concrete and was completed in cooperation with New York State's Department of Housing and Community Renewal's Homes for Working Families Program and the New York City Housing and Development Corporation's Low-Income Affordable Marketplace Program (LAMP). The building will also be a subject of a study by Mt. Sinai School of Medicine on the effects of living in a green building on families who suffer from asthma.

The building will feature an array of sealed turbine components needing no lubrication, each rated at one kilowatt and having a 40- to 50-year life span. The turbines are mounted on its parapet walls, a system recently approved by Con Edison (New York City's power company). On the plus side, small wind power projects can produce "clean" power with no harmful emissions. If the building has a good wind source, the costs of the mini-wind farm may well be offset by the savings in energy off the Con Ed grid.

As we said before, this is breaking new ground. There hasn't been much time to evaluate the project, so no one knows how successful a mini-wind farm will be, how many wind power devices will be needed, what is the best way to site a device, how much weight is ultimately involved, or even a good method to measure the wind on top of a building. There is no good process developed, yet. Since the first tours of The Eltona took place in July 2009, it is too early to tell how successful generating needed power to the building will be, although Blue Sea Development Company, responsible for the building's construction, says it has done enough research to conclude that the effort is worth the investment. It is certainly something to watch.

A slightly different take on GBD is the Green Allowance (GA) Project, founded and led by Paul Reale. It is a very clever project combining economic incentive with limiting the use of scare resources. It is a human "green" project. No, not the Hulk, but rather a project intended to produce a change in behavior. The focus of the project is to encourage children to "help" their parents conserve energy and make a deal to participate in the energy savings. Children will be provided with very specific tips and techniques to educate their parents. Those tips and techniques will not be given rapid-fire to the children, but rather, presented in manageable blocks. The first iteration will be on how to help conserve electricity. Later iterations of the project will be focused on conserving water and other limited resources. The reasoning behind giving children a few things at a time is so they are not overwhelmed with the effort, something that all project managers should take into consideration, whether children are involved or not. Additionally, the GA Project will provide tracking methods on their Web site, http://www.greenallowance.org, so that children can record and track their energy-saving efforts.

The payoff for the children will come in the deal that they make with their parents. As an example, if the monthly electric bill shows a savings of $20 over the previous month when the methods were not implemented, and the children made a deal for 50% of the savings, they would realize a $10 "allowance." The ability to measure an objective is one of the key fundamentals of project management. The ability to show value from a project is just as important.

Another advantage to the GA Project is the fact that the energy companies are just as interested in energy savings as the children and their parents— for the same reason, economics. It is very expensive to upgrade and expand power-producing facilities. In some regulated states, profits are not linked to volume of sales, another incentive for power companies to conserve. Even with the most altruistic intentions, the question "What's in it for me?" (WIIFM) arises. The subtitle to Gary Hirshberg's book *Stirring It Up* is *How to Make Money and Save the World*.[3] Money and sound environmental judgment are not mutually exclusive. As a matter of fact, they are closely linked today.

Besides the product of the project, creating the green allowance, the *project itself,* is also carefully being kept green. The GA Project is dedicated to becoming carbon neutral. Some of the things that Paul has done to reduce his own carbon footprint are: (1) when anyone has to travel to meet customers, they purchase a carbon offset. As we've said before, carbon off- sets may be controversial. In Paul's opinion, "we are living in a world that is carbon intensive. Until that transformation to a carbon neutral society, we have to deal with it. To reach a zero footprint practically, you ultimately have to offset something."[4] It is an opinion the authors share.

Further, it is the continual evaluation of how resources are being used on this project and others that, again, makes the project manager a lead- ing advocate for green. That's what project managers have always done— resource evaluation and efficient usage of the available resources.

Finally, the Green Allowance Project, in effect, is trying to create mil- lions of (budding) project managers among the children it reaches. Each child participates in the mini-project of conserving limited, scarce resources. They will use tools and techniques, manage expectations, look at the actual energy consumption data, and receive feedback in the form of an allowance should the project prove successful.

Examples of other projects that are GBD are forest reclamation, estab- lishing a wildlife preserve, increasing green awareness (global confer- ences), carbon exchange programs (Jet Blue), carbon offsets (TerraPass), and a commuter rail line.

One of the granddaddies of projects that fit in this category is one that many Americans have not yet heard about—DESERTEC. "Our Sun offers a way out: Within the space of six hours, the world's deserts receive more energy than all the people in the world consume in a year."[5] The only question we have to answer is: how can this radiant energy be economically transformed into useful energy and transported to consumers?

The DESERTEC concept provides a solution to this. From the DESERTEC's Red Paper[6]: "In fact it simultaneously tackles efficiently all the global challenges of the upcoming decades mentioned before: shortage of energy, water and food as well as excessive emissions of CO_2. At the same time, this concept offers new options for the prosperity and development of regions that have so far, from an economic point of view, been scarcely developed—as well as promising new opportunities for the economically leading countries."

Studies by the German Aerospace Center (DLR) show that, within 40 years, solar thermal power plants in particular will be capable of generating economically more than half of the electricity needs of the EUMENA region (Europe, the Middle East, North Africa) at that time.

CLEAN ENERGY IS AVAILABLE IN ABUNDANCE IN THE EARTH'S DESERT BELT.

North and south of the equator, deserts span the earth. Over 90% of the world's population could be supplied with clean power from deserts by using technologies that are available today.

In order to meet today's global power demand of 18,000 TeraWatt hours per year, it would suffice to equip about three-thousandths of the world's deserts (about 90,000 square kilometers) with solar collectors of solar thermal power plants. About 20 square meters of desert would be enough to meet the individual power demand of one human being day and night (see later discussion)—all this absolutely CO_2 free. Given the political will, it would be possible to achieve a worldwide realization of the DESERTEC concept in less than 30 years.

The DESERTEC concept will allow most people in the world to access solar and wind power from the energy-rich desert areas. This would be a useful addition to the renewable-energy resources of each region. By using high-voltage direct current (HVDC) transmission lines, it is possible to transfer power with losses of no more than 3% per 1,000 kilometers. Given the relatively high intensity of sunlight in desert regions and the relatively small variations between summer and winter, the benefits of generating electricity in desert regions will more than outweigh the cost of long-distance transmission. More than 90% of the people in the world live within 3,000 kilometers of a desert and may be supplied with solar electricity from there.[7]

GREEN BY PROJECT IMPACT (OR THE LACK THEREOF)

Projects that are green by impact include those that may not have a green outcome, like an electric car, but do have an immediate (positive) impact on their environment. It can be argued that every project has an immediate impact on their environment, and that statement would not be wrong. However, what we are referring to here are those projects that have an immediate and significant impact on their environment. These projects may or not be intended to be green, but by nature, they will significantly affect, positively or negatively, the environment. These are also projects in which both the process and the product will have significant and immediate environmental impact. To clarify let's look closely at a couple of projects—one on the sea and one under the ground.

On the Sea

There is an enormous project being undertaken in the port of Dubai in the United Arab Emirates. The need for the expansion of Dubai's facilities to accommodate an increasing number of cruise ships visiting their port is the driving force behind the project. There was the option of physically changing the harbor, filling, and relocating businesses, thereby reconfiguring the port, or coming up with a new solution. Either way, the project would involve significant impact to the environment of Dubai. The result was to propose a new solution that would not involve reconfiguring the existing port, but rather building a floating cruise ship terminal. Koen Olthuis of Waterstudio.NL, a Dutch architectural firm, came up with a unique solution. Based on technology used in his native Holland, that of floating houses, Koen proposed a triangular floating terminal 300 × 300 × 300 meters. The Dubai government responded with a request that he design a floating terminal 700 × 700 × 700 meters with one corner being 35 meters high. Having that corner so high would allow water taxis to pass underneath the raised lip to enter the inner harbor. The outer edges of the triangle would allow the largest cruise ships to dock. The interior of the terminal would contain retail shops, restaurants, hotel, conference rooms, and more. To give you some perspective on the project, it is like having three supertankers rafted together.

It is easy to see the extent of the immediate environmental impact the project would have. For some environmental activists, this type of development is what Koen calls "scarless." In other words, there is no real impact to the earth as far as filling wetlands, digging foundations, or demolishing existing buildings along the waterfront to make room for such a huge development. To other environmental activists, it will mean disruption of the natural flow of the life in the water surrounding the project. There would be an increase in boat traffic carrying workers to and from the work site. Anchoring mechanisms would have to be secured to the bottom of the sea. There are both positive and negative environmental impacts depending on your point of view. Either way, the project is green by direct impact.

Going Underground

Another infrastructure project that certainly wasn't green focused, but had significant impact to the environment is the Big Dig Project in Boston, Massachusetts. The purpose of the Big Dig was to mitigate the traffic situation in downtown Boston. In 1959, the Central Artery was opened and could comfortably carry about 75,000 vehicles a day. By the early 1990s, it was carrying 200,000 vehicles a day, and by 2010, it was expected to be a stop-and-go traffic jam for 16 hours a day.[8] There was no doubt that a new solution (a project) was needed.

The project had a two-pronged approach: (1) replace the six-lane elevated highway with an 8- to 10-lane underground expressway directly beneath the existing road, and (2) extend the Massachusetts Turnpike through a tunnel beneath South Boston and Boston Harbor to Logan Airport. The first link in the new connection, the Ted Williams Tunnel, was completed under the harbor in 1995.

One can only imagine the environmental impact the project would have, in both immediacy and significance. The southern end of the underground highway was completely rebuilt on six levels, including two subterranean. In South Boston, a mostly underground interchange carries traffic between the Mass Pike and the developing Boston waterfront. Heavy equipment was deployed throughout the project, adding to air quality issues; sediment protection from the digging needed to be put in place, to say nothing of the dredging spoils. However, because a project is green by direct impact doesn't mean it doesn't have significant green accomplishments.

Big Dig Facts

The project placed 3.8 million cubic yards of concrete, enough to build a sidewalk three feet wide and four inches thick from Boston to San Francisco and back three times.

The underground Central Artery will carry about 245,000 vehicles a day by 2010 versus 75,000 a day before.

The project excavated a total of 16 million cubic yards of dirt, enough to fill Foxboro Stadium (where the Patriots football team and Revolution soccer team play) to the rim 15 times.

With the Big Dig, Spectacle Island in Boston Harbor was created when project dirt was used to cap an abandoned landfill. Additionally, clay and dirt from the project was used to cap other abandoned landfills in the area. According to the Massachusetts Transportation Agency (MTA), there was a 12% reduction in carbon monoxide in downtown Boston directly attributed to the project. Additionally, open space was created when the old elevated highway was demolished, and there was an emphasis during the project to keep Boston open for business, protecting the livelihood of the city's merchants. No matter what type of project it is, it is incumbent on the project manager to understand the green aspects of their projects, provide an environmental strategy, view their project through an "environmental lens," and build in "greenality." Like the Big Dig, projects with immediate and significant environmental impacts can result in a positive if properly project managed. The Big Dig has many other interesting project management aspects along the lines of scope control, communications, and contract management—but it would take a separate book (or two) for that. We've limited our coverage to where the Big Dig fits on the spectrum of green.

GREEN BY PRODUCT IMPACT

Projects that are green by product impact are those whose main focus is not green but would have impact not in the project itself, but mainly in the *steady-state operation of the end product.* The product of the project's purpose is not directly related to energy saving, resource protection, and habitat preservation among other things. The main focus of the outcome of these projects is not sustainability or reduction in the Natural Step[9] issues (i.e., biodiversity). However, built in to that operation handoff is the process beyond the project's end. It sounds like a contradiction to the definition of a project, a temporary endeavor with a definitive beginning and end, but we feel that being environmentally responsible means going that extra step to ensure that long-term impacts for the project are considered.

A great example of a project that is "green by indirect impact" is the Beloit Casino Project. The Bad River Band of the Lake Superior Tribe of Chippewa Indians and the St. Croix Chippewa Indians of Wisconsin are proposing a casino complex to be located in the city of Beloit, Wisconsin. Proposed is a casino hotel entertainment complex. Along with the casino itself, the proposal includes a convention center, theater, and year-round water park. One of the more obvious indirect impacts of the project is the fact that it would produce 1,500 jobs during the building of the casino, and 3,000 permanent jobs when it was in operation. Additionally, it would generate hundreds of millions of dollars in economic growth for the area, an area with a demonstrated economic need to both improve and support a better quality of life. That is an effort to improve people's lives, or at the least, "eliminate our contribution to conditions that undermine people's capacity to meet their basic human needs (for example, unsafe working conditions and not enough pay to live on)."[10] Additionally, the tribes' application included a full environmental impact statement based on years of public hearings and archeological surveys in an effort to protect the environment and any cultural heritage that may be disrupted.

Other green by indirect impact projects include projects like the major expansion of a factory or building new facilities, as well as the introduction of a new disposable razor. In fact, one good example, which we've discussed on our EarthPM Web site, is that of the single-serve disposable-pod coffeemakers, such as Tassimo and Keurig—the little nonrecyclable pods or cups that go inside them and then are discarded after seconds of use.

In an article by Scott Kirsner in the *Boston Globe*,[11] the subject of the Keurig coffeemaker and the "K-cups" is discussed. Green Mountain Coffee owns Keurig (they bought it in 2005; to read more go to http://boston.bizjournals.com/boston/stories/2006/05/01/daily33.html).   The article discussed the quandary Green Mountain finds itself in as a "responsible" company with a conscience. In fact, they do work hard on fair trade for the coffee itself.

But the K-cups are another story. They are made from **nonrecyclable materials**. And although the cups themselves are small, their numbers are huge. Last year alone, over 1.6 billion (yes, *billion!*) cups were used. My calculations say that this is *enough K-cups to circle the earth one and a quarter times.* And they all go into landfills after their seconds of use and stay there for hundreds or thousands of years. And that's just Keurig. There is also Tassimo, Senseo, and others. Further, the forecast for K-cup sales is 3 billion in 2010 and 5 billion in 2011. *So now we are talking about a chain of K-cups from 2009, 2010, and 2011 made up of 9 or 10 billion units and circling the earth eight times!*

This has prompted Keurig to make this environmental statement:

KEURIG'S ENVIRONMENTAL STATEMENT:

Sharing Our Commitment for a Better Planet

All of us at Keurig are citizens first and employees second! We are committed as a company to responsible business practices that sustain our environment for all.

In fact, our parent company Green Mountain Coffee Roasters, Inc. (GMCR) is a leader in developing Fair Trade/Organic coffee blends that are great for coffee lovers, coffee growers, and our planet. Also GMCR is repeatedly cited for best practices in business ethics.

As such, we'd like to share what we are doing at Keurig and what we are doing in cooperation with GMCR to build a better world for both gourmet coffee lovers ... and lovers of best practices in corporate responsibility.

Sustainable Packaging

K-Cup Portion Pack Packaging is an area of major environmental concern for all consumer product companies. As the single-cup coffee market and our Keurig brewing systems grow in popularity, we understand that the impact of the K-Cup Portion Pack waste stream is one of our most significant environmental challenges. The K-Cup package is made up of three main elements— the cup itself, a filter and an aluminum foil top. The polyethylene coating of the foil—as well as the process of heat-sealing the various elements—makes recycling difficult.

However, this packaging approach prevents oxygen, light and moisture from degrading the coffee. Without the barrier the packaging materials provide, we could not maintain the quality and freshness of the coffee, which means that all the resources and effort put into growing and roasting great coffee would be wasted. Finding a more environmentally-friendly approach to this packaging challenge is a big priority for us. We are working on a few different fronts to improve the environmental characteristics of the K-Cup system, as well as to mitigate its impact.

Here's what we are doing

We are actively researching alternatives to the K-Cup Portion Pack's petroleum-based materials.

*We are conducting a **Life Cycle Analysis** to help us understand the overall environmental impact of the K-Cup Portion Pack as compared to the use of a typical drip-brewer. There are environmental considerations at every step on the road from "tree to cup". By studying the K-Cup over its entire life cycle, we can more clearly understand how and where we can reduce its footprint.*

We are working to identify the right definition of "environmentally friendly" for all our packaging, including the K-Cup Portion Pack. For example it could mean carbon-neutral, made with renewable materials, recyclable, biodegradable, compostable, petroleum-free, all of the above, or something entirely different. We are researching what is possible today and tomorrow, taking into account the current state of packaging technology, consumer preferences, community infrastructure, performance requirements, and the demands of the marketplace.

We also continue to offer the My K-Cup, a reusable filter cartridge assembly that can be refilled by the consumer, is easily cleaned, and is compatible with all Keurig home brewers sold today.

So we can see that it's the operation (or more succinctly put, the use) of the single-serve coffeemakers that is causing the impact.

GREEN—GENERAL

There are a multitude of projects that we all can name that would seem to be devoid of any green at all: developing a new software release, developing a new curriculum at college, or producing a movie. Even though we don't see them as green projects, we assert that every project has an opportunity to improve its greenality. The project team can still gain insight from this spectrum. Let's take a new software release, for example. They can think of their project as green in general, because the project itself will not have such a tremendous impact, nor will the product. But both will have some impact. The project team can collaborate virtually to save paper and travel, the information technology (IT) departments involved

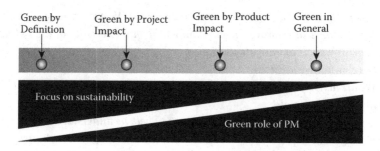

As the project's focus is less and less green, the PM must assert a stronger and stronger role in order to have a positive effect on the sustainability of the project.

FIGURE 4.3
Role of the PM as greenality focus changes.

can "green" their servers, and in general, the team can promote green practices. For their product, they can increase the attractiveness of electronic downloading versus physical distribution, and in physical distribution they can improve the sustainability of the packaging. This is what we mean by green in general.

In Section II, we will explore the tools and techniques first to help identify these opportunities, and second to take advantage of them.

A RAINBOW OF GREEN

We've presented examples along our "Rainbow of Green." What's also important to know is that *the role of the project manager changes* as the focus on green changes. In Figure 4.3, we can see that as the focus on green goes down and the projects move from "Green by Definition" to "Green in General," the project manager will need to take a stronger and stronger role in order to make a difference on these projects. The connection to sustainability will not be as obvious and prevalent in the project, so it will require that increased effort on the part of the project manager.

ENDNOTES

1. The Natural Step, "4 Sustainability Principles," http://www.naturalstep.org/.
2. The Green Project, *Welcome to the Green Project; About.* http://www.thegreenproject.org/.

3. G. Hirshberg, *Stirring It Up: How to Make Money and Save the World* (New York: Hyperion, 2008).

4. Paul Reale, founder and CEO of GreenAllowance, interview, http://www.earthpm.com/interviews/.

5. DESERTEC Foundation, *Red Paper: An Overview of the DESERTEC Concept,* http://www.desertec.org/fileadmin/downloads/DESERTEC_RedPaper_2nd_en.pdf.

6. DESERTEC Foundation Red Paper, *An Overview of the DESERTEC Concept,* http://www.desertec.org/fileadmin/downloads/desertec-foundation_redpaper_3rd-edition_english.pdf , pg. 6]

7. DESERTEC Foundation, *Red Paper: An Overview of the DESERTEC Concept,* http://www.desertec.org/fileadmin/downloads/DESERTEC_RedPaper_2nd_en.pdf.

8. The Massachusetts Department of Transportation, *The Big Dig: Project Background,* http://www.massdot.state.ma.us/Highway/bigdig/.

9. The Natural Step, "4 Sustainability Principles."

10. Ibid.

11. http://www.boston.com/business/articles/2010/01/03/an_environmental_quandary_percolates_at_green_mountain_coffee_roasters.

Section II

Hiking the Project

In every walk with nature one receives far more than he seeks.

John Muir

5

Project Ideation

Every journey begins with the first step. "Hiking" through any project is always a journey, an adventure. *Webster's New Collegiate Dictionary*[1] defines *adventure* as "an undertaking involving danger and unknown risks." It also defines *adventure* as "an exciting or remarkable experience." Sound familiar? Whether projects involve danger or unknown risks depends on the type of project undertaken and the environment in which it's executed, but we can all agree that projects involve risks and they can be an exciting experience. No matter how many projects you have run before, by nature and definition, every project will be different. Sometimes it may be only that the project is taking place in a different time frame than a similar successful project—and even that makes it an adventure. Green project management adds another dimension, *greenality*, to an already complex discipline. One could argue that the greenality of a project adds additional risks, particular challenges, and excitement to the project along with the possibility for an enhanced sense of accomplishment. We think that it's fundamental for PMs to think of this work not as a burden but as an integrated part of their work. If we keep the analogy we often hear of "having too much on our plate," well, we suggest that you think of the green aspect of projects as adding only extra vitamins and minerals to the existing nourishment, and not adding anything bulky to the plate. To reiterate, it is our contention that *all projects* have some green aspect to them; therefore, the greenality of a project is one of the fundamental project characteristics that will be prevalent throughout the project life cycle (see Figure 5.1).

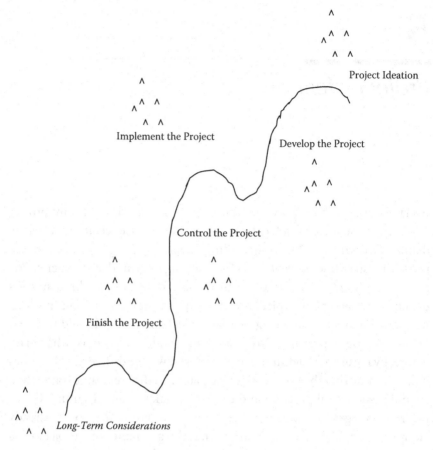

FIGURE 5.1
Hiking the project life cycle.

WHY ARE PROJECTS INITIATED?

The most compelling reason that a project is initiated is *customer demand*. Customer demand, however, may include the demands of a particular organization's large group of customers. An example of that type of demand may be that a group of customers of Sony's PlayStation wanted a better joystick to add to the PlayStation 3, a green-general (G-G) project. It may also be at the suggestion of one customer that an organization responds. An example of that would be the following. A customer of Stonewall Kitchen, a specialty-food manufacturer, enjoys the raspberry jam, but is now intolerant to seeds. The company takes that suggestion, does some market research to see if there is a need for a product like that, and then decides to produce a seedless raspberry jam, the launch of which would be another example of a G-G project. While the project is G-G, the company continues its green efforts. According to Laura Duncan, director of marketing for Stonewall Kitchen, "Stonewall recycled 65% of our wastes, over 2 tons in 2009," including recycling cardboard, metal, plastic, fiber drums, office paper, glass bottles, vegetable oil, and ink cartridges.

Market demand is another of the principal reasons projects are initiated. Something in the market has changed. Market demand is a broader application of customer demand. It differs from customer demand in that it is more of an aggregate demand from all (or most) participants in a market segment. One only has to look at the demand for more-efficient automobiles (hybrids) to see the effect of market demand on car makers. First introduced as a concept car in 1995, Toyota began delivering them to the U.S. market in January 2002, but couldn't fulfill all the Internet orders until mid-2002. As this book goes to press, the demand for the Prius continues to outpace production.[2] The Prius, in addition to being an example of a market-demanded product, is also an example of a project that is Green by Product Impact. And now, we're on the verge of the introduction of the first fully electric cars such as the Chevrolet Volt and the Nissan Leaf.

Projects can be initiated within the business environment: the company's product is obsolete, competition has forced a change, a new "visionary" has taken over the company and wishes to take it in a different direction, or the business is being restructured by merger or acquisition.

Projects can also be initiated because technological advances *force* the company to react, just to keep up. Alternatively, the company may want to be on an industry's leading edge and proactively initiate a new technology. New regulations may be a driving force behind project initiation. New funding may be available for certain new products or services (this is actually the case for many thousands of green projects as we write this book).

With the advent of the Health Insurance Portability and Accountability Act of 1996 (HIPAA), the health care industry has had to initiate many projects. In the telecom business, local number portability (LNP)—the FCC ruling that as a consumer you had the right to keep your same phone number even if you changed carriers—was a stimulus for hundreds of infrastructure projects. No matter what the impetus, organizations must respond to them with projects if they are to survive.

HOW ARE PROJECTS CHOSEN?

Now that we've briefly discussed the "why," we need to look at the "how." Not all identified projects within any organization can be chosen. "All projects should support the organization's strategic goals. The strategic plan of the performing organization should be considered as a factor when making project selection decisions and prioritization."[3] If the company has (as many now do) strategic goals that are tied to climate change and social responsibility, this is a key linkage of which the project manager and team must be aware. Economics, resource availability, timeliness, or ability to execute may influence whether or not a project is accepted. The process of picking a project in some organizations, in spite of all of the great ideas and reasoning, can be complex, vague, inequitable, and downright mysterious. To put it in perspective, however, a project should be chosen for very specific reasons, such as: it satisfies a business or human need, it fits with the strategic plan of the organization, and it has been determined doable (financially, technically). However, there is one more criterion that should be considered: that is, the environmental responsibility of the project, or its ability to satisfy a greenality component, because "a project run with green intent is the right thing to do."[4] As asserted previously and supported by the *PMBOK Guide*, the project should link with the strategic plan of the organization. Any project manager should be able to point "up" to reference their team as to how their particular project contributes to the enterprise vision. Without that, not only will the team be undermotivated, but even if they *are* motivated, they are producing a deliverable that doesn't make a contribution to the organization's *raison d'être*. We assert that greenality must be part of the decision-making process. It is part of the SMARTER (see Figure 5.2) objectives and the stakeholder analysis. It was previously mentioned that stakeholders are becoming increasingly aware of green components in every project undertaken. If consideration of green components is not in the criteria for decision making, then that decision alone could lead to project failure—the inability of the project to meet or exceed customer expectations. Here we include those expectations as outlined in "Surfing the Green Wave" (Section I). Customers increasingly expect your project, and the product of the project, to be green. Decision making is a mental process in which individual project fundamentals are discussed in the context of the project's purpose, and then a selection or selections is/are

Specific
Measurable
Attainable
Related to the Goal
Timely
Environmentally
Responsible

FIGURE 5.2
SMARTER.

made from among those alternatives. So, how do we add a green component to decision-making tools?

DECISION-MAKING TOOLS AND THE GREEN COMPONENT

Because it is a relatively new field, selecting and managing projects with green components throughout the project can require a different—or at least enhanced—decision-making process. The sensitivity around the "conflicting" information about global warming, for instance, creates a different meeting dynamic. To avoid getting bogged down with extraneous information, or baggage, associated with green issues, a particularly constructive decision-making environment must be created.

CREATING THE "GREEN"-FRIENDLY DECISION-MAKING ENVIRONMENT

The first effort to establishing a "green"-friendly environment is to make sure that the objectives are clearly articulated. Being SMARTER (see Figure 5.2) will certainly help that. The objectives should be all of that, and particularly environmentally responsible (ER). Once the objectives, with their ER components, are clearly defined, then the process used to make the decision should be defined and approved by the body. For instance, how will the decisions be made? Via committee, by one designated individual, by an executive? Who else needs to be involved in the decision-making process? Have we identified any one (or more) stakeholder as critical to the decision-making process? Have all those who should be heard in the process been heard? These questions are all considered with the ER in mind. The environmental policy of the enterprise, if it exists, should be ever-present in this process as well.

CHANGING THE WAY PEOPLE THINK ABOUT GREEN

Part of creating a green-friendly decision-making environment is helping the people in the process understand that there is a new way to think about green. Once people realize the truth in that statement, the more creative they will be around green issues, thus the friendlier the environment will be. One way to do that is to have the facts available to be able to challenge those who may have made uniformed or misinformed assumptions. See Chapter 14, "Resource Information," for information on where to find the facts.

Another technique to use to help change the way people think is to reengineer the issue. To decide whether or not a green component exists in the project, assume the scenario that it doesn't and explore the issues caused by not including it in the project. This scenario-based thinking exercise can be an eye opener. Let's use the implementation of a new video game as an example. Again, this is a thinking exercise too. Go to an extreme. Assume that there is *no* green planning or consideration for the project, *no* thought given to green packaging, the product will be deployed in a standard way, and there is no greening of the process. What effect will it have, just on the environment? Start a list of the consequences. On the top of the list will be the thousands or millions, if it is a very popular game, of pounds of plastic packaging, tons of CO_2 generated by the trucks delivering the product, to say nothing of the wasted electricity by the developers leaving lights and computers on over weekends, holidays, overnight. Also, important to note, have we thought about the disposal of the project resources when the project is complete? How about the disposal of the materials of the product itself? The list can be exhaustive, and it will be plain that there certainly *is* a green component (or, more likely, a bunch of them) to the project. Once the green-friendly environment is created, it is time to get into the actual decision-making process. What tools will be most effective for green issues?

It takes about 20 billion barrels of oil to make 5 trillion plastic bags. Americans alone use more than 380 billion polyethylene bags and throw away approximately 100 billion of them per year. Only about 1% of these plastic bags are recycled.

Scientists estimate that it takes 1,000 years for a polyethylene bag to break down, and as polyethylene breaks down, toxic substances leach into the soil and enter the food chain.

—**From ABC.com,** *Good Morning America*

DECISION-MAKING TOOLS

Most of the decision-making tools—Pareto analysis, decision tree, six thinking hats, etc.—can be adapted to include green components in the process. We have listed just a few of our favorites.

Brainstorming

The foundation of *brainstorming* is a free exchange of ideas that are then "boarded" with virtually no screening or judgment. No matter how strange ideas may seem at the time, they should all be boarded for later discussion and screening.

One of our favorite stories we like to tell about brainstorming is "The Polar Bear Story."

> A northern Canadian electric utility company was having problems with lines coming down because of icing. Ice coating the lines made them too heavy and they would collapse, interrupting service and possibly causing harm (fire, shock). So they decided to brainstorm ways to prevent or remove the ice. People in the team started to list ideas, and the moderator recorded them:
>
> - "Teflon coating of wires"
> - "Heating elements around the outside of the cables"
> - And so on
>
> *Jim, one of the team members, shouts out, "Polar bears."*
> *The moderator initially didn't write this down, but then remembered that the rules of brainstorming call for NO ELIMINATION at the EARLY STAGE.*

So she dutifully wrote down "polar bears" on the flip chart. "Next?" she says. A few more ideas come out, and they move to the next state.

The next stage of brainstorming is to go through the ideas and one by one, following them through with "how to implement."

When they got to "polar bears," the moderator dutifully said, "OK, Jim, you had this one, how are polar bears going to help?" Jim shrugs and says, "I dunno, we have polar bears shake the towers, knocking the ice off the wires." The moderator says, "Okaaaay, how do we get the polar bears to be attracted to the towers, Jim?" He shrugs again and says, "Um, how about we, just put big pots of honey at the top of the towers, I guess." So the moderator says, "And how are we supposed to fill those pots of honey, Jim?" Jim says, "Hmmm, I guess just fly some helicopters out and they can ..." Suddenly, an engineer named Tom interrupts. "Wait!" he exclaims. "Don't helicopters have a huge, vibrating downdraft from their blades?" Everyone stopped to consider this point, because they realized that this was the solution to the problem. To this day, this company clears their lines by flying helicopters over the lines—not to fill honey pots, but to directly solve the problem—via a downdraft that shakes the ice free.

What is the moral of the story? You *want* people like Jim in your meeting, and if you are brainstorming, write down *all* of the ideas.

It is therefore important that the group participating in the exercise have a "green advocate" who will represent green thinking. Those ideas generated by the advocate will inevitably lead to others in the group considering and voicing additional green ideas. Until green thinking becomes ingrained, an advocate will have to be used.

Reverse Brainstorming

Because it is sometimes difficult to make decisions on green components for a variety of reasons, *reverse brainstorming* is a good alternative to regular brainstorming. It is similar to reengineering in that instead of solving the problem, you determine how to create the problem. Once all of the ideas are generated as to how to create the problem, or make it worse, then the effort begins as to how to mitigate or reverse the damage. In this case, we would try to come up with all of the ideas that would make the project or its project create as much environmental havoc as possible—and then use that to come up with ideas of how to prevent those things. Influence diagrams are very helpful tools when doing any type of brainstorming (see Figure 5.3).

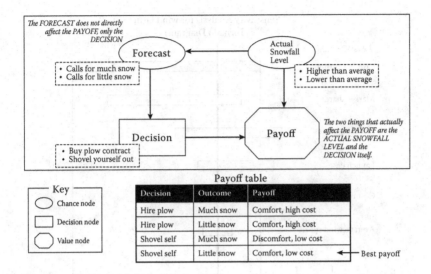

FIGURE 5.3
Influence diagram example.

Force Field Analysis

One of the best tools used to make decisions on green projects is force field analysis, developed by Kurt Lewin, an American social scientist. The reason that it is so effective as a decision-making tool for green projects is that the basis of the force field analysis is that the forces opposed to the project are measured against those that support the project. All forces should be considered including environmental responsibility (see Figure 5.4).

There are also ways to weight or numerically prioritize the forces to be able to make a better decision. It is also a better decision because all of the forces, for and against, are identified. So aside from the high-level project description, how the project fits in with the business strategy of the organization, and any other information collected in relationship to past projects, *green intent* is considered as an input to project ideation. The output, then, would be a project charter that includes the green component.

Cost-Benefit Analysis

Probably one of the more important decision-making tools for including green components is the cost-benefit analysis. The reason that it is such an important tool is within the structure of the analysis—green benefits as well as green costs can be documented. In March 2009, Sheila Blake of the city of Houston presented a cost-benefit analysis for Cool Roof to the EPA

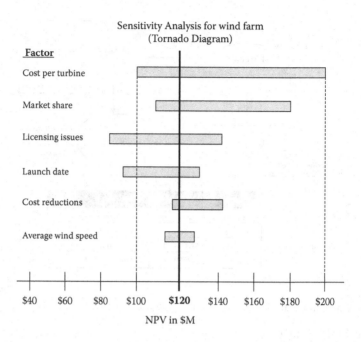

FIGURE 5.4
Sensitivity analysis for wind farm.

Sustainable Communities Conference in Dallas, Texas. The purpose of the cost-benefit analysis was to show that the additional effort required to install new or retrofit existing roofs to make them cooler (therefore more energy efficient) would be offset by savings. Along with adding insulation, the recommendation included the installation of light-colored roofs. According to the presentation, light-colored roofs keep buildings cooler, thereby reducing air-conditioning costs, reducing the need for carbon-based fuels for electrical generation, inhibiting the formation of smog, reducing Urban Heat Island,[5] and also reducing the thermal cycling effect on the life span of the roof. The cost-benefit analysis took into consideration four scenarios: strip retail, three- to five-story office building, apartment building, and a typical unconditioned warehouse space. Two cost aspects were considered, capital investment (comparison of roof costs versus life expectancy) and operational (energy) costs. The resulting analysis showed that, assuming a 15-year life for the roof, a 20% premium in cost, R-11 insulation for a retrofit, and R-19 for a new installation, the savings would be as shown in Table 5.1.

The cost-benefit analysis was an ideal place to include all of the green components. However, only one of the three components was actually

TABLE 5.1

Comparison of Savings by Insulating

Building Type	New	Retrofit
Apartment	$132	$425
Unconditioned warehouse	$0	$0
Strip-retail	$1,077	$1,789
Office	$219	$482

used in the calculations—the energy savings. The other two, the inhibiting of the smog and the reduction of the Urban Heat Island effect, were not quantified as far as we can tell. By putting a price tag on the other two green components, the savings would have been significantly greater. For a complete picture then, all of the green components should be quantified.

Please note that all of this analysis did not even take into consideration the intangibles of marketing advantage, employee morale, and the "right thing to do" aspects of greenality. These may not be visible, and we acknowledge that they are difficult to measure, but they are very much present and real.

Whatever the technique used in making decisions, there are a couple of additional considerations. With every decision there are risks, so a risk analysis should be conducted to ensure that not only project risks are considered, but also the likelihood that they will occur and the consequences. At this stage of the project, it is not a complete risk analysis as that will come later, but it is a consideration. Sources relative to decision-making tools can be found in Chapter 13.

VALIDATION OF THE DECISION

A sanity check for both the decision and the decision-making process is needed. It is a double check to ensure the process used and the decision made to pursue the project were done objectively. For instance, did we consider resources with regard to availability and competency, especially considering the green components of the project? When we considered SMARTER objectives, does this solution match with the considerations, particularly the ER? Looking toward sustainability, does this project meet that objective? Have we evaluated all the alternative project ideas to validate whether or not this project is the best one, again, considering the ER in our objectives as one criterion? Have we tested our assumptions, explored any doubts, and looked to see if we have any blind spots? There are many tools used by project managers to validate decisions: paired comparison, decision trees, multivoting, and Delphi, for instance. *At this point there has been no detailed planning, but there should be validation of decisions based on available information during the decision-making (ideation) stage of the project.*

It is also good to seek out "expert judgment" to help validate the project decision. However, because greenality is a relatively new phenomenon in project management, it may be difficult to find someone who has direct experience. In one sense, project managers are "green" by nature, in that conservation of resource usage and aversion to waste is ingrained in our culture as PMs. Most of our literature, training, and practice is focused on the need to reduce resource usage when we can, to reduce project costs or schedule, while keeping the quality high to meet or exceed stakeholder requirements. So asking another project manager to review your information can help validate (or not) your project decision.

Finally, a good decision-making process, at the least, increases the chances of making the right decision on a project, which increases the chances of project success.

CREATING A GREEN CHARTER

What makes a green charter green? How does it differ from the traditional project charter and how is it the same? The last question is probably easiest to answer because a green charter contains all of the information a traditional charter includes. While there are differing opinions as to exactly what should be included in the project charter, we believe that the traditional project charter should include the following:

- The need (opportunity or threat) the project is addressing
  - Business
    - Strategic
    - Competitive
    - Customer
  - Legal

- Safety
- Technological
- Goal and objectives of the project
- Pro forma time frame
- Pro forma budget
- Project manager's authorization
- Project assumptions and constraints
- Sponsor's signature

The project charter is not (nor should it be) a complex document. In keeping with the simplicity of the document, to make a project charter green all one has to do is add a "green statement" to the document. Examples of green statements to include in a project charter are:

- We are fully committed to include green components when making project decisions.
- A project run with green intent is the right thing to do.[6]
- Begin with the end in mind. But which end? Most project managers think of the "end" of their project as that time when the deliverable is delivered and the customer is happy with that deliverable. In this case, the end is the final disposal of the deliverable as well as the project resources.

Another green statement that has powerful implications is a commitment to spending money on making the project's *process and product* as green as possible. There could be a line item in the pro forma budget allowing for a certain percentage of the final budget to be set aside for greening the project. For example, there could be a line item for greenality assurance testing or consulting for the project product or process. There are a plethora of reputable consulting companies that can assist in providing this type of assurance. We provide some references in Chapter 14.

THE INITIAL PROJECT KICKOFF MEETING

Once the ideation phase is just about complete, there needs to be a way to "get the word out." The best way to do that is a project kickoff meeting.

That meeting will include a subset of the project stakeholders. It is primarily an internal meeting to ensure that the key internal project stakeholders are all aware of the project, the decision-making process involved in choosing the project, the contents of its charter, including the pro forma budget and schedule, and the identified project manager. Also, introducing the greenality commitment is one of the most important functions of the project manager during the initial kickoff meeting.

The initial project kickoff meeting is part of the project process, and therefore should be as green as possible. There are many templates available for a project kickoff meeting, so we will not provide one here; however, we will provide a template to use to ensure that the initial project kickoff meeting is as green as possible.

ACTING ON THE IDEA

Now that the project has been chosen and the charter has been written, it is time for action. It's not that the project can now be executed, because there hasn't been a detailed planning effort. However, now is the time to communicate your decision so that your stakeholders can have a chance to review the project information. Even though the information has been thoroughly reviewed by the team during the decision-making process, it is always a good idea to check with key stakeholders. Their input can be invaluable to the success or failure of a project. Remember, the definition of a stakeholder is anyone who may be affected, positively or negatively, by the project. While that may be an exhaustive list, it is important at this point in the project, to identify those who are key to project success or failure, and have them review the decision as appropriate. Reviewers should include anyone who will be affected by the green components of the project.

TOOLS AND TECHNIQUES

During the project ideation phase, the following tools and techniques may be used to ensure that the project stays focused on greenality:

1. The project charter should include a commitment statement from management and the project sponsor: for example, "[The named project manager], as project manager, shall take all measures available to ensure that the project product as well as the processes used to manage the project meet or exceed the greenality standards established by the environment policy statement of the organization and in particular for this project."

2. The project charter may also include, in the high-level budget, a monetary commitment to greenality: for example, "The organization commits 10% of the total project budget to offset the cost of any greenality efforts."

3. Follow the SMARTER objectives.

GREENALITY OF PROJECT COMMUNICATIONS

Project communications is one area where the project manager has direct influence. Marshall McLuhan, best known for his phrase turned into a book, "The medium is the message," is said to have meant that the message is greatly impacted by the medium. Whether or not that is truly what he meant, we project managers know that the actual words are only a small fraction of the message to be conveyed. The way the message is conveyed is much more important that the words themselves. We believe that the old adage "It's not what you say, but how you say it," holds true when it comes to the greenality of communications. We approach the greenality of communications in two ways: the "spirit" of the way the message is conveyed and the physical medium of the message.

THE SPIRIT OF THE COMMUNICATION

We are not sure which is most important, but we certainly understand that if the message is conveyed in a spirit that is not acceptable to the receiver, the message is lost. This can be especially true with project greenality communications. The subject of "green" can be polarizing, so it is up to the project manager to communicate in ways that allow the message to be heard. What we are saying is because of the sensitivity surrounding "green," the project manager should take additional time and thought when communicating information about the greenality of a project. One simple example is to use the words *climate change* rather than the words *global warming*.

The physical medium of communications is a matter of "walking the walk." If the project manager intends to convey a high sense of greenality in the project, then one of the key processes, communications, should be green. For instance, instead of generating paper reports, use an internal shared drive to hold and update data. Allow access to that drive to all project team members. For the most part, it will be on a read-only basis, but those who need to keep the files updated can have special permission to do so. Those changes must be tracked, however. Another example would be to supply all key team members with an e-reader, allowing them to download and view the latest files without carrying a lot of paper. For more examples of greenality in communications, see Chapter 13, "Tips, Tools, and Techniques to Green."

JEOPARDY AND ESCALATION PROCESSES

We are including a brief section on these two processes because we feel that while they are important to any project, they will be critical to the green project manager. Because green project management is so new, and at times controversial, these processes may be used more frequently. Both of these processes are related, so we have included them under the same heading. A jeopardy process is a process that is put in place at the ideation phase that allows everyone associated with the project to know how a project jeopardy is communicated. A very simple one that we have used before requires three colors to be used for your electronic alert: red, yellow, and green. When an issue arises that will directly affect the project's timeline, costs, quality, or greenality, an alert in red type is used to convey the jeopardy information to upper management. The information in the alert includes: the description of the jeopardy, what area of the project is affected, and possible solutions (if known). The reason for it to be in red is because that alerts upper management that it is an issue that requires immediate attention, usually within 24 hours. An alert in yellow type has the same information as the red alert, except that the issue defined is not immediately affecting the project constraints, but rather is a potential problem, and the response to it can be delayed, usually 48 hours. A message in green type again has the same information as the red and yellow alerts, except it contains an additional piece of information—the solution to the red or yellow jeopardy. So an issue may have two electronic files, one in red type and one in green type; two electronic files, one in yellow type and one in green type; or three electronic files, one in red type, one in yellow type, and one in green type. Always remember that if there isn't a file with green type associated with the electronic files, then the issue hasn't been resolved, or someone forgot to document the resolution, and documenting the resolution is one of the more important project artifacts.

The escalation process contains information as to who to go to in the project when a decision cannot be made at the project manager level. The process, while related to the jeopardy process, can be a multifaceted one. For example, the project manager may be working with a customer who has their own project manager. When the two project managers cannot agree on the disposition of an issue, the escalation process will proceed to the next level of decision maker. Not only that, but it should include all levels above the project manager, even as far as the president of the companies, if that is the ultimate decision maker. It allows the project teams to have a process of escalation in place if needed.

GREENALITY OF SUPPLIERS

The final aspect of the ideation phase is to consider the greenality of your suppliers. This is probably one of the areas where the project manager needs to watch out for greenwashing. Suppliers may portray their green efforts differently than they actually are in order to get your business. So how do you avoid that? One of the more expensive ways is through inspection. If the project requires significant investment with "green" businesses, then the project manager may need to budget money to ensure the greenality of suppliers. Another way to secure information about your suppliers is through expert judgment. Find someone who has used that particular supplier before and learn from them what you can about the greenality. As we become more and more green, greater amounts of information will become available to and through project managers as to the greenality of suppliers. For more on where to find green suppliers, see Chapters 13, "Tips, Tools, and Techniques to Green," and 14, "Resource Information."

ENDNOTES

1. *Webster's New Collegiate Dictionary,* 11th ed., s.v. "adventure."
2. John Voelcker, *2010 Toyota Prius Shortages Ahead Due to Global Demand,* July 13, 2009, http://www.allaboutprius.com/blog/1021476_2010-toyota-prius-shortages-ahead-due-to-global-demand.
3. *A Guide to the Project Management Book of Knowledge,* 4th ed. (Newtown Square, PA: Project Management Institute, 2008), 75.
4. EarthPM, *EarthPM's Five Assertions of Green Project Management,* part of mission statement, 2007 © http://www.earthpm.com.
5. When compared to the surrounding rural areas, urban areas produce a significantly greater amount of heat, thus the name Urban Heat Island. From http://www.epa.gov/hiri/.
6. EarthPM, *EarthPM's Five Assertions.*

6

Developing the Project

The next stop along the project path is the development of the project plan. There are three separate but interconnected elements: project planning, organizing the plan into a cohesive undertaking, and the generation of supporting documentation. These elements are sequential in nature, and each successive element should be thoroughly investigated using the available tools and techniques prior to stepping to the next element. Developing the project plan is where the detailed project definition is accomplished, and without a complete detailed definition, the project is doomed for failure. Remember, like many of the processes in project management, the elements should be iterated and elaborated as necessary as new information about the project or its environment becomes available. And as we know, the environment can be a very changeable thing.

PROJECT PLANNING

This is the important first step in the development of a "green" project plan. As with any project-planning effort, the first action required is to fully understand the nature of the project. Defining **scope**—what the project does and does not include—sets the stage for all future project decisions. If something is defined as out of scope, it would have to be accepted formally into the project via the project's change control processes. If that "something" is sustainability, that may easily be enough of a hurdle to discourage its addition later on. That's why we urge you to put it into the project's scope at this early stage. Just as other business needs are incorporated into the scope of the project, so is the green business need. That is why it is so important to connect the company's commitment to sustainability to the project charter. As we briefly discussed in the Introduction to this book, connecting sustainability to the business needs means going beyond simply paying "lip service" to the environment, or being an "also-ran" part of the Green Wave. It is *good business,* and the green project manager is in the best position to provide that information to the organization, should further convincing be needed. As the *PM Network* article of November 2009, "Green Out," says, "Sustainable IT projects make your company look good, but it's probably the lower energy bills that will get them approved." In that same article, it's pointed out that "six out of seven corporate officers say that the adoption of green technology is more likely a result of escalating energy costs than ecological altruism."[1] The green project manager has at his or her disposal the many books and articles written that say not only that "greenality is free," but that a high greenality score equates to significant cost savings and enhanced bottom line.

For the sake of the rest of this discussion, we'll make an assumption here, and it is a big one. We'll assume that the organization—for either altruistic or economic reasons, or more likely, both—has committed to its projects being green, ostensibly with an environmental management policy that says this definitively. The work isn't done with that declaration. Now it is a matter of assessing what goes into a planning effort for a project and inserting the correct green elements in the appropriate spots. What information will the project manager need to do that? We've already discussed the project charter. Within the charter is a greenality commitment, either commitment verbiage, budgetary commitment, or ideally, both. Additionally, from the project charter, the goals and objectives are defined, a pro forma time frame and budget are communicated, and the project's assumptions and constraints are specified. For project goals and objectives, the environmental responsibility of each has been defined using the SMARTER technique. Those responsibilities are a *direct* input to the project's scope, as supporting detail.

This information, referred to as inputs to define scope (see Section 5.2 of the *PMBOK Guide*), is analyzed using any number of available tools, as well as seeking out technical experts and other green project managers to provide historical information from similar projects and processes to be utilized. Remember, the field of green project management is relatively new; therefore, some of the information used will be based on green *business* practices and will have to be adapted for project management. This is not at all unlike the adaptation PMs make in the realm of quality, where much of the wisdom comes from pioneers of manufacturing and operations and is adapted for project management.

Once the goals and objectives, assumptions and constraints, and high-level budget and schedule are identified, the next step in the process is the detailed planning. Unequivocally, the most important planning tool for the green project manager is the work breakdown schedule (WBS). There are no guarantees for project success or failure. For most projects, especially the more complex projects (and indeed greenality does add a new level of complexity), there are a whole host of issues that will positively and negatively affect the project's objectives. But we can guarantee one thing, and that is: if a complete and thorough WBS is not identified, failure is probably assured. And, the green aspects that must be included in the WBS are part of a complete and thorough WBS. So what is different about a green WBS?

It may help to have a short tutorial of a WBS and how it is constructed. For simplicity, we'll think about a WBS in the form of a top-down flow-chart. Thinking about any WBS requires that the top levels of effort be identified first, and then those levels are "decomposed" further and further until there is a level at which work can be assigned in the form of manageable chunks, or "tasks."

Here is a typical recipe for baking a "standard white cake."

Standard White Cake Recipe

    1 package of white cake mix
    1¼ cups of water
    3 eggs
    2 tablespoons of vegetable oil
    1 teaspoon of vanilla
    ½ teaspoon of almond extract

CREAMY WHITE FROSTING

    1 cup milk
    3 tablespoons of all-purpose flour
    1 cup of butter
    1 cup of powdered sugar
    1 teaspoon of vanilla

CAKE PREPARATION:

Preheat oven to 350°F. Grease and flour two 8- or 9-inch round cake pans.
    Combine cake mix, water, eggs, and oil in large bowl. Beat at medium speed with electric mixer until well blended. Add vanilla and almond extract; mix until well blended. Divide batter evenly between prepared pans.

Bake 30 to 35 minutes or until toothpicks inserted into centers come out clean. Cool in pans on wire racks 10 minutes. Remove cakes from pans to racks; cool completely.

Prepare Creamy White Frosting. Fill and frost cake with frosting.

FROSTING PREPARATION:

1. Combine milk and flour in medium saucepan; cook and stir over low heat until thickened. Cool.
2. Beat butter in large bowl until creamy. Add powdered sugar; beat until fluffy. Blend in vanilla. Add flour mixture; beat until thick and smooth.

As you can see in Figure 6.1, the traditional project "Baking a Cake" is decomposed into its "recipe," ingredients, and equipment. We should think about projects no longer in the traditional sense, but in an expanded green sensibility. The WBS in Figure 6.2 represents a recipe that includes this green sensibility. It is not just a matter of substituting organic ingredients to make the project's product green, but also assessing the project's processes, including the aspects of disposal, to ensure that these processes are *also* green.

Project managers have traditionally (subconsciously, perhaps) considered some of the green aspects of a project's product, because project managers are usually task oriented and focused on preserving scarce project resources. But now we must also be concerned with the greening of the project's processes. Throughout this book, we will be providing tools and techniques for the project manager to use during the greening of a project. There are more included in Chapter 14.

Once the WBS is complete, the "real" reason for a complete and thorough WBS becomes evident. This is the basis for planning the rest of the project. Within the WBS are all of the tasks that have to be performed to ensure that the project meets or exceeds customer expectations. The next steps in the project-planning effort are iterative and cumulative. Each task can now be detailed as to:

- What resources will be required to execute those tasks?
  - Who will do the task?
  - How much will each task cost?
  - How much time will the task require?

1.0 Ingredients
    1.1 Procure eggs
    1.2 Procure flavoring
        1.2.1 Vanilla extract
        1.2.2 Almond extract
    1.3 Procure oils & butter
    1.4 Procure flour
    1.5 Procure sugar
    1.6 Water
2.0 Equipment
    2.1 Procure pans and dishes
        2.1.1 Cake pans
        2.1.2 Mixing bowl
        2.1.3 Medium sauce pan
    2.2 Procure electric mixer
    2.3 Preheat oven
        2.3.1 350 degrees
3.0 Recipe
    3.1 Cake
        3.1.1 Grease and flour cake pans
        3.1.2 Combine cake mix, water, eggs & oil in large bowl
            3.1.2.1 Beat at medium speed with electric mixer
            3.1.2.2 Add vanilla and almond extract; mix
        3.1.3 Divide evenly into cake pans
        3.1.4 Bake at 350 degrees for 30-35 minutes until done
    3.2 Icing
        3.2.1 Combine milk and flour in medium sauce pan
            3.2.1.1 Cook and stir over low heat until thickened
            3.2.1.2 Cool
        3.2.2 Beat butter in large bowl until creamy
        3.2.3 Add powdered sugar and beat until fluffy
        3.2.4 Blend in vanilla
        3.2.5 Add flour mixture and beat until thick and creamy
        3.2.6 Ice cake

FIGURE 6.1
Baking a cake (standard).

1.0 Ingredients
    1.1 Investigate organic eggs
        1.1.1 Procure organic eggs
    1.2 Investigate fair traded flavorings
        1.2.1 Procure fair traded flavoring
            1.2.1.1 Vanilla extract
            1.2.1.2 Almond extract
    1.3 Procure oils & butter

    1.4 Procure flour
    1.5 Procure sugar   } See "Scratch Cake Mix" 3.1.1
    1.6 Water   below for "green" ingredients

2.0 Equipment
    2.1 Procure pans and dishes
        2.1.1 Cake pans
        2.1.2 Mixing bowl
        2.1.3 Medium sauce pan
    2.2 Procure electric mixer
    2.3 Preheat oven
        2.3.1 350 degrees
3.0 Recipe
    3.1 Scratch cake mix
        3.1.1 Procure organic flour, sugar, organic butter, organically fed cow milk, alum free baking powder, sea salt, free trade vanilla, and 3 organic eggs
        3.1.2 Grease and flour cake pans
        3.1.3 Mix together the flour, baking powder and salt; set aside.
        3.1.4 In a large bowl, cream sugar and shortening until light and fluffy
        3.1.5 Add eggs one at a time, beating thoroughly after each addition
        3.1.6 Add flour mixture alternately with milk, beating just to combine
        3.1.7 Stir in vanilla and almond extract
        3.1.8 Divide evenly into cake pans
        3.1.9 Bake at 350 degrees for 40-45 minutes until done
    3.2 Icing
        3.2.1 Combine milk and flour in medium sauce pan
            3.2.1.1 Cook and stir over low heat until thickened
            3.2.1.2 Cool
        3.2.2 Beat butter in large bowl until creamy
        3.2.3 Add powdered sugar and beat until fluffy
        3.2.4 Blend in vanilla
        3.2.5 Add flour mixture and beat until thick and creamy
        3.2.6 Ice cake

FIGURE 6.2
Baking a "green" cake.

- What tasks are affected by other tasks and what tasks can stand alone?
- In what order will the tasks be executed?
- Are there other dependencies besides the obvious between tasks?

We can't stress enough that greenality must be planned into the project. We've said how important it is to get the greenality in the project's scope. However, getting it in is only the first step. The WBS is the place to find the green tasks a home and the proper owners. Once the WBS is defined, while not impossible, it is more difficult to "add" task to the project without impacting the overall schedule, cost, or quality of the project. Let's look in detail at the major planning areas and how they are affected by planning for project greenality.

SUSTAINABILITY AND THE WBS

We'd like to formally introduce sustainability into the disciplined approach of project management. As we defined in Chapter 2, sustainability is not sacrificing the future for the present. It is not only that, but in project management it is the *planning for sustainability* that makes our contribution so important. Therefore, as well as thinking about the WBS in terms of all the tasks necessary to complete the project, we need to take our traditional thinking one step further. There is life after project closeout, and that life makes the difference whether or not the project is truly green or not. Without that further step, green planning of the project could be considered greenwashing, as defined in Chapter 2. A project manager will be able to defend a project from accusations of greenwashing by virtue of a WBS with green intent threaded throughout, rather than glued on at the end.

What does the WBS look like when sustainability is *planned in*? Let's take our simple example of baking a green cake (Figure 6.2) and make sure that sustainability is included in the "recipe." Reviewing the modified recipe for baking a green cake, we can see that there are sustainability issues that should be addressed. Let's look at the pan used to bake the cake. When we purchased the pan, planning to bake a cake in it, what did we consider? Did we consider whether or not we would reuse it? Did we consider what type of materials it was made out of, so it either had a long life or could be recycled? Even if it had a long life, was it recyclable? Did we consider the packaging of the eggs and the vanilla, as well as their manufacturers' commitments to sustainability? Did we buy just enough ingredients to bake the cake or are there waste or storage issues? Did we consider the product? Will it get eaten in the first sitting, or will we have to store it? How will we store it? What kind of material is the storage container made from? Might this require us to power up a refrigerator to "keep" it? It sounds like a lot of things to think about for "just baking a cake," and you're right, it *is*. However, once it is ingrained in our thinking, those issues and decisions we make will become second nature, just as for our experienced readers, the use of a WBS and a Gantt chart have become second nature. And what good will this green planning do? Only time will tell, but economist David Friedman once said, "I'm trying to have everything that I put into the world be something that makes a difference in the way I want to make a difference." Here's our chance as project managers to make that difference.

WHO AND WHAT ARE REQUIRED FOR THE PROJECT

Depending on the nature of the project, **resource planning** includes three major aspects; (1) the people required to do the work, (2) the equipment needed to support the people or the project needs, and (3) the cost of the people and equipment required. There is a direct connection between the resources required and the quality of the project and we'll talk about that aspect, too, in Chapter 7.

GREENING THE PEOPLE

One of the purposes of this book is to instill green into project management so that there is no longer a difference between how we have done projects and how we will provide greenality to projects. It will be one and the same. Planning for greenality will become the "new" project planning. In order to do this, the people you choose for projects need to have some background in green. What we mean by that is that all contributors (stakeholders) to the project are aware of the universality of green, including all of the awareness of the information of the type we provided in Chapter 1. Whether the people agree with the information or not, there must be an understanding that in order to preserve scarce resources, the philosophy of greenality must be seriously considered in project planning and by the people on the project. One of the compelling arguments for greenality is that it is good for the organization's bottom line. As an example, Bristol-Myers-Squibb's IT team found that removing screensavers from all employees' computers in the United States saves about 1.9 million kilowatts of energy and $266,000 annually,[2] a simple fix that saved a significant amount of money. It's that type of green thinking that will improve the bottom line and ensure that greenality is considered when planning a project. Money talks! So, step one in the process of *greening the people* is to have people who are "green aware" on the project. In some instances, the people who need to work on a project are not green aware. One option is to provide some training. Of course, that may affect the project's timeline and costs, a planning consideration and potential addition to the project's WBS. Another option is to hire a green consultant to work with the team during the project, thus potentially increasing the project's cost, and, of course, another addition to the WBS.

GREENING THE SCHEDULE

At this point, the WBS and resource planning are complete. The WBS includes all of the tasks required to properly plan, execute, control, close, and sustain the project. Completing the resources planning allows the project manager to be able to account for the personnel needed to do the tasks. The next step is considering the duration of the defined activities and the order in which those activities are completed in light of both the WBS and the resources needed. Once again, green thinking should be used in determining the duration and sequence, particularly with regard to resource usage.

There are questions to be asked and answered with consideration to the nature of the project, the nature of the resources needed, and the social aspect of the answers to the first two issues. The nature of the project may determine the criticality or urgency of the project. Criticality and urgency may be more prevalent in projects that are green by intent. Not wanting to beat a dead horse, but one of the assertions that we work from says that "project managers must first understand the green aspects of their projects, knowing that knowing that this will better equip them to identify, manage, and respond to project risks."[3] If a project has been identified as green by intent, perhaps there is some urgency to protect a limited, fragile, or critical resource in imminent danger. An example of that would be an environmental project such as the ones that are being prompted by the severe drought conditions in Kenya, Africa.

According to IRIN News, "Humanitarian News and Analysis, a Project of the UN Office of Coordination of Humanitarian Affairs (http://www.irinnews.org/Report.aspx?ReportId=82683), scarce water resources is the reason for escalating violence among the people of northeastern Kenya. It is about gaining access to the limited water and pasture areas. Because of the drought, people are struggling to find water for themselves and their livestock. Consequently, without the water, there will be no food, either." An article on *National Geographic*'s Web site on September 21, 2009 (http://news.nationalgeographic.com/news/2009/09/090921-kenya-animals-drought-water.html), says, "More than sixty African elephants and hundreds of other animals have died so far in Kenya amid the worst drought to hit the country in over a decade. In addition, 30 baby elephants have been reported dead so far this year in Amboseli National Park, farther south. So-called 'long rains' that usually fall in March and April failed this year, and some areas have now been in drought conditions for almost three years. No one knows why the drought has been so bad. Many attribute it to global warming, but others say it is simply part of the long-term weather cycle in East Africa." The need for a water project is critical.

Some of the projects that are going on now and some that we anticipate will start soon are deep-water well construction, irrigation projects, water-processing and -holding facilities, low-water-impact sanitation projects, among others. The green aspects of these projects are obvious. What isn't obvious is their effect on the project management schedule and resources. Project managers will have to make decisions on the project calendars and ask questions like: Will there be any holidays or weekends considered? Will project execution take place 24/7 because of the criticality of the solutions? If it does require 24/7 execution, what will be needed—generators, fuel, lighting, to say nothing of the personnel requirements to both manage and work on the project? One of the authors recently noted that a large highway construction project did much of its work at night, to avoid shutting down the highway during busy times. Makes sense. For night work, large banks of lights were set up to allow the workers to break up pavement, move equipment, and so on. So far so good. However, the banks of lights were observed to be on for long periods of time over several nights where there was no activity—the lights were more of a hazard to oncoming traffic than anything. This same effect—tens of thousands of kilowatt hours of electricity wasted as well as lights burning out because they were lighting up unused equipment—could have been easily avoided with green thinking. What will be the environmental impact of the projects themselves? What are the sustainability issues for the projects?

Returning to the earlier drought issue, it is obvious that these solutions must be permanent, as the long-term forecasts for drought areas are not good. Therefore they have to be planned, designed, and executed with sustainability in mind. Keeping all that in mind, the green project manager also has to focus on making sure that the process around the projects is as green as possible. It now becomes a balancing act to ensure that the necessary tasks are performed with greenality, but yet satisfy the urgency of the project's scheduled tasks.

One doesn't need to consider a project with the sweeping change of addressing drought conditions in Africa. A project like the construction of a wind farm in Maui, still green by intent, is an example that doesn't have the same constraints as the previous example. There are still green schedule techniques to apply. First Wind is a company whose motto is "Clean energy, made here." According to David Ertz, director of project management–east, First Wind likes the challenge of areas where it is more difficult to build wind farms, like the top of a ridge in Maui or the top of a ridge in Maine, rather than the plains of the Midwest, whether or not placing a wind generator on a ridgetop in Maui or in Maine makes it very visible in areas that are noted for their beauty and remoteness. We're saying that wind generators can be attractive but that the attractiveness will be in the eye of the beholder. We can see some green schedule issues that need to be considered when working in challenging areas on projects that are green by intent. With wind energy, the best places to put the generators are places with sustained winds. Those can also be the places where the environment can work against you. One cannot place the blades on top of the tower in windy conditions. It is too dangerous.

Project managers have the opportunity to consider the schedule and application of resources to save money and energy. Even the application of common sense when it comes to working when air conditioning or heating does not need to be used, or handing off work between time zones to remote offices—these things and more can play into the project manager's hand for a greener project.

GREENING THE PROJECT PURCHASING (PROCUREMENT) PROCESS

In most cases, the project will require resources other than people. Those resources sometimes include items to be purchased , like equipment and services, or raw materials. Here is an opportunity for green thinking about the suppliers (vendors) supplying the equipment resources. The U.S. Environmental Protection Agency has produced significant guidelines for green purchasing. We provide information in Chapter 14. The European Union has an extensive eco-labeling program—details are available at http://www.eco-label.com/default.htm.

Again, this is also an opportunity for management to validate their commitment to project greenality. Management should encourage the project manager and the project team to seek out the greener vendors. That commitment may mean that the cost of the purchasing equipment and services from greener vendors may be higher in dollars, but when considering the value of corporate social responsibility (CSR) and how that is viewed by the stakeholders, the benefit may offset the additional cost. Green thinking instilled in management, the project manager, and the project team means that these kinds of offsets will always be considered.

There are several areas of the purchasing process where green thinking can be applied. The first instance is during purchase planning. Using the scope statement, the work breakdown definition, and the schedule, the project manager will have a good idea as to what needs to be purchased and when those purchases need to be made. Looking through their environmental lens, the project manager and team can determine the green alternatives for the project purchases by further defining the project needs, seeking green purchasing experts when appropriate, and particularly using the experience and knowledge of the project team, selected for those very reasons. Something to keep in mind, though, is that even with the best plans of what will be needed for the project, if the vendor cannot supply it when needed, there is a good possibility that the project will not succeed. So again, price and greenality may not be the only determinants. At this point, the project manager and team will have assessed the purchasing alternatives and identified the various sources of equipment and services needed. The results of the purchasing needs definition will be a purchasing requirements document that then can be used for the next step.

The next step is to take the output of the purchase planning—the relevant purchasing documents—and transmit those documents to potential suppliers. As green becomes a way of doing business, suppliers of greener products will become numerous, and prices will become more competitive, as saving in energy costs, for example, are realized by the suppliers. But we assert that this should not be left to chance. This is actually somewhat of a communications issue. Your vendors and suppliers should be very clear on your intent. They should know that green is important to your project. Knowing this, they will proactively offer you green options—or should, if they know their business. Some of the typical documents used to obtain purchase information from suppliers are the invitation to bid, request for proposal, and request for quote. (See Table 6.1 for the differences between each.) Included in the information sent to potential suppliers will be: (1) what will be purchased, (2) when it will be needed, and (3) questions as to what the potential supplier is doing to green their processes and products or services. The project manager and team can request the information from the supplier either via written documentation sent to potential suppliers or with written documentation furnished at a face-to-face meeting. Either way, detailed documents have to be prepared. The level of detail and how much time is spent on those documents depends on the purchase. A purchase that is expensive, has a high degree of technicality, has only a few suppliers, is needed at a specific time in the project schedule, or has

TABLE 6.1

Solicitation Documents

Type	Explanation
Invitation to bid (IFB)	Invitation to participate in sealed bid procurement. It is the initiation of the process. The IFB contains all the information required by a bidder to submit a responsive bid.
Request for quote (RFQ) Request for proposal (RFP)	Originally there was a technical difference between RFQ and RFP. An RFP was used to solicit firm offers and upon acceptance became a contract. The difference between the two has become blurred. Both are used in negotiated acquisitions to communicate requirements to selected contractors to solicit proposals or quotes.

a high environmental impact requires much more time to plan than one that doesn't have the same requirements.

One Sunday edition of the *New York Times* consumes as many as 75,000 trees—projects include reducing paper usage by moving toward electronic media online, electronic document readers, and new technologies.

After considering the information from the various suppliers, the project manager and team can make an informed decision. As a result of that decision there is generally a contract. We are advocating a "greenality clause" in the contract. Should the project manager and team decide to go with a company that has responded with the outline of their green efforts, we believe not only that the green efforts should be captured in the contact body, but that somehow the supplier should be held accountable for the efforts they purported to make. While we will not give legal advice or suggest greenality wording for a contract to make a company accountable for their green efforts, a damage clause may be added in case the company does not fulfill the green part of the contract.

GREENING PROJECT COSTS

We have frequently mentioned cost as a factor to managing projects. It is certainly an important factor in the company's decision to undertake a project. The only caution we have is that at first glance, costs may appear to be much higher when the greenality factor is considered. However, green savings may not be fully realized during these project-planning processes. As we said in Chapter 1, a project with a high greenality score is good for the bottom line. It may require a "deeper dive" into the financials of the project and the project's sustainability to fully realize the real cost savings to the company. There are ways to add greenality to the project costs, and some will be included in Chapter 7, "Executing the Project." However, they are several green costing methods that can be used in the cost-planning stage. In general, moving communications from written on paper to electronic form can save a significant amount of resources. Additionally, doing as much research as possible on the products and services needed to be procured prior to generating any cost figures can save rework and the back-and-forth that sometimes accompanies requests for money, saving time and effort on the project and further reducing limited resource usage.

GREENING PROJECT QUALITY

In Joseph Juran's book *Leadership for Quality*,[4] he talked about "life behind the quality dikes." Among other quality drivers Juran was talking about behind the dikes was a growing concern about damage to the environment and fear of major disasters. This book was published in March 1989 and was a prophecy of what concerns were growing. Frederick Taylor's management system emphasizes a pure science approach to quality, including scientific selection and education of workers. However, today we have a world that, while it is still somewhat science driven, is trying a softer view, giving workers more self-control, self-inspection, and self-directing teams. Much of this can be exemplified by the "Toyota Way" (see Table 6.2). Perhaps not coincidentally, Toyota consistently shows up at or near the top of environmentally minded companies.

This is an advantage to the green project manager who is trying to use the more unempirical approach, like the Natural Step method, as well as the more scientific approach. And, unlike the quality efforts of the 1950s–1990s, the United States can lead rather than follow green quality efforts. To help us understand the future, we need to look at the past.

While the United States led the development of quality control and improvement, most of the quality gurus did not have an audience in the United States. Both Juran and Deming spent considerable time in Japan where their efforts were not only accepted, but rewarded. The Deming Prize for quality excellence was established in Japan in 1951. In contrast, the Malcolm Baldrige National Quality Award was established in 1987. The easiest way to explain green quality is to use Deming's 14 points as a starting place (see Table 6.3).

Again, using another one of the quality guru's approaches, we'll define green quality. David Garvin, in his 1988 book *Managing Quality: The Strategic and Competitive Edge*, defines quality in five dimensions; transcendent, product based, user based, manufacturing based, and value based. We'll use those same criteria to define green quality.

TABLE 6.2

The Toyota Way Illustrated

The Toyota Way
1. Base your management decisions on a long-term philosophy, even at the expense of short-term financial goals.
2. Create a continuous process flow to bring problems to the surface.
3. Use "pull" systems to avoid overproduction.
4. Level out the workload (heijunka).
5. Build a culture of stopping to fix problems, to get quality right the first time.
6. Standardized tasks and processes are the foundation for continuous improvement and employee empowerment.
7. Use visual control so no problems are hidden.
8. Use only reliable, thoroughly tested technology that serves your people and processes.
9. Grow leaders who thoroughly understand the work, live the philosophy, and teach it to others.
10. Develop exceptional people and teams who follow your company's philosophy.
11. Respect your extended network of partners and suppliers by challenging them and helping them improve.
12. Go and see for yourself to thoroughly understand the situation (genchi genbutsu).
13. Make decisions slowly by consensus, thoroughly considering all options; implement decisions rapidly (nemawashi).
14. Become a learning organization through relentless reflection (hansei) and continuous improvement (kaizen).

Note: Adapted from Jeffrey Liker, *The Toyota Way* (New York: McGraw-Hill, 2004).

Transcendent Greenality

Transcendent greenality is something that is not easy to put your finger on, and therefore is difficult to define. However, when you see this particular type of greenality, it becomes apparent. I am going to paraphrase one of my favorite definitions of transcendent quality: "*Greenality* is neither mind nor matter, but a third entity independent of the two ... even though *Greenality* cannot be defined, you know what it is."[5] Because a particular company has a reputation of achieving greenality, that achievement is sometimes translated to all products of that company. In other words, the view of the company's greenality transcends the more fundamental definitions of greenality. If a company has a stellar reputation of being sustainable, including a cute eco-friendly logo, that company may be perceived to have high greenality. We are not saying that the company does not have high greenality, based on other greenality dimensions, just that

TABLE 6.3

Deming and Green Quality

Deming Quality	Green Quality
Create constancy of purpose for improvement of products and services.	Continually look for ways to green the products and the services of the project.
Adopt a new philosophy.	Adopt a new green philosophy and avoid "greenwashing."
Cease dependence on mass inspection.	Plan greenality into the project.
End the practice of awarding business on price tag alone.	Look at more than the cost when awarding business as the true cost considers all of the greenality factors as well.
Improve constantly and forever the system of production and service.	Improve the greenality of the project's processes.
Institute training.	Institute training on greening subjects.
Institute leadership.	True leadership going forward will include a commitment to greenality.
Drive out fear.	It is OK to suggest areas to improve the greenality of a project's product or process.
Break down barriers between staff areas.	Encourage all areas of an organization to pitch in with greenality.
Eliminate slogans, exhortations, and targets for the workforce.	Have greenality be part of the project manager's DNA.
Eliminate numerical quotas.	Do not limit the extent of greenality of a project—green should be in the mind-set of the project team, not a quota to be accomplished.
Remove barriers to pride of workmanship.	There is pride in demonstrating personal commitment to the environment and sustainability.
Institute a vigorous program of education and retraining.	Move from the traditional discipline of project management through the "accidently green" project management to a disciplined green project management.
Take action to accomplish the transformation.	Be part of the green project management movement.

Note: Adapted from W. Edwards Deming, *Out of Crisis,* 9th ed. (Cambridge, MA: MIT Press, 1982), 18–96.

the greenality in this case is based solely on reputation and perhaps the aesthetics of the logo. While transcendent is a dimension of greenality, it may not be prudent to use it as the only measure.

Product-Based Greenality

This is a much more concrete measurement of greenality. It is based on a particular green element contained in the project's product or process. For the project's product, the attribute could be, in the case of an automobile, the ability to switch from electric mode for short-term driving to fossil fuel for longer distances, thereby reducing the fossil fuel component and the carbon footprint of the vehicle. The project manager may have instituted a paperless project policy and is able to measure the cost savings to the project, thus greening the project process.

User-Based Greenality

User-based greenality comes at greenality from a different direction, from the user stakeholder. It is the stakeholder's expectations that drive user-based greenality. It is becoming more and more apparent that greenality will be a differentiator for some users. Similar to transcendent greenality, user-based greenality is in the "eye of the beholder." Stakeholders will look to different products of projects and eventually the processes of the project for greenality efforts before choosing the product. Further, the stakeholders as leaders of the corporation will look to the greenality of the project process before choosing a project.

Manufacturing-Based Greenality

No longer something that has to be inspected in, greenality will become inherent in the entire product life cycle from the planning and design phase, to the manufacturing phase and beyond. The manufacturing process itself will have its own high-greenality measurements. In the design phase, the product specifications will include greenality standards that will be required during the manufacturing phase of the project. Therefore the project product greenality will be measured against those design specifications. Applying the same principle to the project's processes, the process will be designed to include greenality components, and will be measured against those specifications.

Value-Based Greenality

We are already experiencing value-based greenality with organic products from yogurts to cleaning solutions. Consumers are making a choice based on the greenality attributes of certain products and using the cost of those attributes to calculate their own cost-benefit ratios. Granted, some of the attributes that consumers are basing their calculations on may not be clear, but will be refined further and further as more consumers become greenality conscious and more competing companies enter the market place.

RISK AND GREENALITY

What is risk and how does it affect the greenality of the project? Risks are inherent in projects because of the uncertainty that defines a project: a unique undertaking, using and possibly abusing limited resources, an effort being done for the first time, untried and untested. Harold Kerzner, author of dozens of project management books, writes, "Since risk actually constitutes a lack of knowledge of future events, we can define risk as the cumulative effect that these adverse events could have on a project's objectives. Future events (or outcomes) that are favorable are called opportunities; whereas unfavorable events are called risks."[6]

We would like to accomplish two things: identify the potential greenality risks (negative risks), and identify areas for the green project manager to take advantage of opportunities or positive outcomes of risk situations (positive risks). Every day, more and more information is offered relative to green risks in business and then by definition, in projects. We certainly won't be able to cover all of them, so we will highlight some of the green risk and opportunity conditions we feel are of top priority.

As with all project risks, the project manager has to consider both the consequences of the risk occurring and the likelihood of the event. With negative risks, the purpose is to reduce the likelihood of their happening, while with positive risks it is to increase the likelihood of occurrence. Just so we are clear, it is our assertion that not considering the green risks and opportunities of a project is a mistake. Risks can cause havoc in a project, delaying finish dates, using or abusing limited resources, and forcing a change in the project plan. Risk taking can also help to accelerate the schedule, protect the limited resources, and achieve higher greenality.

Recycling one ton of paper saves 17 trees, two barrels of oil, 4,100 kilowatts of energy, 3.2 cubic yards of landfill space, and 60 pounds of air pollution.

The first place to look for project risks is in the objectives and goal of the project. Has the SMARTER technique been used to develop the project objectives? Particularly, has the *environmental responsibility* of those objectives been fully identified? That will go a long way to identifying project green risks. Offshore oil drilling has long been a target for environmentalists. But let's look at it as a project. Until we are independent of fossil fuel, oil and oil exploration will continue. A complete worldwide independence will be highly unlikely. So the demand for oil continues, and offshore drilling will continue. One of the objectives of offshore oil drilling is to distribute the oil. Looking at it from SMARTER, that is specific. We consume approximately 80 million gallons of oil per day, we've been distributing oil from offshore drilling enterprises, and the goal is to supply oil; so we can put a measure on how much we can supply from one offshore rig. It is doable, it is related to the goal, and we know that it has to be done as quickly as possible. That covers SMART, but how about the environmental responsibility? How reliable is the delivery system with respect to environmental damage? What indigenous species could be affected? What type of environmental damage can occur from the piping needed to transport the oil from offshore to a shore-based storage facility? These are just a few of the risks that can affect the greenality of the project, in this case the product of the project. However, these are just the negative risks.

Here are some examples of opportunity (positive risk):

- A vendor offers you a substitute material that is not only cheaper but greener and yet provides exactly the characteristics you need.
- Funding becomes available from the government for your wind turbine development idea.
- You make an altruistic decision to use electric vehicles for your project and at the same time, the manufacturer, based on stimulus money received, offers $1,000-per-vehicle rebates.

Negative risks to the project in its early stages include lack of management commitment, or overt opposition to greenality, lack of an organization-wide environmental policy, and lack of greenality support statement or funding for greenality in the project's charter. One could lead to the other, but the bottom line is that without some sort of commitment, the greenality effort on a project will be greatly inhibited, even if the project manager is an advocate. This is a *huge* risk to project greenality. As goes the management, so goes the project!

Looking at further potential risks on the project, have green techniques as outlined in this chapter been applied to the scheduling and costing estimation process, resource planning, and other aspects of the project management? Have we taken the time to identify, quantify, plan risk responses, and plan the necessary monitoring and controlling process for greenality risks? It used to be that one of the project manager's objectives was to protect the stakeholder's monetary investment in the project. That is now not enough. To paraphrase one of our assertions,[7] "an environmental strategy, including environmental risk management, provides added opportunity for the success of both the project and the project's product."

GREENALITY OUTPUTS
Environmental Management Plan

One of the outputs of developing the project is the environmental management plan (EMP). The EMP is similar in perspective to the quality management plan (QMP), but is specifically focused on the environmental and sustainability aspects of the project. The inputs to that plan are the environmental objectives, environmental policy, and environmental risks. These inputs may be incorporated into other plans, and they are significant enough, given the future of green project management, that they be included in a stand-alone document that serves as an input to the project management plan (PMP). Additionally, like the QMP, the EMP template will include scope, stakeholders, EEVM (earned environmental value management), organizational policies, and risk register, and will use tools similar to those in quality management: benchmarking, cost-benefit analysis, the cost of greenality, etc. The output then would be an EMP that dovetails into all the appropriate other plans, like the QMP, risk management plan, and others.

Another area that is impacted by environmental considerations is the monitoring and controlling of the project. One of the inputs to that area is the PMP, of which the EMP is a part. One of the purposes of monitoring and controlling a project is to compare the environmental objectives/ requirements listed in the project statement of work with actual regulations and when necessary take corrective action to ensure compliance. Another purpose of monitoring and controlling a project is "implementing risk response plans, tracking identified risks, monitoring residual risks, identifying new risks, and evaluating risk process effectiveness throughout the project,"[8] including environmental risks identified earlier in the project development. Nothing would be different for the EMP. It is just that EMP would have to be one of the inputs. EMP may have its own change control process, and is part of the project-integrated change control process, or it may be included only as part of the integrated change control process.

ENDNOTES

1. Sarah Fister Gale, *Green Out,* PM Network, November 2009, Project Management Institute, Newton Square, PA, 43–44.
2. *Go Green at Bristol-Myers-Squibb,* 2009, http://www.bms.com/ sustainability/go_gree n/Pages/default.aspx.
3. *The Five Assertions of EarthPM,* http://www.earthpm.com.
4. J. M. Juran, *Juran on Leadership for Quality,* Free Press (1989).
5. R. M. Pirsig, *Zen and the Art of Motorcycle Maintenance* (New York: Bantam, 1975), 185–213.
6. Harold Kerzner, *Project Management: A Systems Approach to Planning, Scheduling, and Control* (New York: Van Nostrand Reinhold, 1995), 879.
7. *The Five Assertions of EarthPM.*
8. *A Guide to the Project Management Book of Knowledge,* 4th ed. (Newtown Square, PA: Project Management Institute, 2008), 308.

7

Executing the Project

Now that the project has been planned, it is time to implement it. If you're familiar with the S-shaped curve (Figure 7.1) that describes a project's progress over time, we're now at the part of the curve with the steepest slope—where we are expending resources at the fastest rate. There are some additional aspects to consider now that your project has been greened, at least in the planning stages. This is the time when your good intentions are put to the test. A good place to start project implementation is with the project team and the kickoff meeting. Many of the project stakeholders have been involved in the project-planning process, but it is unlikely that they have a view of the entire project. To this point, they have been primarily involved with—and had the limited perspective of—their *own piece*. Not only does the kickoff meeting help the stakeholders with the broader view of the project, it is also a key time to reemphasize the green aspects of the project and how they will be woven through the project's execution, especially considering that we are just at the "incline" of this steep slope.

THE PROJECT TEAM

A core subset of project team members, or in some cases the project manager alone, has been working diligently so far to plan the project. That plan includes identifying all of the tasks needed to accomplish the project's goal and objectives, understanding the dependencies of those tasks and scheduling them, defining the resources and time needed to accomplish the tasks, and costing those tasks resulting in the project's budget and schedule baselines. Now is the time to secure the needed resources,

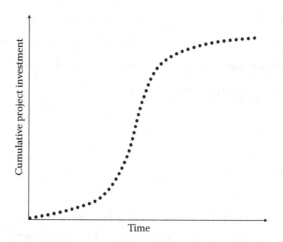

FIGURE 7.1
Classic S-curve: Cumulative project investment over time.

known as the full project team, to ensure that the right people will be available at the right time, within the specified budget, and that they know what they're contributing and how their contribution fits into the overall project's objectives—not only from a green perspective but from an overall project perspective. It would be helpful (but not imperative) for the members of the full team to have some knowledge of greenality and what it takes to green the project and the project processes. It is, however, crucial that the core project team be fully cognizant of the effort to green the project and fully committed to those aspects so that they can help the full team understand the issues. The project team will likely and almost necessarily include a variety of individuals with differing skill sets and differing viewpoints. While the core team may be able to help coach them through some of the greenality issues during the project's implementation, additional education may need to be provided to acquaint the full team with the greenality aspects of the project. There needs to be particular emphasis on how those factors will contribute not only to the success of the project, but to the success of the organization. See Chapter 2 for information regarding the contributions of greenality to success. Additional education will cost more in resources, so additional monies and time should have been set aside during the planning process.

Once the team has been selected (and it may be an iterative process as personnel could change for a variety of reasons during the course of a project), a **kickoff meeting** should be scheduled.

THE KICKOFF MEETING (IMPLEMENTATION)

The kickoff meeting for a new project is your best opportunity to energize the group and establish a common purpose toward completing the work. We've found that a great kickoff is the result of good planning. In fact, the authors have planned and run dozens of kickoff meetings like this all over the globe. It's all about good preparation. After you've done your project preparation work, you need to plan for an effective meeting. *The kickoff meeting will establish whether or not your efforts to green the project and the project's product will be successful.* The project kickoff meeting is the best chance for the project manager to educate project participants in the green aspects of the project and to gain acceptance of those green aspects. In addition to the traditional project management functions of a project kickoff meeting, it is an opportunity for the project manager to establish leadership in and gain buy-in for green methodology.

It is important to establish an agenda with the green aspects of the project clearly articulated, to give attendees a clear understanding of what is to be accomplished and to show a commitment to greenality. Because it is a relatively new concept, greenality needs to be introduced carefully so that the participants are comfortable with the concept. Greenality can be off-putting to some, but our assertion is that "a project run with green intent is the right thing to do, but it also helps the project team do things right."[1] Because greenality may be (falsely) connected to views about climate change and in other ways be considered controversial, the project manager needs to take immediate charge of the meeting to prevent it from getting derailed on a tangent related to climate change. Stakeholders may have strong opinions of both sides of the green issue, and those opinions could easily distract the meeting participants. The fact that the project is considering green issues will energize and motivate a number of people. Walk everyone through the agenda, and explain that there will be time at the end of the meeting to discuss any issues from individual contributors. Stress that this meeting is about making the *project* more efficient. Focus on the fact that this is not about politics or even buying into the assertions of climate change. More than anything this is about running the project more efficiently and considering what affects the project's processes, and that the final outcome will have an "extended family" of stakeholders.

As you walk through the agenda, look for cues to identify possible allies and contributors, and also people who may have been "turned off" by these efforts. By doing this you will be able to better identify those individuals who may need some additional, and perhaps off-line, coaching.

Explicitly define the project goal and objectives referring to SMARTER if necessary. It is also important to introduce the project team, letting each discuss their roles. Ask them each to talk about their expectations of their contributions to greenality. Note that although we focus here on greenality, we realize that this is a general meeting to discuss the project's execution. Still, we insist that this will be the right time to introduce and get buy-in on greenality. There will be additional meetings with individual team members to discuss the contributions of each. *In this meeting, you need to keep the team focused on the project.*

This meeting is the first time many of the team have seen the project in its full context, especially with respect to greenality. The purpose is to establish a baseline project plan, to make sure all of the tasks are included, the right people are assigned, the costs and schedule are reasonable, and that risks are represented. Input requested at this time should be confined to those attributes of the project. Since this is the first time the plan is shared with the entire team, expect changes, controversy, and some pushback. Realize that greenality will be a new concept to some, and therefore may appear to be riskier than prior projects without the greenality component. The project information shared during this meeting is the road map for the project and for project tracking, so it is important to capture all team members' concerns. Other aspects of the project are probably well understood; carefully emphasize greenality, the newest component of the project's plan. There will be a tendency here to wander off track, but again, it is very important to stay focused. Remember to stress that greenality, like quality, must be built in and not "sprayed on" after the project is complete. One technique to keep the team focused is to document greenality concerns in the project's action register. Make sure that you have a category for greenality action items, with some sort of identifier. That way, the project manager can quickly identify those issues related to greenality that need to be addressed. Remember the visual cues you gained earlier during the meeting? Use these to help you assign action items for greenality-related tasks of the project. Using your judgment you could choose to assign a task that has some green focus to the more cynical contributors, thus challenging them and perhaps gaining buy-in through their involvement. Or, you could tap into the energy you noted earlier, and assign a greenality task to one of the most fervent supporters. Depending on the types of issues that arise during the meeting, the project manager may need to convene a separate follow-on greenality educational meeting.

Emphasize that achieving a high level of greenality will be one of the key success factors. Show your enthusiasm for greenality—keeping a good balance between cheerleader and impartial, but well-informed facilitator. Successfully completing a project is a team effort, and the project manager will need the help and commitment from each and every team member. Factors affecting the project's greenality must be communicated by the team members as quickly and effectively as are changes to cost, schedule, or any other of the project's constraints.

After any walk-on items are dealt with, the next agenda item is feedback. The PM will have documented issues and concerns throughout the meeting, and now the meeting is opened up for questions and answers. Make sure that there is time on the agenda for this discussion. If not, the PM may need a follow-up meeting, or staying true to greening the project processes, by greening the project processes themselves, perhaps using shared media tools, such as Sosius, PSODA, SharePoint, Google Groups, wikis, and/or blogs, for continued project discussions. Finally, summarize the meeting, including action items and any follow-up information. The closing should also include when the PM expects to have the first meeting to evaluate the project's progress.

GREENALITY ASSURANCE

Greenality assurance (GA) is treated similarly to ensuring the quality of the project. The PM is trying to ascertain whether or not the defined greenality aspects of the project are being implemented, the greenality of both the project's outcome and project's processes. The first step in the process is to assess the greenality aspects of the project by comparing and mapping these to the organization's environmental management plan. Using the project's sustainability/environmental objectives and risks, along with the organization's environmental policy, the project team can access their effectiveness at any point in time. Along with that, GA could include measurements like earned environmental value management, looking at the specific earned value of the greenality efforts as compared to the actual costs of the green efforts, and the earned value of the greenality efforts as compared to the planned contribution of the greenality effort. It is unlikely that there will be much historical data to review or benchmarks to compare. As the field of green project management matures, that type of data—and improved tools to handle them—will surely become more readily available.

The GA of the project's product can be assessed by comparing the product's green functionality at the various waypoints of the project.

Thinking of the hiking analogy of this part of the book, we can imagine a hiker using a handheld global positioning system (GPS) with programmed waypoints and checking progress along the way as he or she hikes through the project. In this way, it will be easy to check on the success of the hike by comparing progress against the waypoints as well as reconciling supplies and health status as the hiker moves along. Assessing the greenality of the project is relatively the same. At each of the project's milestones set during the planning process, the project manager can assess whether or not the project has reached that point and whether or not it is healthy (on time, in scope, with greenality, and within budget). However, assessing the project's process greenality may not be as easy, because the focus will be on the other, more traditional project constraints of scope, time, and budget. As we've said before, greenality is just as important as any other project constraint, and in fact should already be included in the scope. Because it is a new concept it will be easy to lose focus, and that would be a mistake, as greenality can affect the project's success just as would going over budget or being behind schedule. Without the vigilance of GA, it will be easy to miss the signs that could adversely affect the project.

TRACKING PROJECT PROCESS

In addition to the GA process, there are other, complementary processes that need to be considered. The method to generate the data should have been defined during the planning stage of the project. It is now time to generate data showing that, relative to time, cost, scope, and other project constraints, the project components are being effectively managed. Standard methodology applies to project tracking. The greenality component of the project is one of the many project components that need to be tracked on a regular basis, and should be included as such. No distinction needs to be made, or should be made, between tracking a greenality milestone and a "regular" project milestone. *It is important that greenality be accepted as a natural, excuse the pun, aspect of a project.*

Establishing a good communications plan that includes the greenality aspects is critical. Greenality tracking needs to be included in the progress-reporting mechanisms.

Status and Progress Reporting

Status reporting is reporting on the project's work at a specific point in time. Progress reporting is reporting on the project's work during a specified time period. There are two areas of project status reporting that need to be addressed, the *immediate* and the *timed reporting*. Immediate reporting is communicating to the right people on issues that have an imminent effect on the project's schedule, cost, scope, and/or greenality. In the communication management plan, there is a road map that indicates which stakeholders need to be involved with immediate, critical communications. This should be part of the escalation process and the jeopardy process identified in the planning stage of the project (see Chapter 5), and also spelled out in the project's communications plan. While the information provided can be expanded, the minimum that is needed is

1. Who is receiving the issue and why
2. The issue
3. Who needs to be responded to
4. Which area(s) it is affecting: schedule, scope, cost, greenality
5. Extent of the potential damage to the project
6. Proposed solution (if available) and requested action, including required time to respond
7. If no proposed solution, then what the requested action is

Timed reporting refers to reports that are distributed during a specified time—weekly, monthly, etc.—and is used for both status and progress reporting. A timed report includes information on the project's schedule, cost, scope, and greenality, but we recommend that it be generated to include information on the status and progress of the project's process greenality. Because of the nature of that report, the audience should be limited to the project team and sponsor. The primary purpose for tracking the effect of the greenality efforts of the project's processes is for the project team and sponsor to evaluate whether or not the efforts are achieving the anticipated benefits and exactly what are those benefits. It also gives the team and the project sponsor information that will help to fine-tune the greenality of the project processes to gain maximum value for the efforts.

The nature of the status and progress information and the point in the project's life cycle will determine the frequency of the information distribution. Early in the planning phase of a project and early in the implementation phase of a project more frequent interaction may be required than in later stages of those phases as the planning effort stabilizes and the implementation efforts stabilize. Each project will be different in the frequency of information distribution, but they will all need status and progress information and a communications plan that accounts for all the variables. Because the project progress greenality report (PPGR) is a new reporting mechanism and greenality is a new reporting subject, we recommend that it be done frequently, at least once every two weeks.

USING SOCIAL MEDIA TO GREEN COMMUNICATIONS

One of the fastest-growing and best ways to maintain a "team" flavor to your project—even if the team is geographically dispersed—is social networking. How does social networking help a project manager add greenality to the project? For that answer, we'll look briefly at a few of the more popular general, business-specific, project management–specific, and green project management–specific sites.

Sharing video is one popular means of social networking, and the most popular site by far on which to post videos is YouTube. There are several ways to use this video site to enhance project communications. One way is to use videos of the project to track its progress. If it happens to be a construction project, it would be appropriate to post a video as the major milestones are achieved, the foundation completion as an example. If a picture's worth a thousand words, then a video is worth an order of magnitude more. It will not only keep stakeholders informed, but save an untold number of resource hours having to use traditional communication methods, as well as using a free electronic medium to save financial resources. With a YouTube video, while there is some time used to prepare the message, the total time to prepare and deliver the message will be considerably less than some other communications means, like developing a written report for instance.

Twitter has been characterized as social networking on steroids. It is being used by emergency responders, the president of the United States, NASA, and other organizations. Twitter may seem like overkill, but those organizations are using it to get out their message, so why not the project manager? The 140-character limit to Twitter makes it ideal, in our opinion, for quick communications between project team members. Should the message need to be longer, e-mail is always a good follow-up method, but the "tweet" can alert the team to the issue and that a follow-up is coming. The resulting green savings is obvious.

Probably the best known of the business social networking sites is LinkedIn®. It is one of the oldest, founded in 2002, and widest-reaching social networking sites, due to the variety of groups defined within the site. There are LinkedIn groups and subgroups for almost all relevant business groups. Some examples are:

- Writing—Writing Mafia, Green Communicators, GWEEN (Green Writers Ever Evolving Network)
- Project Management—PMI® Certified PMPs®, Project Management Link, Green PM (subgroup), EarthPM™

How project managers use a communications channel is limited only by their own creativity. It can be used to inform a targeted community about the efforts during the execution of a project. It could be used to find subject matter experts to use to enhance *expert judgment*, a necessary and effective tool for the project manager.

Specifically targeted groups like Gantthead.com (400,000+ members) are additional resources for the project manager. Communications on these types of sites can again enhance the common set of project management tools, and give the project manager further insight into potential issues and opportunities. It can also give the project manager a "sounding board" to discuss potential issues and opportunities within their own project. One of the key tasks during directing and managing the project's execution is training and managing of project staff. Targeted groups can provide additional direction to specific resources designed to help the project manager accomplish those tasks. White papers, helpful Web sites, and online educational opportunities are all part of that direction provided.

Finally, there are sites like Monster.com that can save project management resources. These sites provide immediate information to allow a project manager to screen potential candidates (whether permanent staff or consultants) quickly and effectively. Staffing is another one of those processes that go on during the execution phase of the project plan.

A search of the literature reveals that project managers spend between 60 and 80% of their time doing some sort of communications activity. If using social media can save 20% or more of a project manager's time (a limited project resource), on a large project that could mean a savings of tens of thousands of dollars. Additionally, the use of social networking is taking advantage of electronic media to get out the project's messages, rather than generating paper or traveling to meetings, which reduces the project's carbon footprint. And a side benefit of using social networking to reach out to a variety of people quickly and easily can do one other thing that is very important to the project manager, *reduce risk*!

EXECUTION OF GREENALITY EFFORTS

During this phase of the project, it is important that the greenality efforts outlined and defined in the planning phase are properly executed. This part of the project has much of the excitement and energy on the project. All of the planning efforts are now coming to fruition. It is also a time when the project team's primary focus is on the "product" of the project, that is, more of the functionality of the project, and aspects such as quality assurance and greenality (product or process) tend to get less attention. However, it is a critical time for greenality. Since it is a relatively new concept in a project, if the attention is not put on greenality at this point, the message will be clear that "greenality is not that important." That certainly is not the message that we want to convey. Managing the project's greenality is a necessary part of project management function and must be considered. *As a matter of fact, more emphasis must be placed on greenality for just that reason.* Because it is a relatively new function as we've defined it, it isn't well understood. Special attention has to be placed on greenality so that it is understood and so that the commitment to it remains strong in order for it to succeed. The question then is how to continue to create a strong sense of commitment to greenality for the project's product and processes.

A point to remember when communicating is that there is a variety of social networking sites that can enhance the experience.

For real estate agents, it's "location, location, location." Similarly, for project managers it's "communications, communications, communications"—with the intraproject team, interproject team, and external stakeholders. The alert mechanisms such as the jeopardy and escalation processes are one area of communications that has to be monitored for any changes in the greenality requirements of the project. The immediacy of intrateam communications is crucial to maintaining the focus on the green aspects of the projects. The project team is the first line of defense for protecting the project's greenality. Any issues that arise affecting the project's greenality must *immediately* be brought to the attention of the project manager. Because of the sensitivity of the greenality efforts, failure to immediately report, acknowledge, and resolve such issues could result in the perception that there is a lack of commitment to the effort on the part of the project team. If the team is perceived to lack the commitment, then the project's green efforts can be viewed as insignificant. Here, actions speak louder than words, and your project team is sending "messages," intentionally or not, by their apparent commitment as judged by the larger organization. It's your job as PM to be aware of that implication and to lead the team not only as a project team but as an example.

For the same reason, regular status meetings should be held and will be more frequent during the critical deployments of the greenality aspects of the project. The reason is to closely monitor the greenality efforts of the project to avoid a situation as described earlier. We all know about scope creep. Here we are talking about avoiding *hope creep,* when individuals get behind on their deliverable and "hope" to catch up, and *effort creep,* where individuals are working as hard as they can but cannot get any traction, endangering their deliverable. This is what we're trying to avoid with earlier detection of any issue. Another technique to use when encouraging project communications within the team is to develop an environment where it's okay to pass along bad news. The project manager needs to *always* create a team environment that says it is fine to raise your hand if you are having an issue, but especially with the deployment of any green aspects of the project. It may be a little easier to do that with green issues because they are relatively new and may not be well understood, so questions are natural. Remember, we don't mean to assert that greenality efforts of a project are any more important than the other project execution factors; it is just that we are concentrating on greenality aspects of the project in this book.

WARNING SIGNS OF GREENALITY PROBLEMS

1. Resource Instability: A review of the project's greenality resources can yield an abundance of information about the effectiveness of the project's greenality effort. Attitudes of team members are directly proportional to the project's chances of success. When team members become concerned with the direction of the project, particularly the efforts to green the project's product and processes, they may react in several ways. If the reaction is frustration, that attitude will be transferred to team members' actions and manifest itself in requests by team members to be transferred from the project, absenteeism, and change in mood. Another indication of resource instability is the reduction of funding for project green efforts. A third indicator is a lack of follow-through of the commitments from suppliers. Excuses will be offered for suppliers that do not meet the greenality standards in original agreements.

2. Changes in Strategic Direction: The original commitment by management becomes diminished as the project progresses, especially when the project experiences other difficulties, with cost or schedule for instance. Greenality, because it is a newer effort and therefore doesn't have the longevity of commitment as other aspects of the project, is the first to be cut.

3. Risk versus Reward: Some of the issues of greenality may appear to come at a higher cost. This is particularly evident when the project is viewed from a microlevel. Without considering all of the aspects of the project, the risk of undertaking green efforts in both the project and the project processes may appear not to be an advantage to the organization's return on investment. As a result, greenality may be sacrificed, a mistake in our opinion.

4. Workload Queues: This is covered in detail in Chapter 10, but for now we just want you to be aware of the concept of waste and work piling up in front of one resource on the project as an indicator that the project itself may be experiencing waste (and a lack of greenality).

Project decisions are made in a "global" environment, including emotions and politics. Green efforts are a political hot potato. Arguments are being made by both sides. Although the progreen efforts seem to be succeeding, we think that it is not for the obvious reasons. Green efforts will prove to be good for everyone, the environment, the social responsibility aspect, and *because they will save money in the long run.* The project manager, therefore, must be vigilant, especially during the execution phase of the project, and be aware of the problems that may arise from greenality efforts.

GREENALITY OF SUPPLIERS

During the implementation of the project, the project team will have a chance to monitor the greenality of suppliers of project needs. Project managers don't expend a lot of energy on supplier management. The general thinking is that once the commitment has been made, and contracts and agreements signed, the suppliers will follow the requirements and the project team will track those milestones, deliverables, and quality specified. Greenality efforts are different. As was outlined in the planning process, the depth of a supplier's greenality requirements is limited only by the influence of the project. The more influence the project has to the supplier—monetarily, fit with the supplier's mission, or other reasons—the more influence the project manager will have in requesting that the supplier adhere to greenality efforts defined during the project-planning process. Those requirements were conveyed to the suppliers during the project-planning effort.

The complexity of the greenality request will dictate the depth of monitoring the project team will have to complete. As an example, if the supplier has agreed to electronic invoices, it is very easy to check to see if the supplier is meeting that requirement. However, if the supplier has agreed to reduce its electrical usage, thereby reduce its carbon footprint, the team may need to request a formal report, electronically of course, of their energy reduction efforts. Remember, every project, no matter what its intended goal, and every supplier to the project, although not obvious, has some green aspects. This is one area of the project where greenality efforts may include some additional costs. These costs should be planned in during the supplier selection process, as well as added to the greenality commitments during the budgeting process.

There is a significant body of knowledge in the area of green procurement. See the resources listed in Chapter 14.

CAPTURING GREENALITY LESSONS LEARNED

All project managers know that lessons learned is one of the best ways to avoid problems with future projects. With greenality efforts, lessons learned become even more important, because it is not just about the project product, but also about potential changes to the fundamental methods of managing a project. It is therefore crucial that the project team accurately record lessons learned during the execution of the greenality effort as well as the execution of the project itself. This will be especially important when it is the first time greenality efforts are included in the project.

ENDNOTE

1. EarthPM, *EarthPM's Five Assertions of Green Project Management,* part of mission statement, 2007 ©, http://www.earthpm.com.

8

Taking the Watch (Monitoring and Controlling)

One of the primary duties of the project manager and project management team is to monitor and control the project to ensure that the project plan is being effectively executed. Monitoring includes the processes used to gather, document, and inform about project progress, and controlling is about using that data to make project decisions.

The DIKW Pyramid

We like to say that it is the job of the project manager to *advance* data into information, knowledge, and even wisdom. This is called the knowledge or DIKW pyramid.

Data means bits of project information not organized in any particular way. I picture a phone number, a test measurement, a temperature, and a Web site address thrown haphazardly together in an e-mail.

Information is a state in which there is order to that madness. Now I picture a stakeholder contact list, organized and sorted by internal and external stakeholders, and whether they have high or low risk tolerance, and are in favor of or opposed to the project, associated with all of their contact numbers.

Knowledge is that information leveraged to convey some important meaning. So we may have the information on our stakeholders organized so that we know not only phone numbers and e-mail addresses, but also key behaviors of stakeholders. For instance, we know that when a certain stakeholder calls us, we are dealing with someone whose birthday is tomorrow. A shallow example, perhaps, but it gives you the idea.

Wisdom could be defined as applying *intelligence* (data, information, and knowledge) and *experience* toward the attainment of a common good. We see the PM as gathering all of the intelligence possible, combining it with experience, to get to this stage (at the top of the knowledge pyramid) of wisdom.

The execution of the project plan is now under way as specified in Chapter 7. The project needs to be monitored and controlled, including the green aspects defined in Chapter 6:

- We will be monitoring and controlling the project greenality aspects of:
  - Scope
  - Schedule
  - Costs
  - Quality
  - Risks
  - Performance reporting
  - Procurements
  - Taking appropriate action
    - Corrective
    - Preventative
    - First aid

Without the proper and disciplined monitoring of the project's "health," it would be impossible to ensure that, in fact, the project was on track to successfully meet or exceed stakeholders' expectations. The commitment to greenality is one of those success criteria. Project managers are used to monitoring and controlling traditional project components. We are concentrating on monitoring and controlling the green aspects of the project because the inclusion of green considerations in the project plan is relatively new and therefore could add a layer of complexity. We also feel that this is just another characteristic of viewing the project through an environmental lens. Regardless of how familiar the project manager is with monitoring and controlling the traditional project components, the execution of the project plan including green aspects will be unfamiliar at first. It will take some additional effort beyond that of fundamental project monitoring and controlling. The project management team will be even less familiar with the monitoring and controlling of the project's green aspects. As a result of these uncertainties, a good monitoring and controlling program must be set up and should integrate these green aspects as determined by the project manager and team.

Being educators, we're always pleased when students (experienced project managers *themselves*) bring their own (sometimes comical) views of project management to our courses. One student, for example, shared the "Six REAL Phases of a Project" with our class. This is a tongue-in-cheek look at project management. There are many variations on this "theme," but we like this one.

Phase 1: Enthusiasm
Phase 2: Disillusionment
Phase 3: Panic
Phase 4: Search for the Guilty
Phase 5: Punishment of the Innocent
Phase 6: Praise and Honors for the Nonparticipants

Funny, yes. But it does contain a kernel of truth. Learn a little from this comedy—watch for your project falling into the traps identified by this humorous view—that captures a little bit of truth.

Monitoring and controlling the project's output and processes will certainly help you avoid Phases 2 through 6, at least as just described.

GREENALITY DATA COLLECTION AND ANALYSIS

There are many effective ways to collect data on a project and they all start with *observation*. Simply put, observation is about watching (hopefully previously identified) project indicators. One of those indicators is the set of key project *milestones*. Milestones are those places in the project, single points in time, when the execution of a planned task is complete. Sometimes we call them "anchors" because they hold the schedule to a fixed point, such as the end of a quarter or a date by which proposals are due. From a green perspective, if we were doing a software project, and the recyclable-packaging design was due on the first day of a given month, then that is a milestone, and one of the many milestones the project manager is assessing. As the milestone approaches, the project manager can use a metric of completion to give an indication of project progress. And if it gets to the point where the milestone is not met, it gives the project team a chance to look at all of the constraints and consider replanning. In our example, the team may want to revisit the cost and quality of the packaging at that point in time. The more critical the task, the more frequent and well-publicized the milestones should be. This is particularly true with the green aspects of the project. Because they are relatively new tasks to the project, they should be monitored more closely. Any trade-offs of the green aspect of the packaging to gain time or reduce costs should be vetted against the environmental management plan. Here's where the vigilance piece comes in for greenality—it's the difference between monitor and control versus monitor and *sigh*. Another observation tool is the Earned Environmental Management System, a system outlined in the following paragraphs that can help to determine if there are any variances in particular aspects of the project's greenality. The observation of the health of the project's green aspects, as well as the health of other project aspects, is critical to the success of the project. The aim of conscientious observation is to catch issues that arise *while there is still time to do something about them,* even if it means terminating the project. Those familiar with large government projects are probably aware of the macabre statistics that indicate that even with only 20% of the project complete, if you are behind schedule or above budget, those aspects will likely never recover.

The process of greenality data analysis involves collecting relevant data about the project's greenality efforts and then analyzing it, seeking some reference point as to how effective the efforts have been, if they are being maintained, and deciding whether or not any "course corrections" need to be completed. The data supplied in the process can come from a variety of qualitative and quantitative techniques. Some of the data inputs are relatively accessible. The project's planned schedule and budget are used in the variance analysis process of earned value management (EVM). EVM is not intended to provide detail as to what actions should be taken on a project, but is designed to provide a measurement of whether or not there are any variances in schedule and costs at any point in project execution. Remember what we said earlier about advancing data into information, knowledge, and wisdom? Earned value is a way to do that. See the vignette "A Case for Earned Value" at the end of this chapter for an example of *why* you'd want to use it. In any case, the earned value technique uses as variables earned value (EV) and actual costs (AC) to determine if there is a cost variance, and EV and planned value (PV) to determine if there is a schedule variance. The formula for determining if there is a variance in schedule is SV = EV – PV. A positive or negative SV indicates there is a schedule variance. The formula for determining if there is a budget variance is CV = EV – AC. A positive or negative CV indicates that there is a budget variance. These numbers are not meant to be definitive, but only to alert the project manager that there is a variance and that further study is needed to determine the cause.

Earned environmental value (EEV) is used specifically to determine if there is any variance in the greenality aspects of the project. Why should greenality have its own measurement? It doesn't, not really. Using EEV, the project manager looks at a specific greenality aspect of the project as if looking at a specific task within the work breakdown structure. With the Earned Value Management System (using EV), it is advisable to look at a group of tasks across the project to determine an overall variance view of either schedule or costs. For instance, looking at a group of six tasks at a single point in time shows that some are ahead of schedule, some behind, with a net gain of 0 perhaps. Earned environmental value management (EEVM) is different because of the nature of the tasks involved. Although green must be "built in," many of the green aspects of the task can be separated out, and for monitoring purposes should be managed as such. Also, since they are markedly fewer in number than the rest of the project tasks, analyzing them individually will not be an issue.

Other methods to collect data on projects include interviewing team members to see if there is any effort, feature, or hope creep.[1] Do all team members have traction on their tasks, or are they working as hard as they can and not making any progress (effort creep)? Are there team members who are behind on their tasks and are hoping to catch up (hope creep)? Are there team members who have "gold plated" project requirements, adding features that were not included in the scope of the project (feature creep)?

Watch for attitude issues here, on both sides of the spectrum. That is, there may be those who are highly motivated, green-focused individuals (so-called "tree huggers") who may go overboard on the green aspects of the project, and there may be those who are cynical and hesitant to work on these aspects. Each presents their own set of problems. Be sure that the team has bought into the green aspects of the project and are putting commensurate effort—neither *boycotting* nor *overemphasizing* this work.

Other types of effective methods data for collecting qualitative data on the green aspects of projects are interviews and focus groups. Interviewing and focus groups are most effective because the project manager will be able to evaluate the "sense" by the stakeholders of the effectiveness of the greenality efforts. This is important because initially, there will be resistance to green efforts, accusations of greenwashing and tree-hugging, and a reluctance to institute anything new. Interviews and focus groups will be able to provide data related to the "softer" side of the issues. "How do you really feel about greenality?" Remember, green project management is in its infancy. Perceptions will have to be managed with the same intensity as when project management itself was in its infancy. We found over and over again in our interviews even with project leaders overseeing projects that were green by project intent that they were not always clear on or fully aware of the green aspects of their projects. This surprised us, but in retrospect often this surprised *them* even more! With respect to the project team and other contributors, remember that people have a natural distrust of change, and hesitancy to adopt anything that is new. Initially, the field of project management and project managers themselves were viewed with skepticism, as an added burden, with no value added. That perception has been proven very wrong, as will the current perception of greening a project.

MEASURING THE PERFORMANCE OF GREENALITY

In order to understand the complexity of measuring greenality efforts on a project, it is necessary to look in detail at one of the greenality elements. Nonproduct output (NPO) is one of the elements of greenality the project manager needs to monitor and control. NPO is defined in Chapter 3 as "essentially what is left prior to reuse or recycling, yet after all efforts for redesign and reduction have been exhausted." However, the NPOs we are talking about here are those that have been defined. One example of NPO is the carbon emissions of the project. Once the efforts identified in the project-planning process are implemented, they are monitored via performance measurements. For instance, have the efforts been implemented so that the anticipated remediation has been realized? How does the project manager measure success of that effort? One of the ways is to look at the energy use of the project itself. For instance, how much savings have been realized by the efforts instituted by the project team? Have computers and other power-consuming equipment been turned off at night and on weekends? Have motion-sensing lights been installed in common areas, turning off desk lighting when not needed? Has the office been using natural light when available? Have programmable thermostats been installed in offices (home offices included)?

To do this, one must start somewhere—and that somewhere is an established baseline. If you do nothing else in this area of greenality, at least take the opportunity to baseline a typical project (assuming that there is some kind of vague theme from project to project in your programs and portfolios). We need to have a basis for comparison, so this idea of baselining is extremely important. From that baseline, you can look at your organization's environmental management plan (EMP) or other benchmark and target improvements. You will at least be able to say that you have achieved energy savings of X%, for example, because you can compare it to this baseline.

CONTROLLING THE ISSUES

Should issues arise, and it is inevitable that they will, there has to be some way to control them. It is all about reducing the differences between what is actually occurring with the project and that which has been planned for the project. As outlined previously, there are methods for evaluating the greenality of the project at any one point in time, as well as establishing progress and trends. Some of the issues that will arise can be categorized as being related to the human resources (including effort and hope creep), supplier and equipment needed, costs and budgets, and changes to the project, whether planned scope changes or unplanned scope changes (scope creep and feature creep). All must be identified and controlled in a way to minimize the impact on the project.

Because of the sensitivity of greenality efforts, being new and for the most part sailing in uncharted waters, the project manager must be careful to work to correct the errors in the project, and to avoid going on a "witch hunt." It is very easy for a project manager who is emotionally invested in the greenality of the project to try to single out individuals who are not *as invested*. This may inadvertently cause problems. By doing this, the focus of correcting issues in a process-oriented way, so they do not occur again, is diminished. Also, singling out individuals (or organizations for that matter) will divert from the real issues involved. People have a tendency to grab onto emotional issues. Once that happens, that becomes the only focus, or at least a distracter from the true issues. As a result, innovation and creativity, so important to greenality, become stifled. There is a loss of the "global picture," and short-term results take precedent over long-term gains. Once those issues become public, there is a chance that, while the project may be heading for a successful conclusion, it may be derailed because of emotional issues. This is especially true with the greenality efforts on the project. It is therefore imperative that the issues be separated from the people. Always focus the project team (and *refocus* them if necessary) on their end goal, and the way that this end goal fits into the organization's overall portfolio and mission.

KEEPING ON AN EVEN KEEL

As we've said many times, there are two aspects to green project management: the *product* of the project and the *process* of the project. *Both* need to be controlled in order to keep the project on an even keel, or at least not keeling over too far one way or the other. Remember, dealing with greenality means sailing in heavy winds. One of the ways to manage and control the project's processes is to have periodic process reviews. How are we doing with the process greenality efforts including reducing energy use, using digital information transfer, electronic meetings, and others? As much as is possible, these should be quantifiable measurements, not esoteric assessments. Recall the need for benchmarking mentioned earlier.

Using the data collected during the interview (with team members), review the personnel assignments, how people are feeling, and whether or not there is any hope or effort creep. More frequent reviews should be done early in the project because of uncertainty surrounding project greenality. The project manager will be able not only to assess the team's abilities to execute on project greenality, but also to provide additional coaching to help them understand what is expected. Gaining a better understanding by team members of the greenality efforts on the project will help to get their buy-in. Without the buy-in, the project is likely not to succeed. It is important to note that there are advantages to the individual team members in understanding and committing to the project's greenality efforts. There is a "green wave." Understanding the issues around the wave can give the team members additional insight for the next project, making them better and more competent candidates. Some team members care deeply about the commitment to sustainability. Evaluation of the EEVM data can lead to valuable information relative to how the resources are being utilized. Variations in the schedule and costs of greenality efforts could lead to reallocation of resources. For instance, if the costs of the resources are running below estimates, and the schedule is behind, additional resources could be acquired to help bring the greenality efforts back on schedule. The use of milestones to track green efforts can be a powerful tool to monitor variances and look for future trends.

Here are some examples of green milestones:

- Link from project to organization's EMP established
- External audit(s) of project or product completed
- Periodic review of greenality measurements
- Individual and team recognition of achieving greenality goals/ objectives

CHANGE CONTROL AND GREENALITY

Overall change control is very important to the management of a project. Additionally, there may be other specific change control processes needed on a project depending on its complexity, such as schedule, budget, quality, risk, or other processes. We are advising that, because greenality aspects of project represent a new facet of project management, a specific greenality change control process (GCCP) be adopted for the project (although it needs to be integrated into the project's overall change control process, of course). By defining the GCCP, the project manager has the ability to "set the standard" of control, specifically addressing the issues of how changes are requested, who has the authority to review and recommend changes, and how those changes will be implemented. The purpose of the GCCP is to have a mechanism to record, review, and decide on changes to the project's greenality efforts in a disciplined (project management) manner.

Greenality scope creep can occur if there is overenthusiasm for sustainability or green aspects of the project. Unlike normal scope creep, this may be allowable if the benefit fits with the environmental management policy of the organization. However, the more likely scenario is that there will be a tendency to *reduce* the scope of greenality. "Despite altruistic statements to the contrary, green could be the first to go," says Bas de Baar of Project Shrink (http://softwareprojects.org), "so watch out!" The misconception is that by reducing the scope of greenality, project costs will decrease. As we have pointed out, greenality is free; or rather, by practicing good greenality management, costs to the project, not only for greenality, but for resources in general, will be reduced. Bas also points out that green project management is more "about project *managers* than project *management.*" By this, he means that the control of greenality really is a human thing and not just a project thing. It is going to come down to whether or not the project manager—the *person*—takes control in situations where greenality is slipping.

A change control system specifically targeted to greenality is essential, more to protect the project's greenality than anything else at this point. We are also aware, however, that the view of greenality is going to change. More and more project managers will embrace the concept as it is shown to save and enhance scarce project resources. So, for both reasons, a change control system for greenality should be established. The project manager should require that all changes to greenality follow the change request process. That process provides a written record, and we recommend that an electronic method be established. The change request process includes escalation guidelines, which will tell us, depending on criteria, who in the organization has to approve the request. For instance, there could be a principle in the change request process that states that if there is a limited impact on schedule or cost (less than 5%), then the project manager can approve that request. The system will include a mechanism for recording change requests, and processes for reviewing the change, communicating results of the request, tracking changes that are accepted or put on hold, as well as amending the project plan to include the changes (see Figure 8.1). The mechanism to record the change request will include the following information:

- An information section (requester responsibility)
  - Tracking number
  - Name of requester (could be any stakeholder)
  - Description of change
  - Impact (including criticality) of change as viewed by the requester
    - Also connect the change to the organization's EMP assertions
  - Any alternatives to change that may have been considered

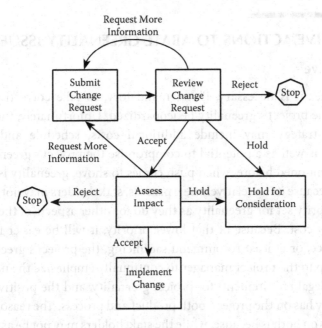

FIGURE 8.1
Change control process.

- Initial review section (project manager or designated agent responsibility)
  - Impact of change as viewed by the project manager (or other designated agent)
  - Recommendations to change committee if there is a change committee
- Final review section (responsibility of final authority on changes)
  - Approval/rejection/hold for further study
  - Reasoning for approval, rejection, or hold
  - If accepted—time frame and priority of implementation

One thing to note here: the change control for greenality could be integrated into the overall change process if that works better for the project team. In either case, be sure that greenality changes are indeed tracked with at least the same intensity as all other project changes.

Using the example of **nonproduct output,** one corrective measure that could be put in place is to add stack scrubbers on smoke stacks to reduce or eliminate harmful substances being released into the atmosphere.

EFFECTIVE ACTIONS TO ABATE GREENALITY ISSUES

Corrective

Sometimes it is necessary, if not mandatory, to take corrective action should the project's greenality be jeopardized. Unfortunately, the impact of that strategy may include additional costs, schedule and quality impacts, as well as a potential to compromise the project's greenality. As we've mentioned before, when push comes to shove, greenality is an easy target. Because it is a relatively new process, stakeholders may not have the same priority set for greenality as they do for other aspects of the project, especially cost. Because of that lower priority, it will be easier for them to sacrifice, or at least recommend sacrificing, the project's greenality. It will be up to the project manager to continually emphasize the need (and perhaps legal requirement) for project greenality, and the positive effects greenality has on the project, both product and process. The reason for the emphasis on both is because, while the stakeholders may not be as familiar with greenality, they will relate to the product before they will relate to the process. But for the project manager, it is a balance of both that will make the project successful in terms of results and resource savings. It will be especially discouraging to successfully manage the green aspects of the project to a point, only to have the savings and success compromised during project execution. One other criterion for corrective action is that it should be done in a procedural way. One of the best ways to ensure that happens is to use an abbreviated plan-do-check-act cycle (sometimes called the Deming cycle or Shewhart cycle; see Figure 8.2). Corrective actions should be planned with a disciplined process, then implemented on a trial basis, evaluated to make sure they solve the problem, and then standardized into the project.

Proactively building greenality into a project is an example of a **preventative strategy**.

Preventative

A much better alternative is to conscientiously monitor the project so that the issues that need to be controlled are identified early enough to use a

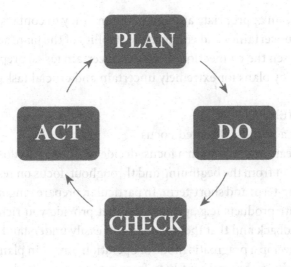

FIGURE 8.2
PDCA cycle.

preventative strategy. While the planning effort is the best place for antici-
pating greenality issues (greenality risks), the environment in which the
project is being executed can and probably will change as the project progresses. The longer the implementation period for the project, the greater
the chance the *project's environment* will change. It is helpful to remember
that the project is being planned, executed, monitored, and controlled in
a dynamic environment, made even more dynamic by the new process of
greenality. One important sphere within that dynamic environment is the
social aspect, one of the issues of sustainability. The balancing act includes
all of those aspects—social, technical, and environmental.

Here are some tips for working in a dynamic environment from NASA:[2]

PLANNING & CONTROL
1. Plan and Control to Accommodate Change
   1.1 Adopt a learning-based planning mind-set: start by defining
       project objectives that are dictated by customer's needs, however,
       don't finalize them before you quickly explore the means and the
       solutions.
   1.2 Start planning early and employ an evolving planning and
       control process: continuously and throughout project life col-
       lect feedback on changes in the environment and in planning
       assumptions, and on project performance.

1.3 Use an appropriate amount of redundancy to contain the impact of uncertainty and enhance the stability of the plan: add reserves; loosen the connections between uncertain tasks; prepare contingency plans for extremely uncertain and crucial tasks.

IMPLEMENTATION
2. Create a Results-Oriented Focus
   2.1 Create and maintain a focus; decide what NOT to do.
   2.2 Right from the beginning and throughout, focus on results—both long-term and short-term. In particular, prepare tangible intermediate products (e.g., prototypes) that provide you rich and quick feedback and that the customer can easily understand and assess.
   2.3 Develop a pragmatic mode of operation: invest in planning yet be ready to respond swiftly to frequent, unanticipated events; identify areas where the search for optimal solutions is worthwhile, but for the rest of the project be ready to embrace "good enough" solutions; for repetitive activities or critical areas (i.e., safety), employ formal/standard work processes; otherwise, employ those that are informal or ad hoc.

ATTITUDE
3. Develop a Will to Win
   3.1 Develop a sense of a mission and "own" the project. (When needed, engage in politics and work hard to sell your project.)
   3.2 When necessary, challenge the status quo and be willing to take calculated risks.
   3.3 Persevere; keep trying until you get it right. Yet, know when it is time to change course or retreat.

PEOPLE & ORGANIZATION
4. Collaborate through Interdependence and Trust
   4.1 Take recruiting very seriously and spend as much energy as possible on getting the right people.
   4.2 Develop trust-based teamwork and make sure that team members feel dependent upon each other and share the conviction that they are mutually responsible for project results.
   4.3 Throughout project life, assess team functioning, ensure its alignment on project objectives, and renew its energy.

COMMUNICATION

5. Pull and Push Information Intensively

5.1 Frequently and vigorously pull and push (ask for and provide) information within and across functions and teams, including all project stakeholders.

5.2 Employ multiple communication mediums; in particular, extensive frequent face-to-face communication and modern information technology.

5.3 Adopt a moving about mode of communication. (Moving about helps you affect project performance by better understanding what is going on and by influencing people's behavior in a timely, natural, and subtle way.)

Purchasing carbon offsets is an example of a Band-Aid. It can be used, not as a substitute for reducing emissions, but as a measure with continuing efforts to reduce carbon emissions.

Band-Aid

Stop the bleeding! The least desirable solution to any project issue is *first aid*. The reason is that this solution is meant to be a stopgap, temporary, sometimes called a work-around. It is not meant to be a permanent solution that goes to the heart of the matter. However, once these "fixes" are in place and the bleeding has stopped, unless there is a conscious effort to return to the scene of the crime, these fixes will remain until they break again. Rather than using this strategy, it is better to take the time to fix it right. Inevitably these temporary measures will fail in the future. A warning about the project's greenality—it is even easier to ignore the permanent solution and let the temporary solution stand, because there will be few stakeholders who will have the same urgency about greenality issues as the green project manager and project team.

A Case for Earned Value

How "DONE" are we?

- Let's say you have a task in a project that involves modifying the boilers in 10 production facilities to make them more energy efficient. You have four weeks to modify these identical boilers. Each boiler is planned to take 20 staff hours—for a total of 200 staff hours, at $50 per hour. In other words you have an overall $10,000 budget for labor. Materials are provided by government stimulus grant money (in the form of boiler upgrade kits) so there are no expected material costs.

- At the halfway point of your schedule (two weeks elapsed), your site managers report the following:
  - Labor use: 120 staff hours, plus $500 in material costs (unexpected purchase of special tools and fittings).
  - Number of boilers installed: 4
- So … how done are we?
  - Are we **40%** done because we have 4 out of 10 boilers completed?
  - Are we **50%** done because we have spent two of our four weeks?
  - Are we **60%** done because we have spent 120 of our 200 staff hours?
  - Are we **65%** done because we have spent $6,500 of our budget of $10,000?
- *You can see that there is ambiguity in the way progress is reported here.* The earned value technique is meant to avoid that ambiguity and report progress in a standardized way, geared toward monetized units.

In this case, we can calculate earned value (EV) as follows:

- Our total budget is 200 staff hours × $50 per hour, or $10,000, or $1,000 per boiler.
- EV = 4 (boilers done) × $1,000 (planned expenditure per boiler) = $4,000
- AC = labor + material costs (which is 120 hours × $50/hr) + $500, or $6,500
- PV = The amount we planned to have spent by the second week = $10,000/2 or $5,000

With these three basic numbers, we can calculate the variances and indices:

- Cost variance (CV) = EV − AC = $4,000 − $6,500 = −$2,500

We are over budget by $2,500!

- Schedule variance (SV) = EV − PV = $4,000 − $5,000 = −$1,000

We are behind schedule by $1,000 (a peculiar way to state schedule, but a standard one).

- Cost performance index (CPI) = EV/AC = $4,000/$6,500 = 0.6153

For each dollar we spent, we are getting only about 62 cents worth of accomplishment.

- Schedule performance index (SPI) = EV/PV = $4,000/$5,000 = 0.8

For each hour we put in, we are completing only 80% of what we had planned.

It's beyond the scope of this book, but we can also use these figures to forecast the completion figures for the project. In this case, for example, we can take our budget at completion (BAC) of $10,000 and divide by the CPI to get our estimate at completion (EAC) to predict our final project cost, given the data at our halfway point. That would be:

- EAC = BAC/CPI = $10,000/0.6153 = $16,252

ENDNOTES

1. Robert K. Wysocki, Robert Beck Jr., and David Beck, *Effective Project Management*, 2nd ed., (New York: Wiley, 2000).
2. Alexander Laufer, "Managing Projects in a Dynamic Environment: Results-Focused Leadership," http://askmagazine.nasa.gov/pdf/pdf19/105553main_19_resources_letterfromeditor.pdf.

Section III

Approaching the Finish Line

It is good to have an end to journey toward, but it is the journey that matters in the end.

Ursula K. LeGuin

9

The Beginning and the End?

Famous Dutch author Harry Mulisch organized one of his more lengthy books, *The Discovery of Heaven*,[1] into four big chunks. He titled them:

The Beginning of the Beginning
The End of the Beginning
The Beginning of the End
The End of the End

HEAVEN ON EARTH

Mulisch provides an interesting way for us to think about his book (which, by the way, has been made into an excellent movie), but it also gives us a way to think about the projects on which we work. Even more important, it's a good way to look at the *products* of the projects on which we work. In fact, we could take a lesson from *The Discovery of Heaven* and apply it to *Earth*. We could say that our projects usually involve only the first two chunks. We take an idea from its inception to the point to which it can be deployed *en masse*—put into operation or the *steady state*. Whether it's a bridge, a sales-training program, a new piece of software, or a wind farm, we, the project manager, get that idea to the steady state. So ironically, we tend to focus *not* on that steady state, but rather on the beginning of the beginning and the end of the beginning—the *getting to* the steady state. Here, in the first two chunks, there are indeed green considerations, but they are focused on the project *itself* and the resources the project team *itself* uses. They are not focused on longer-term issues like what happens to the product as it is manufactured, used, and disposed of.

"Think about it: you may be referred to as a consumer, but there is very little you actually consume—some food, some liquids. Everything else is designed for you to throw away when you are finished with it. But where is "away"? Of course, "away" does not exist. "Away" has gone away.[2]

—William McDonough and Michael Braungart (2002)

But although we do that out of necessity (focus on *getting to the steady state*), the product of the project does *not* stop when we hand it over. The wind farm, or bridge, or even the software release, was made from materials from the earth, has a life, and has an end of life. Its creation has an impact on our surroundings, it has a useful period of operation (during which there are side effects such as consumables and waste), and the final disposal of the product itself has to be considered as well. We assert that the project manager, though not traditionally tasked with doing so, should also be thinking about the last two of Harry Mulisch's chunks: the *beginning of the end* and the *end of the end*.

LIFE CYCLE THINKING BASICS

One man's floor is another man's ceiling …

Figure 9.1 (EPA, 1993) will help get us oriented. In fact, to project managers this chart should look strikingly familiar. It is reflected in the *PMBOK Guide* diagram for any of its 42 processes—inputs, tools and techniques, and outputs. In this case, inputs are raw materials and energy; tools and techniques are the acquisition of those items, manufacturing processes, use/reuse and maintenance, and recycle and waste management. Outputs (other than the product itself, of course) are atmospheric emissions, waterborne and solid wastes, coproducts, and other releases. Perhaps the most important part of this drawing is at the bottom: the system boundary. This will be discussed later when we get into the details of a life cycle assessment (LCA).

At times, there is confusion between LCA and other approaches that are life cycle based (but that someone may also be calling LCA). Simplifications to LCA have been necessary mainly due to the lack of readily available life cycle inventory data, which is needed to model the entire product system. Sometimes it is driven by specific interests.

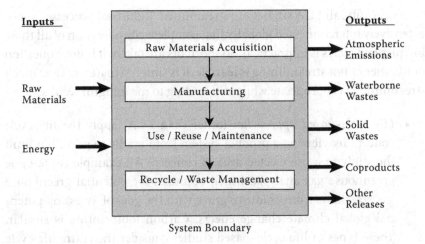

FIGURE 9.1
Inputs and outputs.

- *Life cycle–based approaches* use the life cycle concept to view a product system from cradle to grave but limit the study to a predetermined area of concern, such as energy use, global warming, or material use.
- *Using the life cycle concept, or life cycle thinking,* considers all the interconnected activities within an industrial system from cradle to grave; i.e., it considers the entire product life. The information may be qualitative, or very general quantitative data may be used. The benefit of using life cycle thinking is to help understand the entire life cycle of the product.
- *Life cycle assessment* is a standardized approach to quantifying natural resources used and wastes released to the environment from cradle to grave; to assessing the impact of quantities; and to identifying opportunities to affect environmental improvements.
- *Screening/streamlined LCA* is a simplified application of the LCA methodology in that it is typically a first attempt to collect data and information, e.g., by using generic data, standard modules for transportation or energy production, etc., followed by a simplified assessment.
- *Detailed LCA* is an application of the LCA methodology that uses more comprehensive, quantitative data and incorporates life cycle impact assessment of all relevant environmental aspects. A detailed assessment usually involves multiple iterations of data collection, impact assessment, and scope definition.

Of necessity, all LCA studies are streamlined. Industrial processes are so extensively interconnected globally that complete consideration of all these interdependencies is impractical. So shortcuts are taken. It is not a question of whether or not streamlining is feasible; it is simply a matter of how much streamlining is appropriate while still leading to meaningful results.

- *Life cycle–based approaches* (other than LCA) apply the life cycle concept by viewing a product system from cradle to grave but limit the study to a preselected area of concern. An example is life cycle greenhouse gas analysis, which accounts for potential greenhouse gas emissions from cradle to grave with the goal of assessing potential global climate change effects. Carbon footprinting is similar. These types of life cycle–based studies consider the entire life cycle activities but account only for inputs and outputs of interest.
- *Life cycle management* (LCM) integrates information that is generated by different tools, of which LCA is one. LCA captures environmental information, but information covering other factors, such as costs, performance, risk, community, etc., is also needed. LCM will be covered again later in the discussion. LCA is an effective tool to capture environmental information, but information on other aspects, such as economics and societal needs, is also required. LCM is a term that is growing in popularity and captures the notion of broadening a study's boundaries to help decision makers achieve sustainability goals. The goal of LCM is to integrate information that is generated by different tools to address risk, economics, technological, and social aspects of products, services, and organizations, as well as the environmental aspects. LCM, as with any other project management tool, is applied on a voluntary basis and can be adapted to the specific needs and characteristics of the individual projects and their organizations.

The holistic approach of LCA is the cornerstone of sustainability. LCA is an effective tool for identifying opportunities for continual improvement within industrial operations and for moving us in the right strategic direction.

History is full of stories of notorious cases where "good intentions" have gone wrong (see text box). To keep organizations from choosing practices that might ultimately become environmentally ruinous, a holistic tool is needed.

The Road to (Environmental) Hell Is Paved with Good Intentions.

We have a long history of "solving" one problem by unwittingly creating another—often with even worse long-term consequences. For example, kudzu, an Asian vine, was introduced as a way of preventing erosion in earthworks in the southeastern part of the United States. It now grows unchecked and is considered an invasive pest. In the 1930s and 1940s, many cities thought streetcar tracks and overhead wires were "unsightly." They rushed to replace "old and inefficient" means of transport with fossil-fueled vehicles. Some claim it was all a "Great Streetcar Conspiracy" by carmakers, oil companies, and tire manufacturers seeking a bigger market for their products. Today, the same cities are spending millions to re-establish rail lines in an effort to minimize traffic congestion, reduce air pollution, and curb urban sprawl. Scores of drugs meant to cure ills were later found to cause horrible harm. Thalidomide is the most infamous (and tragic) example. But even medicines as familiar as aspirin have been linked to serious health problems (for example, Reye's syndrome in children). The debate continues over the potential long-term effects of pharmaceuticals in the environment (PIE), while the list of drugs with dubious risk-to-benefit profiles expands each year. Similarly, the long-term risks and benefits of genetically modified (GM) foods and crop-based ethanol fuels continue to be hotly debated.[3]

LIFE CYCLE ASSESSMENT

The basic tool that can be used for holistic life cycle thinking is an LCA (life cycle assessment). LCA enables the estimation of the cumulative environmental impacts, often including impacts that go beyond the boundaries of traditional analyses. By including the impacts throughout the product life cycle, LCA provides a comprehensive view of a product's environmental aspects. It is also valuable in evaluating the many interdependent processes that are involved in a product system. A change to one part of this system may have unintended consequences elsewhere. LCA identifies the potential transfer of environmental impacts from one medium to another (e.g., eliminating air emissions by creating a wastewater effluent instead) and/or from one life cycle stage to another (e.g., from use and reuse of the product to the raw-material acquisition stage). If an LCA were not performed, the transfer might not be recognized and properly included in the analysis because it is outside of the typical scope or focus of product design and selection processes.

In connecting the different parts of the system, many LCAs have led to unexpected and nonintuitive results. This is especially true for products that are sourced from natural, bio-based feed stocks, such as the various products that are being made from corn, including packaging, cups and plates, and bioethanol, to name just a few. These products are often perceived as environmentally superior to comparable products that are made from non-renewable petroleum feed stocks. However, if we look more broadly at the product life cycle, it becomes clear that large amounts of pesticides and fertilizers and land are needed to grow corn. Figure 9.2 shows how fertilizers that are applied to cropland runoff into waterways and end up in the Gulf of Mexico, contributing to the hypoxic Dead Zone (fertilizers cause algae to bloom, then as the algae die, their decay depletes the water of oxygen causing a condition of hypoxia). Yet it is not immediately obvious to connect corn from the upper Midwest of the United States with water pollution problems in the Gulf of Mexico, a thousand miles away. Using a holistic approach to these kinds of analyses highlights how the environmental impacts of alternative products may lead to unanticipated consequences.

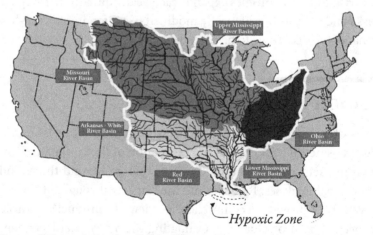

Zone of Hypoxia in the Gulf of Mexico:
Approximately 7,000 square miles
(about the size of Connecticut and Rhode Island combined)

FIGURE 9.2
Zone of hypoxia.

An Example of How One Company Has Used a Life Cycle Perspective in Product Improvement

The Procter & Gamble Company uses the life cycle perspective to improve the environmental profile of their products through holistic innovation. Limiting the analysis to energy usage, a study of their product lines revealed a previously underappreciated value for energy in the use phase (i.e., the heating of water) for the laundry detergents they produce.

According to their calculations, if every U.S. household used cold water for laundry, the energy savings would be 70 to 90 billion kilowatt-hours per year, which is 3% of the nation's total household energy consumption. These savings would translate into 34 million tons of carbon dioxide per year not released into the environment, which is nearly 8% of the Kyoto target for the United States.

LCA was recognized by *Time* magazine as the method behind calculating "Ecological Intelligence," one of "10 Ideas Changing the World Right Now" (March 23, 2009). LCA is the tool that is used to understand the environmental impacts of the products we make and sell. The article says that we can use LCA to "understand the global environmental consequences of our local choices."

So, what is behind this recent growing interest in LCA?

Growing global interest in the life cycle concept can be attributed to four main drivers:

1. Global climate change concerns (or the "Al Gore Effect," popularized by his 2006 documentary *An Inconvenient Truth*)
2. Walmart's planned development of a sustainability index for the products they sell that is intended to include life cycle data
3. The building industry's focus on green buildings and green products (such as the U.S. Green Building Council's LEED standard)
4. General interest by product manufacturers to be considered "green" by their consumers

A BRIEF HISTORY

LCA had its beginnings in the 1960s. Concerns over the limitations of raw materials and energy resources sparked interest in finding ways to account for total energy use and to project future resource supplies and use. In 1969, researchers initiated an internal study for the Coca-Cola Company that laid the foundation for the current methods of life cycle inventory analysis in the United States. In a comparison of different beverage containers to determine which container had the lowest releases to the environment and least affected the supply of natural resources, this study quantified the raw materials and fuels used and the environmental loadings from the manufacturing processes for each container. Other companies in both the United States and Europe performed similar comparative life cycle inventory analyses in the early 1970s.

The process of quantifying the resource use and environmental releases of products became known in the United States as a resource and environmental profile analysis (REPA), while in Europe it was called an Ecobalance. With the formation of public interest groups encouraging industry to ensure the accuracy of information in the public domain, and spurred on by the oil shortages in the early 1970s, a protocol methodology for conducting these studies was developed and further evolved.

From 1975 through the early 1980s, as interest in these comprehensive studies waned because of the fading influence of the oil crisis, environmental concerns shifted to issues of hazardous and household waste management. However, throughout this time, REPAs and Ecoblances continued to be conducted, and the methodology improved through a slow stream of about two studies per year, most of which focused on energy requirements.

When solid waste became a worldwide issue in 1988, LCA again emerged as a tool for analyzing environmental problems. As interest in all areas affecting resources and the environment grew, as with the growing awareness of sustainable development, the methodology for LCA is again being improved. A broad base of consultants and researchers across the globe has been further refining and expanding the methodology. The need to move beyond quantifying, or simply inventorying, resource use and environmental emissions, as is done in a REPA, brought LCA methodology to another point of evolution with the development of life cycle impact assessment methodology.

LCA became popular again in the early 1990s, at first mainly to help support environmental claims that could be directly used by companies in the marketing of their products or services, and indeed this is one use of an LCA. By the same token, a 1999 survey by Rubik and Frankl[4] showed that LCA is most often used for internal purposes such as product improvement, support for strategic choices, and benchmarking. In fact, the best description of an LCA (from the Carnegie-Mellon University site [http://www.eiolca.net/], which provides a free LCA tool) is:

> Life cycle assessment (LCA) is a way to investigate, estimate, and evaluate the environmental burdens caused by a material, product, process, or service throughout its life span. Environmental burdens include the materials and energy resources required to create the product, as well as the wastes and emissions generated during the process. By examining the entire life cycle, one gets a more complete picture of the environmental impact created and the trade-offs in impact from one period of the life cycle to another. Results of LCAs can be useful for identifying areas with high environmental impact, and for evaluating and improving product designs.

STANDARDS FOR LCA

The key organizations working this area are the Society of Environmental Toxicology and Chemistry (SETAC), the United Nations Environment Program (UNEP), and the International Organization for Standardization (ISO). SETAC is an academic society that organizes regular conferences on LCA, particularly on LCA methodology, and it sponsors work groups on unresolved issues. It provides a forum where researchers and industry representatives discuss and exchange ideas on methods development. SETAC published its Code of Practice in 1993. This described the components of the traditional LCA, which we discuss later: goal and scope definition, inventory analysis, impact assessment, and improvement assessment. Starting around 1996, the ISO started to develop LCA standards. They published a series of LCA standards between 1997 and 2000.

ISO established that LCA stands for "life cycle assessment" not "analysis," based on the definition of *analysis* as a strictly quantitative exercise, while an "assessment" also allows for qualitative information in the process.

In 2002, UNEP joined forces with SETAC to launch Life Cycle Initiative, an international partnership. The Life Cycle Initiative's aims consist in putting life cycle thinking into practice and in improving the supporting tools through better data and indicators (see http://lcinitiative.unep.fr/).

The European Commission's Joint Research Centre is supporting the development of recommended international methods, indicators, reference data, and pilot studies to facilitate life cycle thinking in business and public administrations. The focus of the *European Platform on Life Cycle Assessment* is on increased awareness and use through scientific robustness, quality assurance, and consensus building (see http://lct.jrc. ec.europa.eu/eplca).

In 2006, ISO published a second edition of the LCA standards. ISO 14040, *Environmental Management—Life-cycle Assessment—Principles and Framework,* together with ISO 14044, *Environmental Management— Life-cycle Assessment—Requirements and Guidelines,* cancels and replaces the previous LCA standards. The 2006 editions of ISO 14040 and 14044 are mainly focused on readability and consistency; the technical document remains nearly identical to the 1997 editions. ISO standard 14040 describes basic principles and the framework for LCA. Your organization can use it as an overview of the LCA and its applications and limitations. Like the *PMBOK Guide*, these documents do not prescribe methodologies for goal and scope definition, inventory, impact assessment, and interpretation; rather, they provide the framework and clarify the terminology. Also, since these standards must be applicable to a variety of practice areas, they are necessarily rather general in nature. Still, they provide a thorough collection of terms and definitions, the methodological basis, and excellent recommendations for reporting considerations and approaches for critical review. They also provide an appendix describing the application of an example LCA.

CARBON FOOTPRINTING BASED ON LCA

Very recently introduced by Carbon Trust and the BSI (British Standards Institute) is the PAS 2050. The PAS 2050:2008 is a publicly available specification for assessing product life cycle GHG emissions. It is an independent standard, developed with significant input from international stakeholders and experts across academia, business, government, and nongovernmental organizations (NGOs) through two formal consultations and multiple technical working groups. At the time of writing, this standard

TABLE 9.1

Society of Environmental Toxicology and Chemistry Code of Practice

Planning	Statement of objectives
	Definition of the product and its alternatives
	Choice of system boundaries
	Choice of environmental parameters
	Choice of aggregation and evaluation method
	Strategy for data collection
Screening	Preliminary execution of the LCA
	Adjustment of plan
Data collection and data treatment	Measurements, interviews, literature search, theoretical calculations, database search, qualified guessing
	Computation of the inventory table
Evaluation	Classification of the inventory table into impact categories
	Aggregation within the category (characterization)
	Normalization
	Weighting of different categories (valuation)
Improvement assessment	Sensitivity analysis
	Improvement priority and feasibility assessment

was available for free at the following Web site: http://shop.bsigroup.com/en/Browse-by-Sector/Energy--Utilities/PAS-2050/.

PERFORMING AN LCA

As a project manager, you will likely not be the individual performing the LCA, but if possible you should promote its use and get involved. When performing an LCA, take into account the guidelines in Table 9.1, which come from the aforementioned SETAC Code of Practice.

HOW TO PROMOTE THE USE OF AN LCA

If you want to push for an LCA with your sponsors, it's advantageous to know how they can be used and what information and impact it will have on the development of the product or service. Table 9.2, taken from *The Hitch Hiker's Guide to LCA,*[5] can come in handy for "selling" the LCA to your development team.

TABLE 9.2

Promoting Use of LCA

Application	Requirement on Methodology
Decision making, choice between alternative actions/products	Reflection of consequences of contemplated actions
Market communication, e.g., environmental product declaration	Creditability and review process require high transparency
Product development and purchasing (little time on competence of user results)	Results presented with high level of aggregation
Decisions on national level, e.g., on waste treatment strategies	Data representing national averages
Identification of improvement possibilities, own product	Site-specific data

Note: From H. Baumann and A.-M. Tillman, *The Hitch Hiker's Guide to LCA: An Orientation in the Life Cycle Assessment Methodology and Application* (Lund, Sweden: Studentlitteratur AB, 2004). With permission.

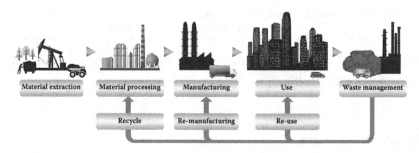

FIGURE 9.3
Environmental impacts.

THE LIFE CYCLE OF THE PRODUCT OF YOUR PROJECT

The product of your project will have different impacts on the environment during different stages of its life. Consider Figure 9.3. The products of some projects will use materials that will have adverse environmental effects when extracted or processed, but when the product is deployed, it may have relatively little effect in its use and may be very easy to recycle or reuse. Aluminum products are an example of this scenario. However, a printer or product powered by disposable batteries will create the bulk of its environmental impact while it is being used by the customer because of its "consumables" (cartridges or batteries).

Let's take the example of a washing machine:

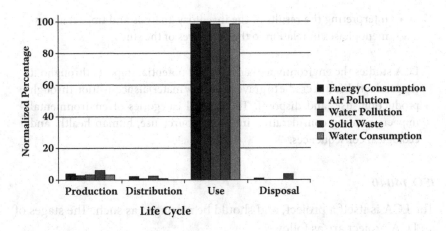

FIGURE 9.4
Environmental impact. From Kadamus, C., *Eco-Design or Greenwashing* (Cambridge, England: Cambridge Consulting, 2009). With permission.

It will be obvious to our readers that a washing machine uses energy and water. There is also, however, solid waste (packaging, end-of-life disposal, and of course the ubiquitous disappearing sock). Most of the environmental impact is during its use (see Figure 9.4). Most of the solid-waste impact comes from the two stages of delivery—first, when the packaging is removed and disposed of, and second, the eventual end-of-life disposal of the machine. The solid-waste levels are indeed significantly higher than other contributors at these stages, but notice that they total less than 15% of the solid waste produced by the washing machine. If this surprises you, a detailed LCA would reveal the packaging for laundry detergents and other consumables that are discarded as the machine is used. This illustrates how careful we must be to consider every aspect of use, and to draw the "system boundary" broadly enough to cover this aspect of the washing machine's use.

LCA Fundamentals

Let's restate the definition of an LCA, this time taking input from ISO 14040:

LCA is a technique for assessing the environmental aspects and potential impacts associated with a product by:

- compiling an inventory of relevant inputs and outputs of a product system;
- evaluating the potential environmental impacts associated with those inputs and outputs;

- interpreting the results of the inventory analysis and impact assessment phases in relation to the objectives of the study.

LCA studies the environmental aspects and potential impacts throughout the product's life (i.e. cradle to grave) from raw materials acquisition through production, use, and disposal. The general categories of environmental impacts needing consideration include resource use, human health, and ecological consequences.

ISO 14040

The LCA is itself a project, and should be managed as such. The stages of an LCA project are as follows:

1. *Goal Definition and Scoping:* Define and describe the product, process or activity. Establish the context in which the assessment is to be made and identify the boundaries and environmental effects to be reviewed for the assessment.
2. *Inventory Analysis:* Identify and quantify energy, water, and materials usage and environmental releases (e.g., air emissions, solid-waste disposal, wastewater discharges).
3. *Impact Assessment:* Assess the potential human and ecological effects of energy, water, and material usage and the environmental releases identified in the inventory analysis.
4. *Interpretation:* Evaluate the results of the inventory analysis and impact assessment to select the preferred product, process, or service with a clear understanding of the uncertainty and the assumptions used to generate the results.

Let's go over each of these in some detail. A great source for a full treatment of this subject, and on which much of this text is based, is the EPA's LCAccess Web site (http://www.epa.gov/nrmrl/lcaccess/).

Goal Definition and Scoping

The objectives of an LCA are to examine systemwide effects on a cradle-to-grave basis, in order to assess all potential impacts to all media. Only through the consideration of the entire suite of issues can potential trade-offs be identified when systems are changed or a selection is made between choices.

LCA has several possible uses, including establishing a baseline of environmental impacts and forming the basis of eco-labeling, but identifying opportunities for improvement is a key application. Used with other information, the results of an LCA can be used to support decision making and provide the basis for achieving sustainability. This is the "begin with the end in mind" philosophy as promoted by Steven Covey. What do you want to get out of the LCA? Following are example outcomes taken from the U.S. EPA, which can help define the goals and scope of an LCA project:

- *Support broad environmental assessments:* The results of an LCA are valuable in understanding the relative environmental burdens resulting from evolutionary changes in given processes, products, or packaging over time; in understanding the relative environmental burdens between alternative processes or materials used to make, distribute, or use the same product; and in comparing the environmental aspects of alternative products that serve the same use.

- *Establish baseline information for a process:* A key application of an LCA is to establish a baseline of information on an entire system given current or predicted practices in the manufacture, use, and disposal of the product or category of products. In some cases, it may suffice to establish a baseline for certain processes associated with a product or package. This baseline would consist of the energy and resource requirements and the environmental loadings from the product or process systems that are analyzed. The baseline information is valuable for initiating improvement analysis by applying specific changes to the baseline system.

- *Rank the relative contribution of individual steps or processes:* The LCA results provide detailed data regarding the individual contributions of each step in the system studied to the total system. The data can provide direction to efforts for change by showing which steps require the most energy or other resources, or which steps contribute the most pollutants. This application is especially relevant for internal industry studies to support decisions on pollution prevention, resource conservation, and waste minimization opportunities.

- *Identify data gaps:* The performance of an LCA for a particular system reveals areas in which data for particular processes are lacking or are of uncertain or questionable quality. Inventory followed by impact assessment aids in identifying areas where data augmentation is appropriate for both stages.

- *Support public policy:* For the public-policy maker, LCA can help broaden the range of environmental issues considered in developing regulations or setting policies.
- *Support product certification:* Product certifications have tended to focus on relatively few criteria. LCA, only when applied using appropriate impact assessment, can provide information on the individual, simultaneous effects of many product attributes.
- *Provide information and direction to decision makers:* LCA can be used to inform industry, government, and consumers on the trade-offs of alternative processes, products, and materials. The data can give industry direction in decisions regarding production materials and processes and create a better-informed public regarding environmental issues and consumer choices.
- *Guide product and process development:* LCA can help guide manufacturers in the development of new products and processes.

Like any project, it's important to identify which of these—or other—goals and outcomes will define success.

Cradle-to-gate boundaries—excluding downstream activities past product manufacture—have been called, and are being called, an LCA. Such cradle-to-gate studies draw the boundary after the product manufacture (see Figure 9.5) stage, *but* claims must relate to what was studied and not be overstated. Such studies are helpful in improving the product supply chain but may miss important impacts that occur at end of life.

Inventory Analysis

The next step is an inventory analysis, or LCI (life cycle inventory), defined by the EPA as a process of quantifying energy and raw material requirements, atmospheric emissions, waterborne emissions, solid wastes, and other releases for the entire life cycle of a product, process, or activity.

The steps for an LCI are as follows:

1. Develop a flow diagram of the processes being evaluated.
2. Develop a data collection plan.
3. Collect data.
4. Evaluate and report results.

The LCI is compiled from a variety of data sources, including:

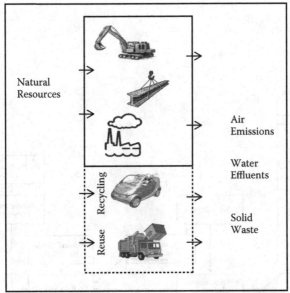

Study Boundary

FIGURE 9.5
Cradle-to-gate boundaries.

- National LCI databases (http://www.nrel.gov/lci) and the Ecoinvent database (http://www.ecoinvent.org)
- Proprietary company data through surveys
- Published data from research by labs and universities
- Public databases, e.g., EPA's Toxics Release Inventory (TRI) and E-Grid
- Estimated data for new products
- LCA practitioner's databases, such as SimaPro and GaBi

Using data that are made available through a public or private database greatly simplifies the inventory process. But the trade-off is the loss of transparency in how the data were collected and modeled.

A "Bar Chart"

Without going into details but in an effort to show how this process can be enlightening, we provide the example flow diagram (Figure 9.6) for a bar of soap (so it's *that* kind of bar chart).

Note the extensive considerations that fall far outside of the normal view of "bar of soap," such as the harvesting and processing of silage, grains,

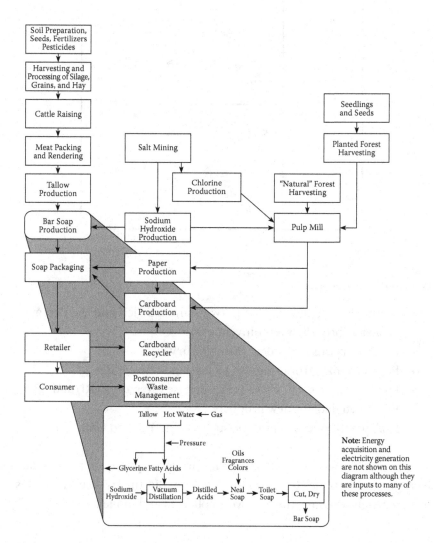

FIGURE 9.6
Flowchart of a bar of soap.

and hay for the livestock that produces the tallow for the soap, and the seedlings that provide the trees, which provide the pulp, which provide the cardboard for the packaging of the soap.

The Life Cycle of a Bar of Soap

A typical bar of soap may seem quite small and insignificant. What impacts can it have? It can have quite a few.

The soap itself:
- Soap tallow: derived from animal fat (farm operations, corn and soybean production, and processing, shipping, meat packing, rendering, etc.)
- Lye: typically from electrochemical treatment of salt (sodium hydroxide, caustic, electricity)
- Perfumes and other chemicals from petroleum and other sources
- Energy: global warming gases, regional pollution impacts
- Water: use and contamination

The packaging:
- Paper and cardboard: trees and logging operations, chipping, shipping; clay for paper, water, energy, and chemicals (chlorine)
- Plastic wrap: petroleum, energy, water, and additives
- Paints and inks: petroleum, dyes, pigments, and inks

Transportation:
- Mining, processing, manufacturing, maintenance, and use of equipment to make and use trucks
- Consumer car to travel to and from store
- Consumer water transfer

Disposal: Most of soap ends up in the sewage water. The paper, plastic, and other wastes end up in landfills; some might be recycled.

These impacts are offset by health benefits and improved longevity of clothes and other products. But the goal should always be to minimize costs and increase benefits from use.

Impact Assessment

This is the *stage most associated with an LCA* and indeed it is the heart of the project. However, without the prior work the project will not have the consideration and thoughtfulness to be effective; it would be like jumping into the Gantt chart for your project without first understanding the objectives and having a charter.

The EPA defines this phase as follows: the impact assessment "is the evaluation of potential human health and environmental impacts of the environmental resources and releases identified during the LCI." Impact assessment should address ecological and human health effects; it should also address resource depletion. Life cycle impact assessment (LCIA) differs from a traditional or "classical" risk assessment. The focus given to risk assessment is a logical one considering it is the bread and butter of the EPA and is a well-established approach to evaluating pollutant and site-specific risk to human health and the environment.

While risk assessment modeling is at the ground level, impact modeling for LCIA is at a higher level of aggregation. For example, emissions of 24,200 pounds of CO_2 and 6.26 pounds of methane would be modeled as follows:

$$CO_2 \text{ GWP (global warming potential) impact factor value} = 1$$

$$\text{Methane GWP impact factor value} = 21$$

(i.e., methane is 21 times more potent than CO_2 as a global warmer)

$$CO_2 \text{ GWP} = 24{,}200 \text{ lb} \times 0.454 \text{ kg/lb} \times 1 = 10{,}900 \text{ kg } CO_2\text{-eq}$$

$$\text{Methane GWP} = 6.26 \text{ lb} \times 0.454 \text{ kg/lb} \times 23 = 65.4 \text{ kg } CO_2\text{-eq}$$

If CO_2 and methane are the only contributors to GWP, then

$$\text{Total GWP} = 10{,}965 \text{ } CO_2\text{-eq}$$

This type of calculation is applied for each impact category. Each life cycle stage as well as the entire life cycle is modeled.

The steps of an LCI, per the EPA, are as follows:

1. *Selection and Definition of Impact Categories:* identifying relevant environmental impact categories (e.g., global warming, acidification, terrestrial toxicity) (see Table 9.3)
2. *Classification:* assigning LCI results to the impact categories (e.g., classifying carbon dioxide emissions to global warming)

TABLE 9.3

Commonly Used Life Cycle Impact Categories

Impact Category	Scale	Examples of LCI Data (i.e., classification)	Common Possible Characterization Factor	Description of Characterization Factor
Global warming	Global	Carbon dioxide (CO_2) Nitrogen dioxide (NO_2) Methane (CH_4) Chlorofluorocarbons (CFCs) Hydrochlorofluorocarbons (HCFCs) Halons Methyl bromide (CH_3Br)	Global warming potential	Converts LCI data to carbon dioxide (CO_2) equivalents Note: global warming potentials can be 50-, 100-, or 500-year potentials.
Stratospheric ozone depletion	Global	Chlorofluorocarbons (CFCs) Hydrochlorofluorocarbons (HCFCs) Halons Methyl bromide (CH_3Br)	Ozone-depleting potential	Converts LCI data to trichlorofluoromethane (CFC-11) equivalents.
Acidification	Regional Local	Sulfur oxides (SO_X) Nitrogen Oxides (NO_X) Hydrochloric acid (HCL) Hydrofluoric acid (HF) Nitrates Ammonia (NH_4)	Acidification potential	Converts LCI data to hydrogen (H+) equivalents.
Eutrophication	Local	Phosphates (PO_4) Nitrogen oxide (NO) Nitrogen dioxide (NO_2) Nitrates Ammonia (NH_4)	Eutrophication potential	Converts LCI data to phosphate (PO_4) equivalents.

Continued

TABLE 9.3 (*Continued*)

Commonly Used Life Cycle Impact Categories

Impact Category	Scale	Examples of LCI Data (i.e., classification)	Common Possible Characterization Factor	Description of Characterization Factor
Photochemical smog	Local	Non-methane hydrocarbon (NMHC)	Photochemical oxidant creation potential	Converts LCI data to ethane (C_2H_6) equivalents.
Terrestrial toxicity	Local	Toxic chemicals with a reported lethal concentration to rodents	LC_{50}	Converts LC_{50} data to equivalents; uses multimedia modeling, exposure pathways.
Aquatic toxicity	Local	Toxic chemicals with a reported lethal concentration to fish	LC_{50}	Converts LC_{50} data to equivalents; uses multimedia modeling, exposure pathways.
Human health	Global Regional Local	Total releases to air, water, and soil	LC_{50}	Converts LC_{50} data to equivalents; uses multimedia modeling, exposure pathways.
Resource depletion	Global Regional Local	Quantity of minerals used Quantity of fossil fuels used	Resource depletion	Converts LCI data to phosphate (PO_4) equivalents.
Land use	Global Regional Local	Quantity disposed of in a landfill or other land modifications	Land availability	Converts mass of solid waste into volume using an estimated density.
Water use	Regional Local	Water used or consumed	Water shortage potential	Converts LCI data to a ratio of quantity of water used versus quantity of resources left in reserve.

3. *Characterization:* modeling LCI impacts within impact categories using science-based conversion factors (e.g., modeling the potential impact of carbon dioxide and methane on global warming)
4. *Normalization:* expressing potential impacts in ways that can be compared (e.g., comparing the global-warming impact of carbon dioxide and methane for the two options)
5. *Grouping:* sorting or ranking the indicators (e.g., sorting the indicators by location: local, regional, and global)
6. *Weighting:* emphasizing the most important potential impacts
7. *Evaluating and Reporting LCIA Results:* gaining a better understanding of the reliability of the LCIA results

Interpretation

Now it's time to take the *carefully* researched and categorized information and convert it *carefully* into knowledge and wisdom. Attempting to "collapse" indicator values to a single score must be done with extreme caution. One could not, for example, easily come up with a way to combine the attributes of Hillsville (see Figure 9.7) into one single score, as shown in the figure, by adding dates to elevation to population to get a total! You would have a number, but it wouldn't have useful meaning or wisdom associated with it. This is why we stress "carefully."

Moving from the results of the impact assessment to a final decision requires additional considerations:

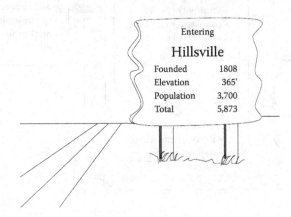

FIGURE 9.7
Welcome to Hillsville.

- Normalization (assessing the relevant potency of the impact)
- Valuation (applying the importance of each impact based on a set of values)
- Uncertainty management (reflecting the variation in the data)

And then, the results apply only to the decision maker who applied the weighting scheme.

Figure 9.8 is a specialized version of the LCA process with a focus on the interpretation portion. The steps in the interpretation are:

1. Identification of the significant issues based on the LCI and LCIA
2. Evaluation that considers completeness, sensitivity, and consistency checks
3. Conclusions, recommendations, and reporting

Step 1 is straightforward and involves highlighting the main issues found in the previous LCA project phases. Step 2 is a "reflection" on the

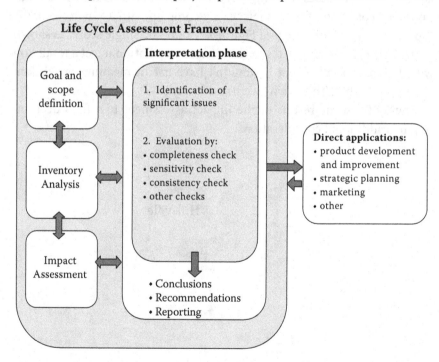

FIGURE 9.8
Life cycle assessment framework. Adapted from ISO® 14040: 2006.

TABLE 9.4

Examples of Checklist Categories and Potential Inconsistencies

Category	Example of Inconsistencies
Data source	Alternative A is based on literature and Alternative B is based on measured data.
Data accuracy	For Alternative A, a detailed process flow diagram is used to develop the LCI data. For Alternative B, limited process information was available and the LCI data was developed for a process that was not described or analyzed in detail.
Data age	Alternative A uses 1980s-era raw materials manufacturing data. Alternative B uses a one-year-old study.
Technical representation	Alternative A is a bench-scale laboratory model. Alternative B is a full-scale production plant operation.
Temporal representation	Data for Alternative A describe a recently developed technology. Alternative B describes a technology mix, including recently built and old plants.
Geographical representation	Data for Alternative A were data from technology employed under European environmental standards. Alternative B used the data from technology employed under U.S. environmental standards.
System boundaries, assumptions, and models	Alternative A uses a global warming potential model based on 50-year potential. Alternative B uses a global warming potential model based on 100-year potential.

work and information that went into the LCA. This is done for full transparency, and identifies areas where there could be inconsistencies in the analysis.

It should include the following checks:

1. Completeness Check: examining the completeness of the study
2. Sensitivity Check: assessing the sensitivity of the significant data elements that influence the results most greatly
3. Consistency Check: evaluating the consistency used to set system boundaries, collect data, make assumptions, and allocate data to impact categories for each alternative. A checklist of potential inconsistencies is provided in Table 9.4.

Step 3 comprises conclusions, recommendations, and reporting. Here the focus is on impartiality and clear communication of the discoveries of the LCA.

As to drawing conclusions, the EPA has this to say:

> A few words of caution should be noted. It is important to draw conclusions and provide recommendations based only on the facts. Understanding and communicating the uncertainties and limitations in the results is equally as important as the final recommendations. In some instances, it may not be clear which product or process is better because of the underlying uncertainties and limitations in the methods used to conduct the LCA or the availability of good data, time, or resources. In this situation, the results of the LCA are still valuable. They can be used to help inform decision-makers about the human health and environmental pros and cons, understanding the significant impacts of each, where they are occurring (locally, regionally, or globally), and the relative magnitude of each type of impact in comparison to each of the proposed alternatives included in the study.[6]

And with respect to making recommendations and reporting, the following recommendation comes from the EPA and ISO:

> LCAs can produce different results even if the same product seems to be the focus of the study. Differences can be caused by a number of factors, including:
> - Different goal statements
> - Different functional units
> - Different boundaries
> - Different assumptions used to model the data

Because of these possible variations, maintaining transparency in how the study was conducted is a critical element in reporting the results.

Reporting the Results

Now that the LCA has been completed, the materials must be assembled into a comprehensive report documenting the study in a clear and organized manner. This will help communicate the results of the assessment fairly, completely, and accurately to others interested in the results. The report presents the results, data, methods, assumptions, and limitations in sufficient detail to allow the reader to comprehend the complexities and trade-offs inherent in the LCA study.

If the results will be reported to someone who was not involved in the LCA study, e.g., third-party stakeholders, this report will serve as a reference document and should be provided to them to help prevent any misrepresentation of the results.

The reference document should consist of the following elements:

1. Administrative information
   a. Name and address of LCA practitioner (person who conducted the LCA study)
   b. Date of report
   c. Other contact information or release information
2. Definition of goal and scope
3. Life cycle inventory analysis (data collection and calculation procedures)
4. Life cycle impact assessment (methodology and results of the impact assessment that was performed)
5. Life cycle interpretation
   a. Results
   b. Assumptions and limitations
   c. Data quality assessment
6. Critical review (internal and external)
   a. Name and affiliation of reviewers
   b. Critical review reports
   c. Responses to recommendations

Note the "critical review." This is an important part of the report. It accommodates the multiple views of peers within and outside the organization to help ensure impartiality and completeness of the analysis.

LCA SOFTWARE TOOLS

A number of commercial software programs and consultants are available to help with conducting an LCA. The two LCA tools most often used are SimaPro and GaBi (see Chapter 14). Almost all of these sources provide life cycle inventory and, with a little practice in using the software, they can make conducting an LCA a fairly straightforward process. The trade-off is that how the data were modeled is not transparent, so the user must trust the modeler. This also makes system comparisons problematic if different data sources are used since it is not easy to determine what assumptions were applied. Still, these LCA tools are very popular, especially among grad students, and the companies are being kept very busy with the demands for their products.

Limitations to Conducting an LCA

- LCA can be very resource and time intensive. As more LCAs are conducted, more data are becoming available, but gathering reliable inventory data can still be difficult.
- Life cycle impact assessment models vary.
- Additional impact data are needed, especially for new frontiers, such as nanotechnology.
- Converting impact results to a single score is a subjective process requiring value judgments. It cannot be done based solely on natural science.
- An LCA study should be used as one component of a more comprehensive decision-making process for assessing the trade-offs with cost and performance facets.
- All assumptions or decisions made throughout the study must be reported. If not, the final results may be taken out of context or misinterpreted.

Maintaining Transparency

It is very important to maintain transparency in reporting an LCA study. This is necessary because it is not a single, prescriptive process. Rather, it involves multiple decision points that can greatly influence the outcome of the LCI and the LCIA. Although it would be best to achieve consensus on the methodology, thereby reducing or eliminating variations in the practice, at this time, the best solution is to maintain transparency and to fully document how the data were calculated. That way, even if others may not agree with the approach, it is at least clear what was done.

Most project managers, by nature, are skeptics. It is not that we do not trust; we do. It is that the accountability of a project lies with us, so we check and check again. Table 9.4 illustrates some of the potential issues that can arise with data, not just LCI data because, with minor alterations, it can be used for the evaluation of any data.

Note: See Chapter 14 for further reading on life cycle assessment. Also, the authors would like to acknowledge and thank Mary Ann Curran, Program Manager, Life Cycle Research, U.S. Environmental Protection

Agency. Mary Ann collaborated with us on this chapter, contributing an important part of the material in it.

ENDNOTES

1. Harry Mulisch, *Discovery of Heaven,* reprinted ed. (New York: Penguin, 1997).
2. William McDonough and Michael Braungart, *Cradle to Cradle: Remaking the Way We Make Things.* (San Francisco: North Point Press, 2002)
3. Richard MacLean, 2009, http://www.competitive-e.com/Current/Good_Intentions_ MacLean_EQM_Winter09-MacLean.pdf.
4. P. Frankl and F. Rubik, *Life-Cycle Assessment (LCA) in Business, An Overview on Drivers, Applications, Issues and Future Perspectives,* Global Nest: the International Journal. 1(3): 189, 1999.
5. H. Baumann and A.-M. Tillman, *The Hitch Hiker's Guide to LCA: An Orientation in Life Cycle Assessment Methodology and Application* (Lund, Sweden: Studentlitteratur AB, 2004).
6. U.S. Environmental Protection Agency, LCA 101, Chapter 5, p. 58, online document, http://www.epa.gov/nrmrl/lcaccess/.

10

Lean Thinking, Muda, and the Four Ls

LEAN THINKING AND YOUR PROJECT

The overarching principle for this section is that Lean thinking can and should be applied to the project itself as well as be folded into the planning for the product of the project. The PM can be a change agent not only for the project but for the long-term effects of the project (the operation of the project's product). In other words, you, the PM, can make a lasting difference for the organization, and even beyond, to the population outside your organization and even beyond this generation.

One of the concepts threaded through Lean thinking is the theory of constraints, which should not be a foreign concept to project managers because it has found its way into project management in the form of critical chain project management and is at the heart of agile methodologies, such as those used in software development (Scrum, XP, DSDM).

As PMs we know that to use the critical chain, we revise the critical path project plan with resource constraints to get the critical chain project plan. Where the critical path is based on task dependencies, the critical chain is based on the additional (and important) information we get when we look at resource dependencies. The critical chain method (as illustrated by Herbie, the slow hiker in Eliyahu Goldratt's *The Goal*[1]) allows us to identify the bottleneck or constrained resource.

For those of you not familiar with *The Goal*, here is a summary of that portion of the book:

> The protagonist of the book, Alex Rogo, takes his son and his son's Boy Scout troop on a hike. The slowest hiker, Herbie, keeps falling behind the rest of the hikers, and the queue in front of him keeps stretching out because the leaders (by definition) are walking much more quickly. The quickest hikers generally have no space between them and the Scout in front of them. Rogo realizes that even if the quickest hikers slow down or stop (to take a breath,

have a snack, or to tie their shoes), they catch up because their average pace is faster than that of the kid in front of them. However, if a Scout who is slower than the hiker in front of him pauses, he never regains his original spacing and the line of hikers continues to expand. Herbie is slowing down the whole group because Rogo (as the responsible adult) has to keep all of the kids in viewing distance and has to call ahead for them to wait. Rogo gets the inspired idea to place Herbie at the front of the line, which solves the problem of keeping the group together, since everyone has to walk as slowly as Herbie does. But he doesn't stop there. To increase the group's rate of speed, he redistributes what Herbie is carrying in his pack (cans of soda, a collapsible steel shovel, and a jar of pickles) into the quickest hikers' backpacks (as well as his own). The lighter load allows Herbie to walk more quickly. Rogo realizes that really, this is *a system of hikers,* hiking the trail *together,* and that any individual hiker's speed is dependent on the hiker's speed in front of him. He further realizes that the changes in pace are statistical fluctuations, and Herbie is the system *constraint.* He has slowed down his speediest hikers, and this intuitively seems quite wrong. However, the *system* is moving at its fastest *collective* rate *because it is moving at the constraint's fastest speed.* So, even though hikers are not individually efficient, *the system's constraint is efficient* and therefore *the system is running at its highest possible efficiency.*[2]

In critical chain project management, we do not have individual safety buffers at each *individual task;* we instead move the buffering to the overall project date, to protect that *team goal.* Progress is measured by the use (or lack thereof) of buffers.

Let's translate this into action.

Here are the "five focusing steps" of the theory of constraints:

1. **Identify the system's constraints.** What's slowing things down? Where is the bottleneck? Here are some triggers that help us identify a constrained resource:
   a. The resource is overloaded.
   b. Work piles up in front of the resource.
   c. Resources downstream from the resource under investigation are idle some of the time.
2. **Decide how to exploit the system's constraints. Make sure there is always work for the constraint to do.** Don't let it fall idle because of lack of resources. This can be accomplished with a (small) "feeding" buffer of work for the constraint. The responsibility of the resources in front of the constraint is to make sure this buffer is always filled with "just enough" work. **Make sure that the constraint works only**

on tasks that improve the process throughput. Cut all unnecessary, nonproductive work from the constraint.

3. **Subordinate everything else to the constraint conclusions from Step 2.** Since the constraints are keeping us from moving toward our goal, all the resources are applied that can assist in breaking them. Here are some examples of subordinating the constraint conclusions:

    a. Resources in front of the constraint can divert some of their excess time reviewing the work in progress they hand off to the constraint, so that the constraint doesn't work on faulty material.

    b. Resources following the constraint should use their slack time to ensure they don't introduce problems that could cause waste from the constraint's output. Remember, wasting output from the constraint, by definition, means wasting throughput of the entire system.

    c. Resources that are nonconstrained can assume some of the constraint's work or alternatively provide assistance that allows the constraint to focus on their throughput—creating work.

4. **Elevate the system's constraints.** If we continue to work toward breaking a constraint (also called elevating a constraint), at some point the constraint will no longer be a constraint. We have broken the constraint. Ways to elevate the system's constraints are:

    a. Improve the system tools, so that resources can work more quickly and accurately.

    b. Improve the training, coaching, mentoring, and community building of the human resources.

    c. Carefully and selectively add new resources.

5. **If the constraint is broken, return to Step 1.** When that happens, there will be another constraint, somewhere else in the system that is limiting progress to the goal. Don't let "inertia" become another constraint. When you solve your worst problem, your next-worst problem gets a promotion, of sorts, and becomes the next big thing you'll work on. The key here is that this is a continuous process.

LEAN METHODS

There are a variety of Lean methods that can be adapted by organizations to become Lean.

What Is Lean?

The following comes from James Womack:[3]

> The core idea is to maximize *customer value* while minimizing waste. Simply, Lean means creating more value for customers with less resources.
>
> A Lean organization understands customer value and focuses its key processes to continuously increase it. The ultimate goal is to provide perfect value to the customer through a perfect value creation process that has zero waste.
>
> To accomplish this, Lean thinking changes the focus of management from optimizing separate technologies, assets, and vertical departments to optimizing the flow of products and services through entire value streams that flow horizontally across technologies, assets, and departments to customers.
>
> Eliminating waste along entire value streams, instead of at isolated points, creates processes that need less human effort, less space, less capital, and less time to make products and services at far less costs and with much fewer defects, compared with traditional business systems. Companies are able to respond to changing customer desires with high variety, high quality, low cost, and with very fast throughput times. Also, information management becomes much simpler and more accurate.

In summary, like the theory of constraints, Lean thinking[4] is about:

- Continuous flow of value
- Value defined by customer
- Value pulled from provider by customer
- All done in search of perfection

A Case Study in Lean Thinking (An Illustration of Lean Thinking Beyond a "Project")

A company we are familiar with uses the world's most advanced technologies for the manufacturing of infrared optics elements including: spherical, aspherical and diffracted optical components; mirrors; metallic optics; and windows. These products are used in electro-optical systems, military, homeland security, commercial, and industrial applications, ranging from night vision equipment to industrial metal processing. The demand for this type of optics is increasing, and the company wanted to increase its production capabilities as quickly as possible. As you know, the setup of a new or improved manufacturing line is a *project*. The ongoing running of the manufacturing line is an *operation*. As the pieces of major manufacturing equipment started to arrive, they were installed at the most convenient location available at that time. The location of the machines themselves was not considered part of the original project, and handover to operations occurred. At the time, the team was considering applying Lean thinking to revise their manufacturing process. Lean thinking design called for the equipment to be relocated for reduced waste and improved efficiency and throughput. Had the project delivery considered this up front, the savings could have been instituted a year earlier at minimum.

This case helps illustrate the importance of connecting the project team's thinking with the long-term operation of the deliverable of the product, in this case, a manufacturing line.

Wastes

What are these wastes? The idea of the importance of eliminating waste was popularized as part of the Toyota Production System (TPS), and the identification of "The Seven Wastes." Muda is Japanese for waste—you will sometimes find this information referred to as the Seven Mudas.

Here, in general, are the Seven Wastes.

1. Overproduction: Simply put, overproduction means producing an item for a process before it is actually required. Overproduction is highly costly to a process because it prohibits the smooth flow of materials or services and will tend to degrade quality and productivity. This is why the Toyota Production System is referred to as "just in time" (JIT), because every item is made just as it is needed. Overproduction is sometimes referred to as "just in case." Working on a just-in-case basis creates unnecessarily long lead times, results in unneeded storage costs, and makes it more difficult for the process to detect defects. One way to find out where overproduction is "hiding" is to turn off the supply to the system and see where the inventory is built up.

2. Waiting: If goods are not moving or being processed by the system, the waste of waiting occurs. Amazingly, the vast majority of a product's life in traditional batch-and-queue manufacture will be spent

waiting to be processed in some way. Waiting can be caused by bad material flow, or production runs that are too long, or long distances between operations. A cure to this is to link the processes together (à la Goldratt) so that one process feeds directly into another.

3. Transporting: Moving product between processes incurs cost and adds no value to the operation. Excessive movement and handling may cause damage or decay in quality. This can be difficult to reduce, but mapping product or operations flows can make this easier to visualize.

4. Inappropriate Processing: In some cases, systems use expensive or unnecessarily high-precision equipment where simpler equipment or operations would be sufficient. In some cases, investing in smaller, more flexible equipment or operations, or creating manufacturing cells and combining steps can reduce the waste of inappropriate processing.

5. Unnecessary Inventory: Excess inventory—which makes us feel safe—tends to hide problems with a system. These problems should be identified and resolved in order to improve operating performance. Work in process (WIP), as stated previously, is a direct result of overproduction and waiting. This WIP takes up floor space and can interfere with good communications by "numbing" the real problems of the system.

6. Unnecessary or Excess Motion: The classic industrial engineers will be familiar with this form of muda. This waste is related to the human-machine interface and is seen in bending, lifting, stretching, reaching, and walking. Activities with excessive motion should be analyzed and redesigned for improvement—and this should be done with the system personnel for ideal effectiveness and buy-in.

7. Defects: Having a direct impact on the bottom line, defects have a high cost to organizations. We know this as project managers when we study the cost of quality. These costs come from rework or scrap, lost customers, and even lawsuits. There is, of course, opportunity to reduce defects at many facilities through involvement of employees, and continuous process improvement (kaizen).

A New Waste?

One further Muda has been added in some treatments of this subject. For example, current Lean thinking is that underutilization of employees is the eighth waste. This waste refers to not capitalizing on employees' creativity—and proposes that organizations can eliminate the other seven wastes more effectively if they better utilize their employees.

These wastes apply mainly to manufacturing. How might they apply to, say, software development? Mary Poppendieck translates this for us next.

The Basic Principles of Lean Development[5]

- Add nothing but value (eliminate waste)
- Center on the people who add value
- Flow value from demand (delay commitment)
- Optimize across organizations

The Seven Wastes of Software Development

- Overproduction = Extra Features
- Inventory = Requirements
- Extra Processing Steps = Extra Steps
- Motion = Finding Information
- Defects = Defects Not Caught by Tests
- Waiting = Waiting, Including Customers
- Transportation = Handoffs

What do we do about these wastes in software development? Agile methods, such as extreme programming, address these wastes as shown in Table 10.1.[6]

TABLE 10.1

Wastes in Software Development

Waste in Software Development	How Extreme Programming Addresses Wastes
Extra features	Develop only for today's stories.
Requirements	Story cards are detailed only for the current iteration.
Extra steps	Code directly from stories: get verbal clarification directly from customers.
Finding information	Have everyone in the same room, customers included.
Defects not caught by tests	Test first, both developer tests and customer tests.
Waiting, including customers	Deliver in smaller increments.
Handoffs	Developers work directly with customers.

Note: Adapted from Mary Poppendieck, *Principles of Lean Thinking,* http://www.poppendieck.com/papers, 2002. With permission.

TABLE 10.2

Manufacturing and Service Wastes

Waste Type	Manufacturing Section Wastes	Service Sector Wastes
Defects	Scrap, rework, replacement production, reinspection	Order entry, design, engineering errors
Waiting	Stock-outs, lot processing delays, equipment downtime, capacity bottlenecks	System downtime, response time, approvals
Overproduction	Manufacturing items for which there are no orders	Printing paperwork, purchasing items before they are needed, processing paperwork before the next person is ready for it
Transportation	Transporting WIP long distances, tracking to and from an off-site storage facility	Multiple sites outside of walking distance, off-site training
Inventory	Excess raw material, WIP, or unfinished goods	Office supplies, sales literature, and reports
Complexity	More parts, process steps, or time than necessary to meet customer needs	Reentry of data, extra copies, excessive reporting, etc.
Unused creativity	Lost time, ideas, skills, improvements, and suggestions from employees	Limited tools or authority available to employees to carry out basic tasks

Note: Courtesy of the U.S. EPA.

What about the service sector? The EPA has looked at the seven wastes and produced the listing in Table 10.2, which shows them for both the manufacturing and service sectors.

Table 10.3 from the EPA summarizes many of these methods and tools. Remember, these are typically applied to operations—the steady-state application of your project's product. However you should still consider applying them in your project for the direct environmental impact and benefit, and you'll want to understand these to have better connection points to your handoff to operations when that occurs.

TABLE 10.3

Environmental Benefits of Lean

Lean Method	Potential Environmental Benefits
Kaizan rapid improvement events	Continued improvement culture focused on eliminating wastes
	Uncovering and eliminating hidden wastes and waste-generating activities
	Quick, sustained results without significant capital investment
5S or 6S	Decreased lighting, energy needs when windows are cleaned and equipment is painted light colors
	Spills, leaks noticed quickly
	Decreased potential for accidents and spills with clearly marked and obstacle-free thoroughfares
	Reduced contamination of product, resulting in fewer product defects (which reduces energy and resource needs; avoids waste)
	Reduced floor space needed for operations storage; potential decrease in energy needs
	Less unneeded consumption of materials and chemicals when equipment, parts, and materials are organized, easy to find; less need for disposal of expired chemicals
	Visual clues that can raise awareness of waste-handling/management procedures, workplace hazards, and emergency response procedures
Cellular manufacturing	Elimination of overproduction, thereby reducing wastes and the use of energy and raw materials
	Fewer defects from processing and product changeovers, which reduces energy and resource needs and avoids waste
	Noticing defects earlier, preventing wastes
	Less use of materials and energy (per unit of production) with right-sized equipment
	Less floor space needed; potential decrease in energy use and less need to construct new facilities
	Easier to focus on equipment maintenance, pollution prevention
Just-in-time/*kanban*	Eliminates overproduction, thereby reducing wastes and the use of energy and raw materials
	Less in-process and postprocess inventory needed; avoids potential waste from damaged, spoiled, or deteriorated products
	Frequent inventory turns, which can eliminate need to degrease metal parts

Continued

TABLE 10.3 (*Continued*)

Environmental Benefits of Lean

Lean Method	Potential Environmental Benefits
	Less floor space needed; potential decrease in energy use and less need to construct new facilities
	Can facilitate worker-led process improvements
	Less excess inventory, which reduces energy use associated with transport and reorganization of unsold inventory
Total production maintenance (TPM)	Fewer defects, which reduces energy and resources needed and avoids waste
	Increased longevity of equipment, which decreases need for replacement equipment and associated environmental impacts (energy, raw materials, etc.)
	Decreased number and severity of spills, leaks, and upset conditions; less solid and hazardous wastes
Six Sigma	Fewer defects, which reduces energy and resources needed and avoids wastes
	Focusing attention on reducing the conditions that result in accidents, spills, and malfunctions, thereby reducing solid and hazardous wastes
	Improving product durability and reliability, which can increase product life span, reducing environmental impact of meeting customer needs
Preproduction planning (3P)	Eliminating waste at product and process design stage, similar to "design for environment" methods
	Using nature (inherently waste free) as a design model
	Right-sized equipment, which lowers material and energy requirements for production
	Reducing the complexity of the production process ("design for manufacturability"), which can eliminate or streamline process steps; targeting environmentally sensitive processes elimination, since they are often time, resource, and capital intense
	Less-complex product designs, which can use fewer parts and fewer types of material, increasing the ease of disassembly and recycling
Lean enterprise supplier networks	Magnification of environmental benefits of Lean production (reduced waste through fewer defects, less scrap, less energy usage, etc.) across the network
	Environmental benefits are more broadly realized by introducing Lean to existing suppliers rather than finding new, already Lean suppliers

Note: Courtesy of the U.S. EPA.

A Case Study in Waste (An Illustration of Waste Involved in the Production of Cola Cans in the UK)

First of all, note that a beverage can is more expensive than the beverage. Here's what happens on its journey to deliver your beverage to you:

1. Bauxite is mined in Australia.
2. Bauxite is trucked to chemical reduction mill; each ton of bauxite becomes half a ton of aluminum oxide.
3. Aluminum oxide is loaded on an ore carrier and shipped to Scandinavia (where there is cheap hydroelectric power).
4. A smelter in Scandinavia turns each ton of aluminum oxide into a quarter ton of aluminum ingots.
5. Ingots are shipped to Germany, heated to 900°F and rolled to ⅛ inch.
6. Sheets of aluminum are shipped to another factory (in Germany or another country) and cold-rolled to become $^1/_{10}$ original thickness.
7. This aluminum is sent to England where sheets are punched and rolled into cans.
8. Cans are washed, dried, and painted with a base coat.
9. Cans are painted with specific product branding and labeling.
10. Cans are lacquered, flanged, sprayed inside with protective coating, and inspected.
11. Cans are palletized, fork lifted, and warehoused until needed.
12. When needed, they are shipped to a bottler, washed and cleaned, and finally filled with beverage (this involves the mixing of syrup, water, carbon dioxide, phosphorous, and caffeine).
13. Filled cans are sealed with a pop-top and inserted into cardboard cartons, with matching color and proper promotional labeling.
14. Cartons are palletized again and shipped to regional warehouses and then to supermarkets.
15. A typical can is purchased within three days, consumed within minutes, and discarded in about one second.

The cartons come from forest pulp that may have originated anywhere from Sweden or Siberia to the old-growth, virgin forests of British Columbia that are the home of grizzly bears, wolverines, otters, and eagles. Beet fields in France provide the sugar, which undergoes significant trucking, milling, refining, and shipping. The phosphorus comes from the U.S. state of Idaho, where it is excavated from deep open-pit mines—a process that also unearths cadmium and radioactive thorium. Round-the-clock, the mining company in Idaho uses the same amount of electricity as a city of 100,000 people in order produce food-grade phosphorous. The caffeine is shipped from a chemical manufacturer to the syrup manufacturer in England. In England, consumers discard 84% of all cans, which means that the overall rate of aluminum waste, after counting production losses, is 88%. The United States still gets three-fifths of its aluminum from virgin ore, at twenty times the energy intensity of recycled aluminum, and throws away enough aluminum to replace its entire commercial aircraft fleet every three months.

We realize that this is a manufacturing process—an *operation,* and not a project—but we think it illustrates where a PM may be able to have a say in the reduction of waste, if the PM can become a change agent in the creation of the manufacturing process or if the PM can set an example in their projects that can be emulated by operations planning people in the organization.

5S[7]

Let's look at one of these Lean methods, "5S." This method actually focuses on a well-lit, well-labeled, well-cleaned workplace. We all sense that we'd work more efficiently (and have less waste) if our activities were more effective because, for example, we can see what we're doing, know where all of the components for the work are located, and don't have to look for documents or other items that are buried under other documents or items. The 5S method, which is Japanese in origin, uses these 5 "S" words (starting with S in Japanese and in loosely translated English):

Seiri → Sort
Seiton → Straighten
Seiso → Shine
Seiketsu → Standardize
Shitsuke → Sustain

Let's look at these in some detail (Figure 10.1):

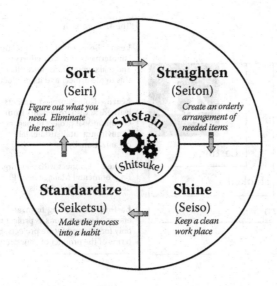

FIGURE 10.1
The five Ss.

Sort: Clearly distinguish between components that are needed in a work area and components that are not, thereby eliminating sources of clutter and unwanted items.

Straighten: Place items in the work area in a logical arrangement, and establish intuitive use guidelines; make the location visible and self-explanatory, so everyone knows what goes where.

Shine: This refers literally to the cleanliness of floors, tools, machines, and equipment in the workplace, and incorporates cleanliness into regular work duties.

Standardize: Defines the standard activities, procedures, schedules, and persons responsible for keeping the workplace clean and organized. As project managers, we're familiar with our tools for this, such as a work breakdown schedule (WBS), a schedule, and a responsibility assignment matrix (RAM).

Sustain: Make 5S an ingrained habit, spread the program to other functional and physical areas, and make it a company-wide routine.

Again, 5S is one of the many Lean methods favored by organizations. Refer to Table 10.3 for a survey of the many others, and we urge you to understand how your organization uses these in the larger sense for operations.

The 4L Approach

Lean – Be aware of your operational counterparts and their efforts to reduce waste and make operations more efficient. Apply this to the project and its product.

Learn – Collect project artifacts, lessons learned, and share benefits from the community of project managers with respect to environmental/sustainability. Grow organizationally.

Linked – Connect with your organization's Environmental Management Plan and break down organizational walls.

Lasting – Think long-term, and of the lasting effects of your actions as project manager, not only for this and future projects, but also in terms of the product of your project.

FIGURE 10.2
The 4L approach.

Summary—The 4L Approach

To wrap up this section as well as to integrate other portions of our book, we provide the 4L approach. The 4 Ls (lean, learn, linked, and lasting) describe how these aspects generally associated with operations can indeed be linked to the project and to the project managers and their team.

See Figure 10.2—this is self-explanatory.

ENDNOTES

1. Eliyahu M. Goldratt, *The Goal: A Process of Ongoing Improvement* (Great Barrington, MA: North River Press, 1992).
2. Eliyahu M. Goldratt, *The Goal,* http://www.vimeo.com/6440653.
3. James P. Womack, *What Is Lean?* Lean Enterprise Institute, http://www.lean.org/WhatsLean/.
4. James P. Womack and Daniel T. Jones, *Lean Thinking: Banish Waste and Create Wealth in Your Corporation* (New York: Simon & Schuster, 1996).
5. Mary Poppendieck, *Principles of Lean Thinking,* http://www.poppendieck.com/papers/LeanThinking.pdf, 2002.
6. Ibid.
7. U.S. Environmental Protection Agency, *Lean Manufacturing and the Environment,* 2009, http://www.epa.gov/lean/thinking/index.htm.

11

At the Top of Their Game

Who are the companies that have planned and are achieving their goals of greenality? _How_ are they achieving those goals? What lessons in greenality can the project manager take away from the efforts of business—at the organizational and project level? We've always asserted that project management is a microcosm of business. Running a project is like running a business. There is a mission, goals, budgets, and other constraints that both "business leaders" managing a business and project managers running projects have to take into account. Projects can be small or can cost hundreds of millions of dollars and anywhere in between. Project managers have the responsibilities that corporate leaders of big business have; as a matter of fact, project managers of large-scale, costly projects have bigger budgets than many _countries_. The parallels are both significant and obvious to us. As mentioned before, it has always been our assertion that project management is a microcosm of business; and to take it one step further, project management is a breeding ground for good corporate leadership because of the parallels of managing a business and running a project. When we look at companies that model the best of green behavior, we look at all of the aspects of the triple bottom line—people, profit, as well as the environment. We believe the companies that we are highlighting are examples of the best of the best, and have successfully _balanced profit with their commitment to their employees and customers, and the environment._ We should point out that in our research, we came across dozens and dozens of excellent projects at scores of companies, but it's beyond the scope of the book—and less productive for the reader—to simply survey their green projects. Again, focusing on the assertion that projects are a microcosm of business, by modeling projects after these green business leaders PMs will get the biggest "bang" for their green efforts.

PATAGONIA

One of the companies that immediately comes to mind when we think of green is Patagonia. Patagonia is a $316 million-a-year, privately owned company based in Ventura, California. We've worn their "plastic" fleeces for many years. But it's certainly not all about recycling with Patagonia. Their mission statement says: *"Build the best product, cause no unnecessary harm, use business to inspire and implement solutions to the environmental crisis."*[1] That mission statement tells only part of Patagonia's story. Principle 4 of the Natural Step[2] states that in response to the conditions that undermine the capacity of people to meet their needs, companies need to eliminate their contribution to those conditions. As an example, companies must eliminate unsafe working conditions.Through their social responsibility manager, presently Nicolle Bassett, Patagonia does just that. In an industry know for unsavory practices like subpar wages, extremely long workweeks, unsafe working conditions, and even child labor (does the word sweatshop come to mind?), Patagonia has seized the initiative and instituted its own set of rules.

Fair Labor Association is a nonprofit organization dedicated to ending sweatshop conditions in factories worldwide. Their mission is to protect workers' rights and improve working conditions.

In the late 1990s, Patagonia instituted social auditing, where third-party auditors under the direction of the social responsibility manager audit Patagonia's foreign and domestic production facilities to assure compliance with the Fair Labor Association's[3] recommendations. Their code of conduct requires their contractors to comply with local law, but even if the local law allows, they will work with no factory that employs workers under 15, the minimum age acceptable to the International Labor Organization. Patagonia even goes as far as to publish their list of factories so that they can be scrutinized by any agency, stakeholder, or customer who wants information.

It is clear that environmentalism is in Patagonia's DNA just as it should be in a project manager's DNA. Using some of the methods that Patagonia uses can enhance the project manager's ability to view their projects through an environmental lens. According to their Web site, "Our definition of quality includes a mandate for building products and working with processes that cause the least harm to the environment. We evaluate raw materials, invest in innovative technologies, rigorously police our waste and use a portion of our sales to support groups working to make a real difference. We acknowledge that the wild world we love best is disappearing. That is why those of us who work here share a strong commitment to protecting undomesticated lands and waters. We believe in using business to inspire solutions to the environmental crisis."[4] Patagonia has an active recycling program for their worn-out clothing, either at Patagonia retailers or through a mail-order program. Patagonia is a cofounder of the Conservation Alliance, which is dedicated to encouraging other companies in the outdoor industry to give money to environmental organizations and to become more involved in environmental work. There are now 155 members of the Alliance. Twice yearly the Alliance donates 100% of its membership dues to grassroots environmental groups working to protect threatened wild lands and biodiversity. In 2009 it disbursed $900,000, and since its founding in 1989, the Alliance has contributed more than $8 million to conservation projects throughout North America.

Patagonia also strives to make their buildings as green as possible. Their Reno Service Center was built in 1996 at a cost of $19 million. According to the company, while it costs more to build, the 30–35% energy savings accomplished with the new building will pay for the green innovations within three to five years. Some of the innovations are insulation and window glass made of recycled material, motion-sensing lighting systems, radiant heating systems, and a bio-filtration system that separates oil from water runoff from roofs and parking lots. The carpeting and countertops are made from 100% recycled material, and the building is old growth free. In 1998, Patagonia became the first California company to buy all of its electric power from newly constructed renewable energy sources and utilize solar panels in some of their stores to generate electricity. These green initiatives can enhance the project manager's long-term thinking and avail themselves of the rising "green wave."

Also, and not unimportant, Patagonia has done a good job of making their environmental lessons learned available. As we covered on our EarthPM blog (http://www.earthpm.com), the "Footprint Chronicles" provide extensive video and text content about Patagonia's supply chain and are not shy about pointing out the shortcomings of either their projects or products with respect to sustainability issues.

TIMBERLAND

Timberland, established in 1955 as the Abington Shoe Company, became the Timberland Company in 1978, headquartered in Stratham, New Hampshire. Its revenues in 2009 were $1.4 billion. The Timberland Company designs, engineers, markets, distributes, and sells premium-quality footwear, apparel, and accessories for men, women, and children, and the products are sold worldwide through independent retailers, department stores, and sports stores as well as their own Timberland retail locations. Timberland committed to "Doing Well and Doing Good" by delivering world-class products, making a difference in the world community, and creating value for shareholders, employees, and consumers around the world. Their mission is "to equip people to make a difference in their world, and to make it better." They have a four-pronged approach:

- People
- Values
  - Humanity
  - Humility
  - Integrity
  - Excellence
- Purpose
- Passion

Operating by these principles is a good way to have a cohesive and productive project team.

In November 2009, Timberland launched a global campaign called "Don't Tell Us It Can't Be Done," in an effort to encourage the establishment of meaningful emissions standards from the UN Climate Change Conference. Known for their environmental stewardship, Timberland encouraged the citizens of the world to challenge their leaders to set standards for emissions. Unfortunately, that was far from accomplished. But Timberland continues to do what it can to reduce its own carbon footprint by improving lighting designs, using renewable energy resources, and building to LEED (Leadership in Energy and Environmental Design; see Chapter 14 for more detail on LEED) specifications.

As a direct correlation between profits and the environment, Timberland relies on outdoor activity; therefore climate change will adversely affect their business. So what specifically are they doing to understand their own carbon footprint?

- Timberland is partnering with factories to help them reduce emissions that come from the manufacturing of products.
- Timberland has designed a tool called the Green Index® that gives consumers information about the environmental footprint of footwear. This tool also allows designers to choose less-carbon-intensive materials.
- Timberland is working closely with transportation vendors to make changes in how and where product is shipped.
- And, while it's not easy to quantify how this fits in to its footprint, even indirectly, Timberland also takes seriously the opportunity to advocate for public policy changes that benefit the environment and to engage consumers through online conversations at http://www.earthkeeper.com.

Timberland has achieved a 27% reduction in emissions (attributable to its owned and operated facilities and employee travel) since 2006 due to efficiency improvements, renewable-energy development, and employee engagement. In this time, Timberland has built three renewable-energy systems including transitioning one of its largest and most polluting facilities over to renewable energy, a comprehensive program for engaging employees in reducing individual emissions, and the first certified LEED retail store in the world. A key part of Timberland's strategy is setting boundaries for its own carbon footprint by laying out a comprehensive reduction plan, which will include verifying greenhouse gas inventory through a third-party vendor, reducing energy demand through efficiency improvements, purchasing clean, renewable energy whenever possible, generating its own renewable energy on-site, and when necessary, purchasing renewable-energy credits and offsets to offset emissions and develop local renewable-energy projects.

Probably one of the more interesting of the initiatives, the Green Index, deserves a closer look. Timberland's Green Index score provides information to the consumer similar to that provided on food labels. Consumers, once they understand what they are looking at, will easily be able to distinguish which products are better suited for the environmentally conscious. The Green Index scoring is based on areas within their design and manufacturing. What it also does is allow the company to view their products

Green Index®		3*
Factors	**Lower Impact**	**Higher Impact**
Climate Impact	0-------2----------------------10	
	Greenhouse Gas Emissions	
Chemicals Used	0-------------------------------10	
	Hazardous, PVCs, etc	
Resource Consumption	0-----------------------8------10	
	Reduced by recycled, organic, renewable	
* 2+0+8/3 = 3 (average)		

FIGURE 11.1
Sample of Green Index card.

through an environmental lens and determine what projects can be instituted to improve the score. Take the example from their Web site;[5] their product would have a Green Index tag, similar to the one in Figure 11.1.

Project managers could use something similar to what we call "greenality" in order to rate how their projects are using the green tools and techniques available to them. See Chapter 13 for greenality measurement and more tips, tools, and techniques for greening your projects.

INTERFACE

While some people sweep environmental issues under the carpet, one flooring company has been highly regarded in its environmental efforts. That company is Interface. Ray Anderson, leader of Interface and a *Time* magazine "Hero of the Environment,"[6] works with a strict sense of what sustainability means. It's all about "taking nothing from the earth that is not rapidly and naturally renewable, and doing no harm to the biosphere," says Anderson in an article in *Inc.* magazine.[7]

Interface provides a great example of EarthPM's[8] and Green to Gold's[9] assertions about doing the right thing being good not only for the planet but also for the company's bottom line. Although originally working on sustainability as part of its "policy" only to comply with the law,

Anderson began to ask questions about Interface's overall impact—and when he heard it, he became alarmed. He challenged his engineers to initiate projects to reduce impact, reduce waste, and improve the bottom line.

The company started with projects focused on waste reduction, considering the reuse of everything from carpet scraps to industrial effluent, which immediately led to savings—more than $60 million in the first three years. So the projects have yielded green as well as improvements in sustainability. According to the article, from a standing start in 1994 Interface is on track to be sustainable by 2020. And even though that article is from 2006, a more recent interview[10] from November 2009 has Anderson not only saying that they are still on target for 2020, but reaffirming the connection of environmental green and income green: "Over fifteen years we've demonstrated that sustainability is a better way to a bigger and more legitimate profit." He goes on to talk about four major points regarding his environmental efforts at Interface, which we paraphrase here:

1. Products are the best they've ever been. Sustainability is a wellspring of innovation.
2. Our people are galvanized around our mission, owing to a sense of higher purpose and self-actualization that comes when you focus on something bigger than yourself.
3. The goodwill of the marketplace is tremendous, winning business for Interface because customers align with a company that is trying to do the right thing by our environment.
4. Interface serves as a good example of a company that "gets" sustainability. You can see it in their mission statement:

VISION

To be the first company that, by its deeds, shows the entire industrial world what sustainability is in all its dimensions: People, process, product, place and profits—by 2020—and in doing so we will become restorative through the power of influence.

Interface is so well-admired in this area that they have established a consulting arm to help others understand the issues and start their journey toward sustainability, and has started a nonprofit community online. See http://missionzero.org/about.

GOOGLE

When we think of Google, we think first of a search engine but shortly realize that it is more than that. But even thinking of it as "only" a search engine, the question comes to mind, how can *that* be green? First of all, Google—founded in 1998 by Stanford PhD students Larry Page and Sergey Brin, and headquartered in Mountain View, California—is a business juggernaut with first-quarter revenues in 2010 at almost $7 billion. They have offices around the world developing a variety of applications including patent searches, news, maps, trends, instant messaging, and YouTube, among others. So with all of this technology (some of which, such as providing directions and maps, clearly has a green impact of its own) what else are they doing to *be* green?

One of the applications that could be of immediate use to project managers is Google's PowerMeter application. It is a free electrical monitoring application that can utilize information from a "smart meter" or consumer-owned electricity management device and provides visual information about electrical usage directly to the consumer's personalized Google home page. Consumers will have access to this personal-use data to better be able to manage, monitor, and control their electrical usage. Using these data, project managers can help to lead projects to more effectively and efficiently use electricity, a limited resource.

Another initiative (we'll call it a project) Google has undertaken is "efficient computing":

> In the time it takes to do a Google search, your own personal computer will likely use more energy than we will use to answer your query. (We [at Google] care about that too, and in 2007 co-founded the Climate Savers Computing Initiative, a non-profit organization committed to making all computers more energy efficient.)[11]

Google is obviously computer intensive, like many of us have come to be, except on a much, much larger scale. However, we can use lessons learned from their efforts and apply them, with scalability, to our efforts. Google is using a five-step approach to their "initiative": (1) making their servers more efficient, (2) making their data centers more efficient, (3) managing their water usage, (4) retiring their servers in a sustainable manner, and (5) working with other members of their community for an "efficient and clean energy future."

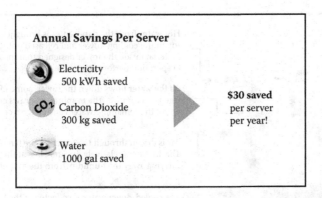

FIGURE 11.2
Annual savings per server (courtesy of Google).

According to Google's Web site, "Up to a third of total energy consumed by a typical server is wasted before reaching the computing components. The majority of these losses occur when converting electricity from one kind to another. The power supply, which converts the AC voltage coming from a standard outlet to a set of low DC voltages, is where most of the energy is lost."[12] Therefore, scrutiny of the efficiencies of their servers is paramount. The goal is to either increase the efficiency of their present servers or replace them with more-efficient ones (see Figure 11.2). For the project manager, if servers are part of the project, or even the process, efficiency may be a key part of saving scarce resources.

"Reducing the environmental footprint of our data centers starts with reducing their electricity consumption."[13] Power and cooling are the major factors in energy use of data centers. In a 2007 report, the U.S. EPA confirmed this sad state and estimated the average energy overhead of current data centers at 96%.[14] Google's data centers are now using the evaporation process, similar to nuclear power plant cooling towers, to provide additional cooling. By using cooling towers, Google's goal is to reduce the time the chillers have to run, thereby reducing the energy consumption of the chillers. Figure 11.3 shows a simple representation of how a cooling tower works.

The third step in their initiative is to look at water usage in their facilities. "On average, two gallons of water is consumed for every kilowatt-hour of electricity produced in the U.S."[15] When you think about how many data centers there are and how much energy they produce, that is a lot of water. To reduce water usage, Google is instituting water-recycling efforts. Their goal is to provide recycled water in 80% of their facilities by this year (2010).

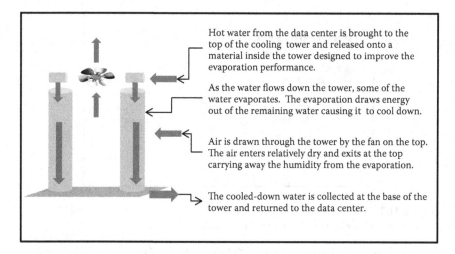

Hot water from the data center is brought to the top of the cooling tower and released onto a material inside the tower designed to improve the evaporation performance.

As the water flows down the tower, some of the water evaporates. The evaporation draws energy out of the remaining water causing it to cool down.

Air is drawn through the tower by the fan on the top. The air enters relatively dry and exits at the top carrying away the humidity from the evaporation.

The cooled-down water is collected at the base of the tower and returned to the data center.

FIGURE 11.3
Representation of cooling tower (courtesy of Google).

The fourth effort for Google is sustainability around their disposal of electronics (see Figure 11.4). Their goal is that 100% of their servers are either reused or recycled. As we have stated before, there is a huge problem in this country, and spilling over to other countries, with the disposal of electronic equipment. With Google's efforts along with their fifth step in

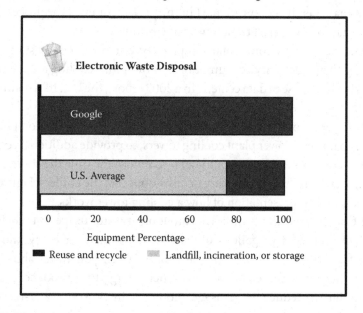

FIGURE 11.4
Electronic waste disposal (courtesy of Google).

the process, there is hope that we all can be more conscious and conscientious with our electronic disposal.

Google's last effort, and one of the most important, is to partner with their community and translate their efforts into a broader application, industry wide. They realize, as we do, that one company can make a difference, but the real reward will come when those efforts are applied in a broader sense. We believe that project managers, thinking of the greenality of their projects and processes, will be the leaders of that effort.

OFFICE DEPOT

Does Office Depot immediately come to mind when you think about green initiatives? It didn't to us either. However, their motto is "Buy Green, Be Green, Sell Green." So how do they intend to live up to their motto?

Buying Green

When Office Depot talks about buying green they are looking at three aspects: (1) sourcing greener office products, (2) buying paper from certified "responsibly managed forests," and (3) buying greener office products for their own internal use. You see, there is a parallel to our assertions about projects. Here, the internally used office products are akin to the project itself being as green as possible.

The company has produced a Green Buyer's Guide (http://www.officedepot.com/promo.do?file=/guides/buygreen/buygreen.jsp) that covers products from paper with recycled content, to green desk accessories made from recycled material, to products using nontoxic glues and inks, to nontoxic cleaning supplies, to HEPA air cleaners. The guide contains a plethora of information on how to green a project. We particularly like this quote from their Web site: "But while we know bold moves are sometimes necessary, we believe the long-term path to sustainability is through more companies, including our own, making small every day purchasing decisions with the environment as a consideration. As discussed in our Green Buyer's Guide, we think an incremental approach to green purchasing will grow markets for sustainable products more successfully than a purist one, where only greenest products are seen as 'good enough.'"

Being Green

Again, Office Depot has three aspects to their program: (1) reducing wastes and recycling, (2) reducing energy and greenhouse gases from their facilities and greening their building, and (3) reducing fuel and greenhouse gases from their transportation. They also realize that while some efforts require initial investment, there is payoff at the back end, like reduced energy costs that, in the long run, can significantly increase their bottom line.

As a major retailer, Office Depot generates an abundance of paper and corrugated cardboard. They have put significant effort into their recycling efforts and achieved the following:

- Increased recycling of paper and cardboard by 21% from 19,000 tons to 23,000 tons
- Implemented basic paper recycling at all stores where they have back haul to cross-dock (the ability to unload incoming materials and directly load them on outgoing transport without storage in between)
- Rolled out an innovative fixture refurbishment and reuse program through which, they estimate, they reused over 1,800 tons of store fixtures; also started buying refurbished shopping carts for use in their stores

What accomplished these results? Is it the driving vision of leadership? Yes. But also, important to note, projects, and of course, project managers who were able to draw their authority from that enterprise vision. Not counting their fixture reuse program, Office Depot has recycled over 26,000 tons of material and continues to find ways to increase that effort.

There are two ways to improve the greenness of one's facilities: reduce energy and GHGE from existing buildings, and build greener new buildings. Office Depot has done both. In 2007 they joined the U.S. Green Building Council (USGBC), the first office supply products company to do so, and also joined the LEED for Retail Prototype pilot, a program for retailers who plan to pursue certification across multiple locations, not just one. In 2008 they opened their first LEED Gold–certified retail operation in Austin, Texas, which was designed to use less energy and water in the daily operations and leave a much smaller environmental footprint.

FIGURE 11.5
Certified SmartWay®.

According to Office Depot, more than half of their annual revenue in North America, their primary market, is generated through deliveries. Therefore a huge impact on their bottom line can be made by more-efficient vehicles. By the end of 2007, they had calculated their carbon emissions from deliveries, reduced their carbon emissions for two consecutive years (11.8% reduction in 2006 and 9.6% reduction in 2007), and had a substantial fleet of fuel-efficient Sprinter vans. Sprinter vans are designed and powered by Mercedes-Benz and assembled in the United States by Freightliner. Office Depot is also an active partner in the U.S. EPA's SmartWay Transportation Partnership, and based on their leadership efforts in 2007, Office Depot was awarded a SmartWay Environmental Excellence Award (see Figure 11.5).

Selling Green

Office Depot has approached selling green by delivering innovative green solutions to their contract customer, direct customer, and retail customers, and by selling greener paper. For those innovative solutions, they provide a Green Book catalog and their designated green Web site at http://www.officedepot.com/yourgreeneroffice.

Corporate Social Responsibility

To round out their green efforts, one only has to look to their core values: inclusion, innovation, and customer focus. Office Depot is committed to recruiting a workforce that reflects the communities in which they do business and providing a work environment based on honesty and mutual respect. Further, they want to ensure that all people-related decisions are made objectively, based on merit, and they will utilize a base of diverse suppliers. As incentive, their managers at all levels are accountable for implementing those core values.

MICROSOFT®

What They Do for Us

It goes without saying that Microsoft through its founder has shown an ultimate commitment to corporate social responsibility. Using their significant resources, founder Bill Gates and his wife, Melinda, created a foundation to help all people lead healthy, productive lives. From the foundation's Web site: "In developing countries, we focus on improving people's health and giving them the chance to lift themselves out of hunger and extreme poverty. In the United States, we seek to ensure that all people—especially those with the fewest resources—have access to the opportunities they need to succeed in school and life."

Microsoft's commitment to corporate citizenship is to be accountable to their millions of customers and stakeholders around the world. While working to meet the needs of their customers and stakeholders, Microsoft is committed to creating value for their partners, employees, and wider society, and to managing their business sustainably.

In addition to corporate citizenship, business sustainability is a focus for their green project managers. According to Microsoft, they "are committed to software and technology innovation that helps people and organizations around the world improve the environment. Our goals are to reduce the impact of our operations and products and to drive responsible environmental leadership." So, like Google, Microsoft is information technologically driven and also active in the global community, as indicated by their participation in the UN's Climate Change Conference in Copenhagen (COP15). Arguably, different people received different messages from COP15, but the issue here is not the outcome but rather the participation by Microsoft. They were clearly in support of the effort, addressing issues and providing technology experts. Microsoft envisions a scenario where technology can offer software tools to help increase energy efficiency, used to accelerate the research and development of clean-energy sources, and provides decision-making tools to better predict the impact of climate change. All noble efforts, but what concrete green measures are they undertaking?

One of their efforts is to reduce energy consumption and carbon emissions. As mentioned previously, virtualization can save energy. Microsoft's virtualization enables multiple operating systems to run on a single server with the potential to reduce energy costs as much as 90%. Their Windows Vista and Windows 7 have built-in power management systems that can be used to reduce power consumption. In Windows 7, power management is on by default. Microsoft Dynamics AX is a powerful comprehensive business management solution software package that now includes an "Environmental Sustainability Dashboard" to help customers track their carbon footprint (energy usage and GHGE). By having that data, companies can better monitoring and controlling their capabilities. For more information on this, you can read "Microsoft Dynamics AX Helps Businesses Track Their 'Green' Performance—Today and Tomorrow" at http://download.microsoft.com/download/1/f/c/1fc5528b-70cc-4b74-aff0-582af019c9d2/EMA and Dashboard Article.docx.

What They Are Doing for Themselves (and Us)

That's what they can do for us. What are they doing to green themselves? One of their major initiatives is to reduce waste on their campus in Redmond, Washington. One of the innovations was to move to use compostable materials as much as possible. Doing that, according to Francois Ajenstat, environmental sustainability manager, "reduced our waste on campus by 50%." The prime ingredients for their compostable materials are corn and potatoes. Microsoft was the first corporate account in North America to receive the Green Restaurant Certification (http://www.dine-green.com). Additionally, they are recycling their kitchen grease for use as biodiesel for their on-campus vehicles. One of the unique ways Microsoft is reducing their carbon footprint is by using what they call "connector buses." The connector buses pick up employees from their neighborhoods and deliver them to a transportation center where hybrid cars take them to their buildings, thus eliminating the need to use individual cars and also reducing the need to cover over large areas of green space for parking lots. And the buildings that the employees are delivered to are LEED Certified and use approximately "20% of the energy of traditional building," says Rob Bernard, chief environmental strategist.

As mentioned before, data centers are both huge power drains and areas for the largest improvement in energy savings through consolidation and virtualization. Just to give you some perspective on usage, Arne Josefsberg, general manager of infrastructure services, says "half a billion unique customers access our data centers every month." In Ireland, for example, Microsoft's data center is using what Michael Manos, senior director of data services, calls "air-side economization." The data center utilizes Ireland's unique cool climate by using outside air to cool their data center.

We have provided information on a very few of the many companies who are looking at their projects through an environmental lens and more. The information is intended to give you examples of ways to help green your projects and organizations, and to be able to view your projects through the environmental lens that makes these companies so effective in their efforts.

GENERAL ELECTRIC

A discussion of companies that are at the top of their "green" game would not be complete without a discussion of GE and ecomagination. Who can forget the catchy ads and imbedded messages? But it is certainly more than just catchy ads; ecomagination is a program that is consistent with GE's mission "to earn the best possible returns for our shareowners by solving big problems like improving energy efficiency and reducing environmental impact."[16] With its roots in the Edison General Electric Company, founded in 1890 by Thomas Edison, GE is today a company with revenues for the first quarter of 2010 of $36.8 billion, with a worldwide workforce of more than 300,000 employees.

So how are they "greening" themselves? As we've said before, greening is about sustainability, and sustainability includes the triple bottom line—people, profits, and planet. Solar energy plays a large role in the reduction of GE's energy costs (profits) and reducing their carbon footprint (planet). According to their Web site (http://www.ge.com/innovation/ghg/index.html), GE has invested more than $2 billion to date in an effort to reduce greenhouse gas emissions (GHGE). Their solar project, beginning at their world headquarters in Fairfield, Connecticut, is slated to advance to 30 worldwide locations. At the headquarters, GE installed 168 kilowatts of solar generating capability. Since they are deploying their own technology, it is also an example of a company "walking the walk."

In addition to the solar initiative, GE has more than 84 projects scheduled to change out their old lighting with new, more energy-efficient T5 and T8 bulbs (LED tube lights). These projects will reduce energy costs (profits), reduce their carbon footprint (planet), and where they have been installed so far, provide better lighting for employees (people). The third major project that GE has undertaken for the last 15 years has been their support of a "Pollution Prevention/Energy Efficiency Team" that includes six engineers and chemists focused on cost-effective reduction of GE's "environmental releases and greenhouse gases."

So what is GE doing for us?

> Good citizenship is our way of life. A natural part of what we do at GE.
>
> **Bob Corcoran**
> *Vice President—Corporate Citizenship*

They are being good corporate citizens with green projects like:

- They are helping in health care in Cambodia by donating critical medical equipment.
- In 2008, GE and the GE Foundation donated $1.2 million to address the crisis in Darfur and more than $5 million in assistance to the region.

> Africa is a continent where we can help people with some of our most innovative products.
>
> **Brackett Dennison III**
> *Senior Vice President and General Counsel*

An important part of the commitment was $500,000 in health care equipment to support International Medical Corps's efforts in Darfur, the Central African Republic (CAR), and Chad. Learn firsthand the difference these donations are having on a population in the middle of a humanitarian crisis by going to http://gereports.com/ges-medical-equipment-hits-the-ground-in-africa.

GE certainly is a diverse company. One of their products, Centricity Electronic Medical Records (EMR), is helping hospitals and physicians provide better health care by being able to quickly and accurately access patients' medical records (people). For the planet, GE produces emission-monitoring equipment and emission control technology. It is also one of the largest suppliers of wind turbines in the world. According to a December 2009 press release, "GE Receives $1.4 Billion Contract to Supply Turbines for Largest Wind Farm Ever Built in the US—Caithness Energy's Oregon Wind Farm to Use GE's Advanced 2.5xl Machines."[17] The project, to be

TABLE 11.1

Ecomagination Goals

2008	2010	2012
Reduce GHG intensity 30% (goal achieved)	Double R&D to $1.5 billion	Reduce water usage 20% (absolute)
	Strive to grow revenues $25 billion	Reduce GHG 1% (absolute)

Note: Courtesy of General Electric.

constructed in Shepherds Flats, Oregon, approximately 140 miles east of Portland, Oregon, is scheduled to begin in the second half of 2010 and be completed two years later. The project is definitely "green by intent."

There is no doubt that GE has a green focus. It has not always been that way, but there are few companies that have been around as long as GE that can say they have always had a green focus.

Ecomagination

Ecomagination is a business strategy designed to drive innovation and the growth of profitable environmental solutions while engaging stakeholders. We invest in innovation through both our own R&D efforts and outside venture capital investments. The resulting products enable GE and our customers to reduce emissions while generating revenue from their sale. Combining profits and energy savings, we continue to invest in environmental solutions, perpetuating the cycle.[18]

See Table 11.1 for a list of the ecomagination goals.

————————

STEWARD ADVANCED MATERIALS—HOME OF "THE TOXIN TERMINATOR"

Green is not just about making or saving energy; it's also about toxicity— reducing it, preventing it, and even *removing* it. And here's a story about a powerful powder that can help remove toxicity. Imagine a powder that has been engineered for extreme absorption. This powder—not imagined but *real*, produced by Steward Advanced Materials, and winner of the Grand Award in Green Technology from *Popular Science* magazine—can get mercury-contaminated water 100 times as clean as any other method at about half the cost. A *single teaspoon* of this powder has the *same surface area as a football field*. Yes, that's extreme absorbency. The silica-based powder is further engineered with sulfur atoms so that when a mercury-tainted liquid is encountered by the powder (or the other way around), the mercury bonds with the sulfur to form a stable powder that is safe for landfills. Normally, mercury has to go through an expensive separate step to be neutralized.

This product, called SAMMS, has successfully cleaned wastewater at coal plants, an offshore oil rig, and a chemical manufacturer. The product holds promise for other materials, including the possibility of cleaning up radioactive wastes by swapping out the sulfur with other atoms to do that type of work.

We'd like to end this chapter with a story about SunChips snacks from their Web site (http://sunchips.com/). While they are a part of a large conglomerate, Frito-Lay PepsiCo, they do live up to their name.

SUN CHIPS

SunChips snacks are now being made with the help of solar energy at their manufacturing facility in Modesto, California, one of eight locations where SunChips snacks are made. To capture this solar energy, a solar collector field was built by American Energy Assets for Frito-Lay covering four acres of land and accommodating 57,969 square feet of net collector aperture area. Prior to construction, the installation design was reviewed and confirmed to be sound by the National Renewable Energy Laboratory. The solar collector system is up and running with a total generating capacity of 14,700MM BTU/yr.

Solar Collector Technology

This ecofriendly process is explained further on the SunChips Web site:

> A solar collector field is comprised of a huge array of concave mirrors. These mirrors track the position of the sun throughout the day, focusing the sun's energy on a black tube that runs along the focus of the array. This black tube is surrounded by a second glass tube that protects it from the air, allowing it to absorb solar energy more effectively. As super heated water

passes through the black tube, the solar energy heats it up even more to an incredible 450°F. This water then runs through a boiler system that uses its heat to generate steam, which helps to cook the wheat and heat the cooking oil used in our SunChips manufacturing process. Cooled water then flows back through the tube to the solar concentrator field to repeat the process. The amount of thermal energy produced by our solar field is significant relative to the amount of energy needed to make SunChips snacks. Thermal energy is one form of energy needed to run a SunChips manufacturing line demanding 2.4MM BTU/hr. The annual thermal energy demand is approximately 14,600MM BTU. This is the approximate annual thermal energy output of the solar collector field at Modesto.[19]

SUMMARY

From air carriers who provide a means for passengers to negate their carbon use on each trip (and back that up with their own corporate greenality), to large organizations that make the environment a priority, to snack manufacturers who power their entire factories on solar panels, to companies that focus on toxic cleanups, these organizations are all at the top of their game.

ENDNOTES

1. Patagonia, mission statement, http://www.patagonia.com/web/us/contribution/.
2. The Natural Step, *Principle Four*, http://www.naturalstep.org/~natural/the-system-conditions.
3. Fair Labor Association, *Code of Conduct*, http://www.fairlabor.org/.
4. Patagonia, *Environmentalism: What We Do*, http://www.patagonia.com/web/us.
5. http://tbl.imageg.net/include/csr_reports/Timberlands_Green_Index_Program_2009_report.pdf.
6. William McDonough, "Ray Anderson: Heroes of the Environment," *Time* magazine online, October 17, 2007, http://www.time.com/time/specials/2007/article/0,28804,1663317_1663322_1669929,00.html.
7. Richard Todd, "The Sustainable Industrialist: Ray Anderson of Interface," Inc. magazine online, November 1, 2006, http://www.inc.com/magazine/20061101/green50_industrialist.html.
8. EarthPM, *EarthPM's Five Assertions of Green Project Management*, part of mission statement, 2007 http://www.earthpm.com.

9. Daniel C. Esty and Andrew S. Winston, *Green to Gold: How Smart Companies Use Environmental Strategy to Innovate, Create Value, and Build Competitive Advantage* (New Haven, CT: Yale University Press, 2007).

10. Tom Konrad, CFA, *Interview with Ray Anderson, of Interface Inc.,* Alternate Energy Stocks online, November 13, 2009, http://www.altenergystocks.com/archives/2009/11/post_10.html.

11. Google, http://www.google.com/corporate/green/datacenters/.

12. Ibid.

13. Ibid.

14. Report to Congress on Server and Data Center Energy Efficiency Public Law 109-431, U.S. Environmental Protection Agency ENERGY STAR Program, August 2, 2007.

15. P. Torcellini, N. Long, and R. Judkoff, *Consumptive Water Use for U.S. Power Production,* National Renewable Energy Laboratory, NREL/TP-550-33905, December 2003.

16. Jeffrey R. Immelt, chairman of the board and CEO, and Steven M. Fludder, vice president, ecomagination, Letter to Investors and Stakeholders, 2010, http://ge.ecomagination.com/annual-reports/letter-to-stakeholders.html.

17. GE Energy, press release, December 10, 2009, http://gepower.com/about/press/en/2009_press/121009.htm).

18. GE ecomagination Web site, http://ge.ecomagination.com/.

19. SunChips Web site, http://www.sunchips.com/resources/pdf/solarbackground.pdf.

12

Enabling Green to Earn You "Green"

Project managers are generally pragmatic individuals who want you to "show them the money" when it comes to efforts involving limited resources. How can project managers show that "going green" is not a monetary drain, but rather, instead of adding cost to the project may even be saving the project money? After all, saving a project's limited funds is one of those things in the DNA of project managers.

GREEN GOVERNMENT PURCHASING—EPA

Because of the profound influence it has on the purchasing for projects that are government related, we want to provide a summary of the U.S. Environmental Protection Agency's green purchasing guidelines. Additionally, in its guiding principles it contains a particular perspective on greenality and green products, as well as some definitions that will help the project manager in establishing a baseline understanding of greenality. The complete information can be found on the EPA's Web site at http://www.epa.gov/epp.

We should point out that similar excellent information is available from other governmental sources. The EU's Global Public Procurement guidelines are described this way: "a process whereby public authorities seek to procure goods, services and works with a reduced environmental impact throughout their life cycle when compared to goods, services and works with the same primary function that would otherwise be procured." To see how well this is working, a recent study of the effect of GPP can be found at http://ec.europa.eu/environment/gpp/pdf/statistical_data.pdf.

History of the U.S. EPA's EPP

In 1998, former President Clinton signed an executive order (EO13101). That order was titled "Greening the Government through Waste Prevention, Recycling and Federal Acquisition." That led to a few revisions and other executive orders, which led to where we are today, and that is the "final guidance" for "acquisition of environmentally preferable products and services." It further defines "environmentally preferable" as "products or services that have a lesser or reduced effect on human health and the environment when compared with competing products or services that serve the same purpose. This comparison may consider raw materials acquisition, production, manufacturing, packaging, distribution, reuse, operation, maintenance or disposal of the product or service." The point of the final guidance is to provide agencies within the federal government and those doing business with the government) some criteria to help them to make their purchasing decisions more green. The guidelines do not provide specificity related to individual products or services, however there is an extensive list of resources in Chapter 14.

Federal purchasing, while recognizing the definition of "environmentally preferable," will likely require the consideration of different environmental factors, as appropriate, for different situations. The guidance applies to all acquisition types, from supplies and services to buildings and systems. It also provides a guiding principle and framework for the implementation of environmentally preferable purchasing. While the target audience is federal agencies, the information should be considered by entities in the private sector that do business with the federal government. It not only tries to promote preferable purchasing, but also encourages companies to purchase products based on "renewable agricultural or forestry materials."

The EPA has developed five guiding principles.

Principle 1. Environment + Price + Performance = Environmentally Preferable Purchasing

We have always asserted that project managers must view their projects through an environmental lens. Therefore, we are in total agreement with the EPA when they say that "environmental considerations should become part of normal purchasing practice, consistent with such traditional factors as product safety, price, performance, and availability." The earlier this is driven in, the more opportunity there is to take advantage of environmentally preferable purchasing. In order to fully realize the opportunities, the thinking must be applied during the concept stages of the project, not just at the implementation stage. Remember, in both large and small projects there could be tens, hundreds, and even thousands of components that should be evaluated per this guideline.

Principle 2. Pollution Prevention

We also agree that consideration of the environmental preference should begin early in the process, probably at the project ideation stage, "rooted in the ethic of pollution prevention."

The Department of Defense integrates pollution prevention into all of its major weapons system acquisition programs. For example, the New Attack Submarine (NSSN) Program has worked to include environmental considerations in all phases of the submarine's life cycle, from initial design to eventual disposal some 30 or more years later.

By considering all viable environmental alternatives during the design phase, the NSSN Program identified a number of options that will result in benefits. Just a few examples are listed below:

1. A redesigned nuclear reactor core will eliminate the need for refueling and disposal of spent nuclear fuel, while achieving a multi-million dollar cost avoidance.
2. A 31 percent reduction in the number of paints and coatings used in manufacturing the NSSN while ensuring that all of the selected paints satisfy applicable performance and environmental requirements.
3. A 61 percent reduction in the number of adhesive products to be used on the NSSN compared to the number required for previous submarine classes.
4. An 80 percent reduction in the number of solvents and cleaners.
5. Research and development effort to identify and test a biodegradable hydraulic fluid for submarines to replace the current toxic mineral oil-based fluid.

By recognizing early on that the key to reducing environmental impact throughout the ship's life cycle is pollution prevention and hazardous material control and management, the NSSN Program was able to design a submarine that meets strict safety and performance requirements, achieves significant cost savings, and minimizes risk to the environment.

Principle 3. Life Cycle Perspective/Multiple Attributes

This is our favorite of the five guiding principles. For further details, see Chapter 9. Green project managers must view their projects beyond the traditional product (project) handoff. They must be thinking about the total spectrum from development to disposal and what environmental impacts are associated with each stage. Besides the life cycle perspective, there is the aspect of multiple attributes. According to the EPA, "a product or service's environmental preferability is a function of multiple attributes."

From the perspective of multiple attributes, it makes sense to look at the full spectrum: energy efficiency, reduced toxicity, and reduced impact on fragile ecosystems. Because of the interrelationship between attributes, not considering all of them at the same time could potentially have negative effects on any one. The EPA also points out, however, that a final decision could be based on a single attribute because it distinguishes a particular product or service in a specific category. The point is that the project manager should consider multiple attributes and impacts when making project decisions.

Principle 4. Comparison of Environmental Impacts

As with any decision made by the project manager, there will be trade-offs. No matter which decision-making tools project managers use, it all comes down to comparison of the best alternative for the job. Making decisions on environmental impacts is no different. The EPA suggests that when comparing environmental impacts, the following be taken into consideration: "reversibility and geographical impacts, the degree of difference among competing products or services, and the overriding importance of protecting human health." Additionally, the EPA states that "in determining environmental preferability, Executive agency personnel might need to compare the various environmental impacts among competing products or services. For example, would the reduced energy requirements of one product be more important than the water pollution reductions associated with the use of a competing product? The ideal option would be a product that optimized energy efficiency *and* minimized water pollution. When this is not possible, however, Executive agency personnel will have to choose between the two attributes. It is important to consider both the nature of the environmental impact and the degree of difference among competing products."

List of High-Priority Human Health Stressors
(not in any order of importance):

- Ambient air pollutants
- Hazardous air pollutants
- Indoor air pollution
- Occupational exposure to chemicals
- Bioaccumulative pollutants

There is no widely accepted hierarchy that ranks the attributes or environmental impacts that are most important. There are three factors to consider that may help the project manager in the decision-making process.

a. Recovery time and geographical scale: How quickly can the environmental effect recover, and how widespread is the problem?
b. As mentioned previously, what are the differing attributes of the products or services under consideration?
c. Protecting human life is of the utmost importance.

Principle 5. Environmental Performance Information

It is imperative that the information used in the purchasing decision be complete, accurate, and relevant to the environmental performance of the products and services under consideration. That statement seems like it should be taken for granted, but with so many companies greenwashing their products and services, it must be explicitly stated. Again, it may seem obvious, but how the information is conveyed can go a long way in determining the validity of the data. For instance, manufacturers' information may be more suspect than information compiled by a third party like Consumer Reports or Energy Star (which in 2009 celebrated 10 years in existence).

A better understanding of the federal guidelines will allow project managers to take full advantage of any grants, rebates, or any other types of incentives that may be offered, thus significantly reducing costs (one of those scarce resources).

GRANTS AND REBATES

We are adding a disclaimer that says that while we are providing some information, it certainly isn't exhaustive. We have provided links to Web sites, and recommended books and articles for further investigation. Additionally, the grants and rebates that we found during the researching for our book are based on the latest information as of the publishing of our book. We are positive that more and more (rather than fewer) grants and rebates will be available in the future. Additionally, research by our readers will be helpful as will our continued research that will be made available on our Web site (http://www.earthpm.com).

What Is Available?

There is a surprisingly large amount of money that has been set aside for green improvements. The good news is that the key word in all of this is *projects*. We looked at the first half a page of Senate Bill S. 1436, Energy and Water Development and Related Agencies Appropriations Act of 2010, a $34 billion-plus appropriations bill, and found the word *projects* mentioned 14 times. This bill alone provided more than $34 billion dollars in funding, the bulk of it going to projects!

The American Recovery and Reinvestment Act (ARRA) and Green

The ARRA, signed in 2009, totaled $787 billion to stimulate the economy. A good portion of that money revolves around green projects. (See Figure 12.1.)

All states are benefiting in some way or another. Here is an example of just one way New Jersey and its businesses and citizens are benefiting from the green aspects of ARRA.[1]

> Thus far, there is a total of $75 million dollars appropriated to help state and local government with their green energy efficiency efforts. There is $61 million in direct grants from the US Department of Energy to counties based on population and energy consumption, $10 million available to

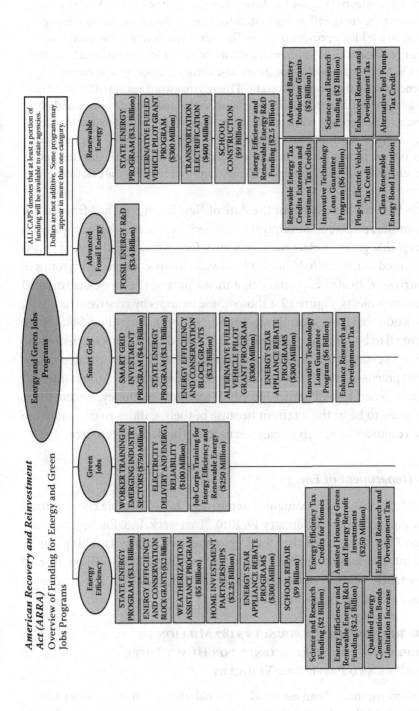

American Recovery and Reinvestment Act (ARRA)
Overview of Funding for Energy and Green Jobs Programs

Energy and Green Jobs Programs

ALL CAPS denotes that at least a portion of funding will be available to state agencies.

Dollars are not additive. Some programs may appear in more than one category.

Energy Efficiency

STATE ENERGY PROGRAM ($3.1 Billion)

ENERGY EFFICIENCY AND CONSERVATION BLOCK GRANTS ($3.2 Billion)

WEATHERIZATION ASSISTANCE PROGRAM ($5 Billion)

HOME INVESTMENT PARTNERSHIPS ($2.25 Billion)

ENERGY STAR APPLIANCE REBATE PROGRAMS ($300 Million)

SCHOOL REPAIR ($9 Billion)

Energy Efficiency Tax Credits for Homes

Assisted Housing Green and Energy Retrofit Investments ($250 Million)

Enhanced Research and Development Tax

Science and Research Funding ($2 Billion)

Energy Efficiency and Renewable Energy R&D Funding ($2.5 Billion)

Qualified Energy Conservation Bonds Limitation Increase

Green Jobs

WORKER TRAINING IN EMERGING INDUSTRY SECTORS ($750 Million)

ELECTRICITY DELIVERY AND ENERGY RELIABILITY ($100 Million)

Job Corps Training for Energy Efficiency and Renewable Energy ($250 Million)

Smart Grid

SMART GRID INVESTMENT PROGRAM ($4.5 Billion)

STATE ENERGY PROGRAM ($3.1 Billion)

ENERGY EFFICIENCY AND CONSERVATION BLOCK GRANTS ($3.2 Billion)

ALTERNATIVE FUELED VEHICLE PILOT GRANT PROGRAM ($300 Million)

ENERGY STAR APPLIANCE REBATE PROGRAMS ($500 Million)

Innovative Technology Loan Guarantee Program ($6 Billion)

Enhance Research and Development Tax

Advanced Fossil Energy

FOSSIL ENERGY R&D ($3.4 Billion)

Renewable Energy

STATE ENERGY PROGRAM ($3.1 Billion)

ALTERNATIVE FUELED VEHICLE PILOT GRANT PROGRAM ($300 Million)

TRANSPORTATION ELECTRIFICATION ($400 Million)

SCHOOL CONSTRUCTION ($9 Billion)

Energy Efficiency and Renewable Energy R&D Funding ($2.5 Billion)

Advanced Battery Production Grants ($2 Billion)

Science and Research Funding ($2 Billion)

Enhanced Research and Development Tax

Alternative Fuel Pumps Tax Credit

Renewable Energy Tax Credits Extension and Investment Tax Credits

Innovative Technology Loan Guarantee Program ($6 Billion)

Plug-In Electric Vehicle Tax Credit

Clean Renewable Energy Bond Limitation

FIGURE 12.1
ARRA chart (courtesy of U.S. EPA).

those counties not eligible for direct grants, and an additional $4 million to improve the energy efficiency of state facilities. In addition, the State Energy Program (SEP) is providing $73 million to "expand renewable energy and energy efficiency." $15 million is to be made available as grants and loans to public and private entities for "renewable energy technology and energy efficiency/alternative energy **projects**." [There's that word again!] $15 million is to be made available for low interest loans so that individuals can make their homes more energy efficient. Another $20.56 million is awarded to state agencies for renewable energy and energy efficiency **projects**. $17 million for oil and propane customers of municipality owned electric utilities, and another $4 million for energy efficiency improvements for state facilities.

This $148 million is just for the state of New Jersey, and just from one of the stimulus packages. Multiply that by the 50 states, and there are projects to keep U.S. green project managers busy for several decades. And this is not limited to the United States. Worldwide, many countries (or groups of countries) instituted bailouts with a major part of the money earmarked for green projects. Figure 12.2 shows these bailouts by relative size.

We know that these gigantic amounts of money in the trillion-$U.S. range are not all to be spent on green efforts, but a good part of this money will be spent on sustainability and environmental projects. Demonstrated efforts toward green—the entire spectrum of green, from green by project intent to green in general—will garner incredible amounts of money. Project managers need to be in the forefront because of their abilities to efficiently use those resources, of which money seems to be the decisive resource.

U.S. Department of Energy

According to Kelly Vaughn, reporting for Greenbiz.com (http://www.greenbiz.com) on January 19, 2010, "Last week, U.S. Energy Secretary Steven Chu announced that the Department of Energy is taking aim at the long-overlooked trucking industry, awarding $115 million toward 'super truck' efficiency projects." On January 11, 2010, U.S. Department of Energy issued the following statement

SECRETARY CHU ANNOUNCES $187 MILLION TO IMPROVE VEHICLE EFFICIENCY FOR HEAVY-DUTY TRUCKS AND PASSENGER VEHICLES

Columbus, Ind.—At an event today in Columbus, Indiana, Secretary Chu announced the selection of nine projects totaling more than $187 million

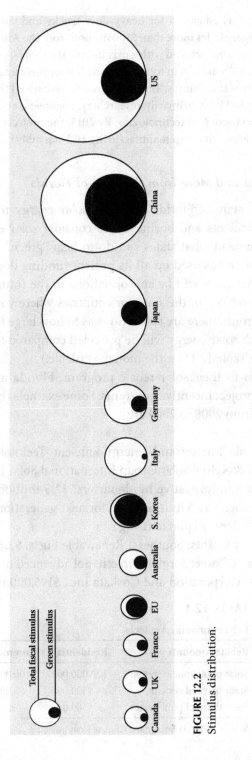

FIGURE 12.2
Stimulus distribution.

to improve fuel efficiency for heavy-duty trucks and passenger vehicles. The funding includes more than $100 million from the American Recovery and Reinvestment Act, and with a private cost share of 50 percent, will support nearly $375 million in total research, development and demonstration projects across the country. The nine winners have stated their projects will create over 500 jobs, primarily researchers, engineers, and managers who will develop these new technologies. By 2015, the projects expect to create over 6,000 jobs—many in manufacturing and assembly.[2]

Solar Rebates and More from the State of Florida

In 2006, the state of Florida created a solar energy rebate program to encourage residents and businesses to consider solar energy. Florida is a good example of what states can do to help "green" our energy. Even though the state has used up all its present funding doesn't preclude the possibility that there will be appropriations in the future, and it's worth looking into rebates in the states or countries where you live. Of course, like any program, there are restrictions as to how large the system should be, how much solar energy will be provided compared to existing energy use, etc. (See Table 12.1[3] for the money available.)

In addition to their solar rebate program, Florida also offers several other green project incentive programs. Some examples of those programs and awards from 2008 to 2009 are

1. Renewable Energy and Energy-Efficient Technology Grants: The Willard & Kelsey Solar Group International Solar Park manufacturing and administrative headquarters, $2.5 million; the ARI Green Energy Inc., a $2.5 million grant for next-generation small wind generator systems manufacturing site
2. Bioenergy Grants: Southeast Renewable Fuels, $2.5 million for construction of sweet sorghum to ethanol advanced biorefinery; Florida Crystals Corporation and Coskata Inc., $195,000 in partial funding

TABLE 12.1

Rebate Amounts Available

Rebate Amounts	Residential	Commercial
Solar photovoltaic system	$20,000.00	$100,000.00
Solar thermal system	$500.00	$5,000.00
Solar thermal pool heater	$100.00	n/a

Source: Florida Energy and Climate Commission.

for engineering for commercial-scale biomass to liquid fuels plant and eucalyptus energy plantation

3. Green Government Grants Program: The Florida Energy and Climate Commission can award grants to municipalities, counties, and school districts to "develop and implement 'green' government programs," programs defined as cost-efficient solutions that reduce greenhouse gases, improve quality of life, and strengthen the state's economy—in other words, adhere to the triple bottom line concept

4. Renewable Tax Credit Program: Provisions for sales tax exemptions, made by possible by the 2006 Florida Energy Act, for both individuals and corporations who are promoting "infrastructure development that supports hydrogen and biofuels technologies," such as hydrogen-powered vehicles and fueling stations, and "infrastructure, transportation, distribution, and storage" of biodiesel and ethanol

Energy Providers

In a clever approach, an increasing number of energy providers (utility companies) are offering incentives for those who want to conserve energy. At first blush it looks like an altruistic gesture by the utilities to discourage energy usage, therefore decreasing their profits. However, it is more of a combination of two circumstances; increasing infrastructure is prohibitively expensive and, for the most part, utility companies' profits are regulated. In the long run, reducing energy usage is not only good for the consumer, but good for the utility companies, too. So how can the project manager take advantage of these types of savings?

For project managers in the new-home construction business, the answer is an easy one. There is a 30% of cost tax credit for green-saving devices like geothermal heat pumps, wind turbines, and solar panels. Commercial applications can be a little more complex.

In Austin, Texas, Austin Energy has a comprehensive program[4] that offers rebates for "interior or qualifying exterior lighting, building envelope, air conditioning, motors, variable frequency drives and other technologies." It provides incentives up to $100,000 for commercial energy management. In addition, it provides incentives up to $200,000 for data center improvements such as "retrofitted server virtualization, Massive Array Idle Array Disc (MAID) storage systems, and Uninterruptable Power Supply (UPS), chillers/cooling towers, and thermal energy storage systems."

Energy Audits

The authors recently had personal experience with this, taking advantage of a home energy audit provided by the local gas utility. The energy audit was a personalized one-hour-plus expert assessment of the author's home opportunities to save energy, and included a detailed survey of air leaks accomplished by a blower door test (see Figure 12.3 and vignette). A full report of savings opportunities was generated, and several discounted services were identified. In particular, insulation above a sunroom and garage were recommended, at a subsidized cost, with 75% of the cost borne by the electric and gas utilities. The two top opportunities (attic door and chimney vent) would prevent a combined 1,000 cubic feet per minute of airflow (heat loss) and pay for themselves almost immediately. There are

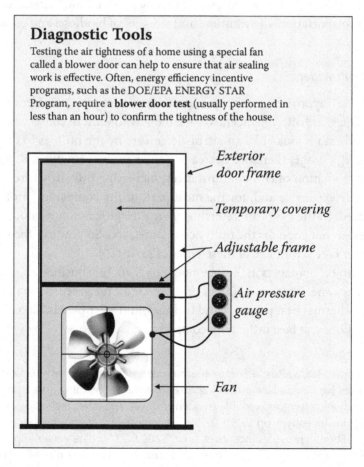

FIGURE 12.3
Diagnostic tools.

more than just electrical utilities providing incentives for green projects. Southern California Gas Company (SCGC)[5] breaks their rebate structure down to an industry basis.

How a Blower Door Test Works

A blower door is a powerful fan that mounts into the frame of an exterior door. The fan pulls air out of the house, lowering the air pressure inside. The higher outside air pressure then flows in through all unsealed cracks and openings. The auditors may use a smoke pencil to detect air leaks. These tests determine the air infiltration rate of a building.

Blower doors consist of a frame and flexible panel that fit in a doorway, a variable-speed fan, a pressure gauge to measure the pressure differences inside and outside the home, and an airflow manometer and hoses for measuring airflow.

For the Hotel and Lodging Industry, SCGC provides three programs:

1. Express Efficiency Rebate Program—for boilers/storage hot water heaters, tankless water heaters, pool heaters and other equipment
2. Commercial Foodservice Rebate Program—for cooking equipment and other foodservice equipment
3. Business Energy Efficiency Program—for dryers in in-house laundries, waste water recycling systems, and highly efficient ozone laundry systems. (Ozone is produced via an electrically charged system and then is injected into the wash water where it acts as a powerful oxidizing agent to breakdown the dirt on clothes.[6])

Some of these incentives are based on purchasing more energy-efficient equipment, some on previous heating units used versus units saved, and some on linear foot or square foot depending on the type of insulation. No matter how the savings are calculated, it translates into real money savings, and real money savings reduce the project's outlays.

ACTIONS UNDERTAKEN

So how much money are some companies saving with their projects?

Bank of America

Bank of America undertook a project to use lighter-weight paper, thus reducing the basic weight of its ATM receipts from 20 pounds to 15 pounds. That project not only saved paper, but also gained the bank additional savings in transportation, storage, and handling costs, to the tune of *$500,000 per year.*[7]

Apple Corporation[8]

Like many companies, Apple Corporation has a "go green" campaign. One of the projects Apple undertook was to reduce the size of their products, making them thinner and smaller. According to their Web site, from their new iMAC computer products alone they were able to mine "10,000 metric tons of material—the equivalent of 7,200 Toyota Priuses—for every one million iMAC computers sold." Another project was to reduce their packaging by 40% between 2006 and 2009. The result has been "shipping 50% more boxes in each airline container, saving the equivalent of one 747 flight for every 32,000 boxes shipped."

Schneider National

A nonprofit organization known as VICS, the Voluntary Interindustry Commerce Solutions Association, designed a program called the Empty Miles Service, which has proved to be beneficial both environmentally and monetarily for Macy's and many other companies. VICS identified the economic and environmental issues associated with trucking companies that ship retail goods to a desired location and travel the return trip with an empty load. The organization designed a program that allows trucking companies, like Schneider National, to post trucking routes and identify which return routes will be empty. Retailers like Macy's have taken advantage of the program and receive more competitive rates from Schneider National now because other retailers are paying for a load to be shipped on the trucker's return route. Macy's has identified certain routes that Schneider regularly travels, and other companies have the opportunity to fill the empty loads. Schneider now works with Macy's and nearly 30 other companies, since its 2009 launch of the Empty Miles Service.[9]

Schneider has also launched an initiative (project) to reduce their contributions to GHGs and in one year have eliminated 61.65 tons of carbon, 1.47 tons of nitrous oxide, and 5,554 gallons of diesel fuel.[10] At $3.00 per gallon, that is $16,662 per year right to the bottom line, to say nothing of the environmental savings.

Lockheed Martin[11]

Lockheed Martin has a four-pronged approach to "going green." All of the projects they are engaged in have a significant impact on the environment, but just as significant on people and the bottom line (profit). They are undertaking a balanced program consisting of projects for their buildings, IT activities, renewable energy, and purchasing renewable energy credits.

To date, eight Lockheed Martin buildings have achieved the U.S. Green Building Council's LEED certification, and an additional 20 Lockheed Martin buildings have registered for various levels of the certification. In addition, Lockheed Martin has implemented energy management systems in a number of their locations.

For example, in Camden, Arkansas, Lockheed Martin Missiles and Fire Control implemented a building energy management system that uses a software system to control lighting and air conditioning. The system led to *$209,124* in reduced costs and lowered demand for power, which resulted in a savings of 2,332 metric tons of carbon dioxide. At the Missile and Fire Control facility in Orlando, Florida, lighting upgrades at the facility have saved *$308,451,* and a reduced demand for power resulted in a savings of 2,511 metric tons of carbon dioxide.

To "green" their IT efforts, Lockheed Martin has identified information technology as a tremendous opportunity for reducing energy usage. In the past two years, Lockheed Martin has embarked on a server virtualization program that saved the corporation *$1.2 million* in business costs. By eliminating the use of 1,700 computing servers, the corporation saved more than 11 million kilowatt-hours of electricity, reducing carbon emissions by 7,000 metric tons. The corporation is committed to enhancing efficiency by consolidating data centers, exploiting intelligent software to manage IT resource capacity, using Energy Star rated power and cooling systems, and improving critical data center support processes and tools.

To mitigate the risks of volatile fossil fuel prices, Lockheed Martin also is increasing its use of renewable-energy sources, including the sun, wind, moving water, organic plant and waste material (biomass), and the earth's heat (geothermal). In 2008, the corporation began operating its first biomass boiler system, a project that was initiated to reduce business costs and has yielded tremendous environmental benefits as well. Today, the biomass boiler system provides steam for heating and process needs at the 1.8-million-square-feet Lockheed Martin facility in Owego, New York. The system is expected to decrease the facility's carbon footprint by 9,000 metric tons a year.

Across the country at a Lockheed Martin facility in Sunnyvale, California, an on-site solar plant designed to reduce energy usage is expected to generate savings of 1.3 million kilowatt-hours of energy per year.

And finally, in 2009, Lockheed Martin purchased 98,063,334 kilowatt-hours of green power, which represents 5% of the corporation's total electricity usage. According to EPA calculations, Lockheed Martin's green power purchase is the equivalent of purchasing enough electricity to power nearly 9,768 average American homes annually or the equivalent of avoiding the carbon dioxide (CO_2) emissions of nearly 12,898 passenger vehicles per year.

Raytheon

A large amount of Raytheon's GHG emissions come from their energy consumption. The major energy consumer for Raytheon is their IT department. The company therefore decided to focus their "green effort" projects on their data centers, where space and power constraints offered opportunities.

As part of the project, Raytheon virtualized or decommissioned 1,300 servers, and established common database services to reduce system acquisition, power and cooling costs, which enabled them to avoid building a major data center despite a 25% growth in capacity demand, according to Rick Swanborg, in a June 29, 2009, online article in *Computer World*. Further, said Swanborg, the green IT projects saved more than *$11 million* in 2008, and Raytheon exceeded its goal by realizing a 38% cut by 2008.[12]

University of Michigan

Most colleges and universities are reevaluating their expenses these days to make the limited available resources more effective. The University of Michigan–Ann Arbor, like all colleges and universities, use a large amount of electricity to operate thousands of servers on their computer network. One of the projects U of M undertook was to reduce the power usage of their servers. The first thing they looked at was whether or not they could do some data center consolidation, and found that they could. The second part of the project was then to virtualize their servers, so they have offered the community what they call "Virtualization as a Service (VaaS)."

Each server on U-M's campus consumes power to operate and cool the server, which represents a huge opportunity to reduce electricity use and associated costs. To get an idea of the impact VaaS consider that servers run 24 hours a day, 7 days a week, totaling 8,760 hours/year of energy consumption. U-M's hourly cost of power is $0.087/kWhr. The average server has a power rating of .350 kW.

Annual Cost to Power Server = 8,760 × 0.087 × .350
Annual Cost to Power Server = $266.74
Average Annual Cooling Cost to Power Server = $533.48 (depending on datacenter cooling efficiency or Power Utilization Efficiency – PUE)
Average Total Annual Cost to Power Server = $800.22

Multiplying the average total cost to power a physical server by the thousands of servers across U of M, illustrates the significant cost savings potential. Consider that VaaS has a **consolidation ratio of 40:1 (40 physical servers can be consolidated to run on 1 physical server)** and the long-term energy- and costs-savings become apparent.[13]

We realize that virtualization may not be an application conducive with all data centers because of the trade-offs involved with availability, recoverability, etc., but it is a consideration for projects that are very data intensive.

Quickies

Liberty Mutual: promotes by enforcing and rewarding employees who turn off lights whenever possible, keep a sweater at their desk, turn off the photocopier at night, make use of the shredding bins throughout the building, consolidate office supply orders, and carpool whenever possible.

Staples: limits the top speed of its delivery trucks to 60 mph, which saves more than 500,000 gallons of diesel fuel per year.

Abbott Laboratories: achieved carbon-neutral status with their U.S. fleet of 6,500 vehicles by providing employees with fuel-efficient hybrid vehicles; this has helped them reduce gas consumption by 400,000 gallons per year. Abbott has also revised the packaging of their products in 2008, which resulted in cutting their plastic usage by 2.7 million pounds.

These are just some of the examples of projects and the companies that undertook them in order to save *money.*

DuPont

According to "Chemical Reaction," a March 22, 2007, article by Nicholas Varchaver, *Fortune* senior writer, "$5 billion of its [DuPont's] $29 billion in revenue comes from sustainable products. These can be pure-green materials, such as bio-PDO, a corn-based substance that can be turned into a fiber for suits or carpets or even made into deicing solutions for airplanes. Or they can be products such as Tyvek—a chemically based material that dates to the 1950s—that can be used in new ways to improve energy efficiency."[14] This is a great example of projects that include green by intent and green by impact.

Portsmouth Brewery

A downtown Portsmouth, New Hampshire, brewery has undertaken a project to compost 100% of their food wastes and paper products. While undertaking the environmentally friendly project, we believe an underlying objective is to reduce disposal costs. Trash pickup, especially for businesses, is going to get only more expensive in the future. If business owners can find alternative methods to dispose of their waste products at little to no cost, it will translate directly to the bottom line as well as saving scarce resources like landfill space.

The Kohler Company

The Kohler Company[15] is offering a product called the "waterless urinal." While not a particularly pleasant topic, the interesting thing is that, according to their literature, it could save as much as 40,000 gallons of water per year per urinal installed. Roughly translated, that could save a commercial user in San Diego, California, or Garland, Texas, approximately $200 per year per application. At approximately $947 per urinal, about $500 more than a low-flow urinal, the payback period is about two and a half years. However in most cities, sewer rates are based on a percentage of water usage, so in New York City, for example, the combined rate is about $361 per year for 40,000 gallons of water used, so the payback period is considerably less, to say nothing of the limited resources saved.

These are just a few examples of money saved by "Enabling Green to Earn You 'Green.'" You can see that some of the efforts will require up-front money to save on the back end. Some of the initiatives, however, do not require any investment and reap rewards directly to the bottom line. Additionally, we'd like to remind you that sometimes it is not just the savings in dollars that tell the entire story. For more information on how you, as a project manager, leader of a project team, part of a larger organization, and personally, can contribute to protection of scarce resources, see Chapter 13.

ENDNOTES

1. http://www.njcleanenergy.com/files/file/program_updates/ARRA%20Fact%20 Sheet%20-%2010-19-09%20-%20final.pdf.
2. Kelly Vaughn, With Money on the Table, What's the Best Move for Green Trucking? http://www.greenbiz.com/blog/2010/01/19/money-table-whats-best-move-green-trucking#ixzz0p455UeVl
3. http://myfloridaclimate.com/climate_quick_links/florida_energy_climate_ commission/grants_solar_rebates_incentives.
4. http://www.austinenergy.com/index.htm.
5. http://www.socalgas.com/business/rebates/industry/hotelsLodging.html.
6. http://www.schiff-consulting.com/Ozone_in_laundry_washing.html.
7. http://www.nrdc.org/cities/living/paper/companies.asp.
8. http://www.apple.com/environment.
9. http://www.vics.org/docs/home/pdf/Macys_Schneider_National_Empty_Miles_ Service_101209_FINAL_med.pdf.
10. Ibid.
11. Lockheed Martin, http://www.lockheedmartin.com.
12. http://www.environmentalleader.com/2009/07/01/raytheon-meets-green-goals-with-it-help/.
13. http://www.climatesavers.umich.edu/downloads/DC-SR_casestudies.pdf.
14. http://money.cnn.com/magazines/fortune/fortune_archive/2007/04/02/8403424/ index.htm.
15. Kohler, http://www.kohler.com.

Section IV

Crossing the Finish Line

We are judged by what we finish, not what we start.

Anonymous

13

Tips, Tools, and Techniques to Green (A Green Project Manager's Toolbox)

There are many ways for the project manager to use a variety of tools and techniques to make their project product and process, project team, office, organization, and themselves greener. We're sure that many of you have thought about it. As stated in Section IV's opening quote, what you finish is what counts. You're not helping reduce your carbon footprint if you think about going to recycled paper in your office—only if you actually make the change. Realizing that this book is for the project managers of the world, one of the things we have tried to do with it is to save the valuable resource called "project manager" by researching and providing information on greening projects—so *you* can focus on your projects and take advantage of *our* research. We have defined some of the terms necessary and provided a road map for traversing a project and making that journey greener. The following is information we've collected along the way to help the project manager realize significant greenality on their projects. While certainly not exhaustive (there is enough information out there for several more books), these suggestions (tips, tools, and techniques) should make the project manager's job a little easier. In Chapter 14 we will provide additional information in the form of Web sites, books, and articles for an even deeper dive into the world of green project management.

The following are suggestions to help the projects become greener.

1. These techniques come from **Bruce Alyward**, PSODA (http://www.psoda.com), a company that provides a suite of tools for program and project management as a fully hosted service, aka software

as a service. Bruce suggests that three of the biggest carbon impacts that a project can have are:

a. Traveling to meetings: Traveling to meetings can have both an impact on the environment (think planes, trains, and automobiles) and a cost in terms of travel times. The farther you have to go, the higher these impacts will be. With the speed and reliability of modern data connections, voice over IP (VoIP) and video over IP technologies, it is possible to hold virtual meetings between multiple parties with very little cost overhead and no traveling time involved. An added advantage of using some of the teleconferencing technologies is that you can record the sessions for anybody who could not make the meeting and for archiving electronically. There are even technologies available now that will give you a 3D view of a person on the other side of the world, although that might be a bit extreme for most project meetings.

b. Couriering or posting documents to all the stakeholders: Moving paper documents around can have almost as big an impact on the environment, and on the project budget for that matter. We've been talking about running a paperless office for a long time, but we still insist on printing and couriering (or posting) documents to each other. So we are cutting down trees to print on and we are using fuel to move those pieces of paper around the place. And the project is paying good money for this! A virtual project folder (for example, *Psoda*) allows you to securely store all of your project information in one central location and share that information in a controlled fashion with all of your stakeholders and team members. This means that everybody will have access to the latest version of a document and you don't have to keep track of who has what version. You use a lot less paper (and printer ink), reduce the impact on the environment because you are not sending the paper all over the country (or world), and save on the courier costs. You have the added benefits of improving the transparency on your projects, and the virtual project folder can automatically track all of the changes for governance. If you are running multiple projects, then a system like Psoda can automatically roll up information from the individual projects to provide a program or portfolio management view, saving you the time and effort of writing up those monthly reports.

c. Running servers in your data center to host the project data: You can deploy a virtual project database in one of two ways: a new server in your own data center or on a shared hosting environment (also known as *software as a service* or *cloud computing*). Deploying a new server in your own data center (even if it is a virtualized server) will have an additional cost in providing administrator staff and training them to maintain that server. You will also be increasing the overall carbon footprint of your data center. If you use a shared hosting environment, then the carbon footprint of those servers will be shared across all of the organizations using the shared infrastructure. In the case of Psoda, this would mean that your organization will have only 1/100th of the footprint compared to deploying your own server.

2. Here are some tips from **Wayne Turmel**, host of the popular podcast, *The Cranky Middle Manager* and president of www. greatwebmeetings.com:

a. Collaboration Tools: The obvious way they can "green a project" is by reducing travel; of course the finance people probably made that decision before the project manager had a chance to make it a conscious choice. Used properly, you can eliminate some meetings all together, but can certainly do more prework and follow-up using a thoughtful combination of both synchronous and asynchronous tools. Additionally, by using asynchronous tools like shared documents and wikis, you can save a lot of printing costs by ensuring version control and doing only what's really necessary.

b. To make collaboration tools more effective, take the time for the social niceties. Help teammates get to know each other. Trust is built on mutual goals, mutual respect, and mutual competence. If you don't allow people to develop human trusting communications, you will pay for it in broken commitments, missed timelines, and being on the wrong end of priorities. It's not wasted time—necessarily.

c. Use a *variety* of tools. Sometimes you want to see the person's face, so use a webcam (Skype or some other video service). Other times a quick, just-in-time message is what you're looking for— so IM them. An important suggestion is to (with the appropriate permission) record Web meetings and conference calls. Learn what's at your disposal and coach your team and your managers and employees to use them effectively. Track usage and if they're not using a tool you've paid for, find out why.

d. Encourage use of shared files and asynchronous tools. Free tools like NING and GoogleDocs (see Chapter 14) are amazing and free or very low cost. Microsoft's SharePoint is a much maligned tool. Take the time to learn it, integrate it with your e-mail and other tools, then create incentives for people to adapt it. Technology isn't the answer. *Using* technology strategically is the answer.

e. Communication is more than just data transfer. Context and interpretation are what make it knowledge.

f. Share the leadership of web meetings and conference calls so everyone develops the capability to be proactive.

3. Google Ideas (for information on Google's green initiatives, go to http://www.google.com/corporate/green/index.html): Google has some great ideas that they have instituted at their Mountain View, California, campus that other companies could easily adopt.

a. There are shared bicycles scattered among their buildings for employees to use on short trips around the campus.

b. They offer extensive shuttle service around the Bay Area, reducing the need for employees to use their own cars to commute. The shuttles are biodiesel fueled.

c. The wastes from their cafeterias are separated and the organic component goes to composting. They have reduced the use of disposable utensils, and those that are disposable are compostable.

d. They offer a car-sharing program that is free to employees, and provide a fleet of eight plug-in hybrid vehicles that can be parked under a solar-panel carport made available.

e. Sustainable building materials that are environmentally friendly and healthier for employees are used in the construction of the buildings. They include products designed never to end up in landfills, fresh-air ventilation, natural light, and PVC- and formaldehyde-free materials whenever possible.

f. Google chefs are committed to using as many local, organic, sustainable ingredients as possible. Café 150, for example, sources ingredients for everything on the menu from within 150 miles. They also have a seasonal farmers market in Mountain View and an organic garden right in their main courtyard.

g. They partner with several residential solar companies to offer discounts to employees who want to go solar at home.

h. (This one will not be for all organizations.) Google, for the past two years has rented approximately 200 goats to trim the grass at some of its corporate fields. For about the same cost as mowing, the goats are quieter and provide free fertilizer. See show at: http://googleblog.blogspot.com/2010/04/goats-are-baaaahk.html.

4. SMARTER Computing—Symantec's Green IT Report, Survey Results 2009[1] in the key findings state:

- Green IT is now an "essential."
- Green IT budgets are rising.
- IT is willing to pay a premium for green equipment.
- IT is at the heart of enterprise green efforts.
- Green IT initiatives are more of a priority.

a. Collect as much data as possible on existing computing, power usage, cooling requirements, necessary sizing as well as growth potential, new technologies available, optional methods to collect and store data, etc. We've always said that the planning effort of any project is commensurate with the size of the project. Computing to an organization may be one of their largest expenses; therefore, planning an organization's computing needs is a *major* project and requires a substantial planning effort.

b. When designing new data centers or upgrading existing data centers, make sure that the new servers are the most efficient to extract the maximum performance per wattage of electricity consumed.

c. Design ahead so as to allow for growth.

d. Data centers should have the same consideration as any other building. They should be designed to reduce environmental impact using natural light, high-efficiency lighting, motion-sensing lighting and heating controls, and power management software to monitor and control energy usage.

e. Switch to laptop computers rather than desktops as they require less energy.

f. Run your laptop and other rechargeable devices on battery power as much as possible to reduce your consumption of electricity and extend the life of your batteries.

g. Choose networked digital storage devices for archiving files. Network storage drives hold much more information with less manufactured material and can be configured for automatic backing up of information. Plus, they reduce the time required to search for needed files, thus reducing the energy needed.

   h.   Use multifunctional devices.
5. Green Your Office/Organization

If each of the UK's 10 million office workers **used one fewer staple a day,** that could save 120 tons of steel a year.

---

   a.   Use digital media for your information, calendars, and to-do list, and your communications, telephone, and e-mail.
   b.   Use copy machine and ink or toner cartridge manufacturers for cartridge recycling. Most manufacturers offer a discount on new cartridges by recycling old ones. If they don't, request that discount or switch manufacturers to one that does!
   c.   Purchase recycled (or at least partially recycled) paper.
   d.   Use a water cooler and encourage reusable water bottles.
   e.   If you do need to use paper, use both front and back before recycling.
   f.   Consider new available software such as Greenprint (http://www.printgreener.com) that reduces the number of blank or nearly blank pages you print.
   g.   An alternative to recycling paper (or necessity in some cases) is document shredding. Shredded documents may be able to be used as packing material for the shipping department.
   h.   Encourage establishing an environmental policy. Volunteer to lead the effort if necessary.
   i.   Recycle or donate old computers, cell phones, digital cameras, rechargeable batteries, and eyeglasses. Senior citizen centers and battered women shelters are good places to donate old cell phones, and service providers like Verizon and their HopeLine program facilitate this for you; schools are good places to donate old computers and photographic equipment; some local clubs (http://www.lionsclubs.org/) and most opticians accept old or no-longer-needed eyeglasses for redistribution.

For a third year in a row, Verizon Wireless collected more than 1 million no-longer-used wireless phones through its HopeLine program. Throughout 2009, consumers and businesses donated nearly 1.1 million phones. With the help of these donations, the HopeLine program awarded $1.6 million in cash grants to domestic violence prevention and awareness programs and donated 23,000 phones with 69 free minutes of service to almost 600 shelters nationwide.

---

j. Encourage your organization to purchase equipment that is Energy Star compliant.

k. Consider eco-friendly packaging material and encourage your suppliers to use them. Example: http://www.geami.com/.

l. Use a "stapleless" stapler. The Greenlok Stapleless Stapler, available from the Green Stationery Company (http://www.greenstat.co.uk/), punches two small tabs into the paper, which simultaneously fold over and create a "paper staple."

m. Consider stopping the magazines that you don't regularly read, perhaps instead getting key articles from an RSS reader—saving you time and providing you with fresher, more concentrated information.

n. Check your purchases of supplies for your project and your office with Greenguard (http://www.greenguard.org) to ensure they are not those that are laden with volatile organic compounds (VOCs).

o. Find some eco-office tips for your particular situation at the David Suzuki Foundation's "Nature Challenge" (http://www.davidsuzuki.org/NatureChallenge/).

p. Sign others up! You can start by simply sharing these tips with your colleagues.

6. Green Your Project

a. Add a section for *environmental impact* to your project management tools, like charter, risk management, action plans, or vendor specifications.

b. Make environmental impact a criterion for decision making or project solutions.

c. Ask the environmental and sustainability questions at every stage of the project management process. Work toward applying green thinking to all aspects of the project itself as well as to the project management techniques.

d. Once "green" thinking becomes part of the DNA of your project, start using it as it applies to project resources, people, equipment, and other materials needed.

e. Consider the old PM adage, "the right people in the right place at the right time."

f. Clearly identify any "team leaders"—and empower them—and let these leaders' responsibilities be known—so that you, as the project manager, don't have to micromanage the project people resources, saving your limited resources.

g. Make sure that anyone else critical to the project—suppliers, IT, etc.—are clearly identified and in the "digital" communications loop.

h. Determine the risks of just-in-time equipment needs versus inventory. This can make a big difference in the usage of project management resources.

i. As mentioned throughout, green as much as your project material needs as possible.

j. Equipment transportation costs and transportation methods themselves are very resource intensive. Combine shipments when possible. That will require thinking about what will be required when and trade-offs between just-in-time and inventory.

k. As mentioned, transportation is resource intensive. Another way to minimize the impact is to make sure that delivery trucks are never empty on return trips. This will probably take collaborative efforts between projects, organizations, companies, and industries. It may be beyond the project manager, but is something to think about.

l. Use digital media for project communications.

7. Green Your Team

a. Consider using freelancers and subcontractors who work from home. Additionally, consider telecommuting (full-time or at least part-time) for your team members.

b. If telecommuting is not an option, consider flexible hours so that team members are commuting at off-peak hours saving having to sit in traffic.

c. When building your team, consider the schedule and choose your team members appropriately to minimize overtime and its added energy consumption.

d. Consider some incentives for "green" efforts by team members. Movie and concert tickets or other services make good "green" incentives (rather than disposable goods like T-shirts or buttons) and are an inexpensive way to get your "green" message out to the organization.

e. Help your team find more tips at this site sponsored by the Discovery channel: http://planetgreen.discovery.com/go-green/green-index/.

f. Have your team turn off equipment, especially computers, at the end of the day. Unplug when possible to avoid "phantom power," the drain that occurs even when televisions, computers, and chargers (even when not in use) remain plugged in. Set up computers to hibernate when not in use during the day.

8. Green Your Travel

a. Don't have your hotel sheets and towels changed every day. Every couple of days is probably fine.

b. Turn out the lights, air conditioning, and computers when you leave your room.

c. Use direct flights whenever possible. While it may cost a little more, it will save you time (your limited resource) and also save on energy. Take-offs particularly use a lot of fuel.

d. Use shared rides, buses, and shuttles, to save energy.

If two people share a ride, the gas mileage is doubled, if three people share a ride, you triple it!

---

9. Green Yourself

a. Bring your lunch rather than going out.

b. Repurpose unused printouts for note sheets.

c. Use washable items, like coffee mugs (take reusable ones to Starbucks, Dunkin' Donuts, etc.) rather than paper cups and plastic utensils.

d. Get your kids involved in saving you money and energy! Green Allowance has programs to "recruit" your children to help (http://greenallowance.org).

e. Check out a wealth of green ideas for individuals and homes at http://www.recycleworks.org/.

ENDNOTE

1. Symantec Corporation, Symantec 2009 Worldwide Green IT Report, press release, http://www.symantec.com/about/news/resources/press_kits/detail.jsp?pkid=greenitreport.

14

Resource Information

BOOKS WE THINK YOU SHOULD READ OR REFERENCE

Daniel C. Esty and Andrew S. Winston, *Green to Gold: How Smart Companies Use Environmental Strategy to Innovate, Create Value, and Build Competitive Advantage* (New Haven, CT: Yale University Press, 2007)

Thomas L. Friedman, *Hot, Flat, and Crowded: Why We Need a Green Revolution—and How It Can Renew America* (New York: Macmillan, 2008)

Gil Friend, *The Truth about Green Business* (Upper Saddle River, NJ: FT Press, 2009)

Gary Hirshberg, *Stirring It Up, How to Make Money and Save the World* (New York: Hyperion, 2008)

Kathy Schwalbe, *Information Technology Project Management*, 6th edition (Boston: Course Technology, 2010)

SUGGESTED READING ON LIFE CYCLE ASSESSMENT

H. Baumann and A.-M. Tillman, *The Hitch Hiker's Guide to LCA: An Orientation in Life Cycle Assessment Methodology and Application* (Lund, Sweden: Studentlitteratur AB, 2004)

M. A. Curran (ed.), *Environmental Life Cycle Assessment* (New York: McGraw-Hill, 1996)

M. A. Curran, "Human Ecology: Life Cycle Assessment," *Encyclopedia of Ecology*, 5 vols. (Oxford: Elsevier, 2008)

J. Fava, R. Denison, B. Jones, M. A. Curran, B. Vigon, S. Sulke, and J. Barnum (eds.), *A Technical Framework for Life Cycle Assessments* (Brussels, Belgium: Society of Environmental Toxicology and Chemistry, 1990)

Daniel Goleman, *Ecological Intelligence* (New York: Broadway Books, 2009)

J. Guinee (ed.), *Handbook of Life Cycle Assessment: An Operational Guide to the ISO Standards* (Heidelberg: Springer Berlin, 2001)

R. Horne, T. Grant, and K. Verghese, *Life Cycle Assessment: Principles, Practice and Prospects* (Collingwood, Victoria, Australia: CSIRO, 2009)

ISO 14040 Environmental Management—LCA—Principles and Framework (Geneva, Switzerland: International Standards Organization, 2006)

U.S. Environmental Protection Agency, *Life Cycle Assessment: Principles and Practice,* EPA/600/R-06/060 (Washington, DC: EPA, 2006), available online at http://ww.epa.gov/ORD/NRMRL/lcaccess

COLLABORATION TOOLS AND RESOURCES

Basecamp
   http://www.basecamp.com
Blog posting with a summary of many collaborative project management tools:
   http://www.pluggd.in/online-project-management-software-web-based-297/
GoogleDocs
   http://docs.google.com/
NING
   http://www.ning.com/
Open WorkBench
   http://www.openworkbench.org/
Planzone
   http://www.planzone.com
PSoda
   http://www.psoda.com/cms.php/home

SOSIUS
http://www.sosius.com

RESOURCE FOR IMPROVING TEAM COLLABORATION USING WEB-BASED MEDIA

http://www.greatwebmeetings.com/

GREEN EFFORTS BY COMPANIES AND OTHER ORGANIZATIONS—A SAMPLER

Most companies are riding the green wave by undertaking efforts to increase their greenality. We've highlighted several companies who are "at the top of their game" in Chapter 11. Here are those, and some more that we found during our research that are making significant progress. This list is—as advertised—a sampler, and certainly not exhaustive. It's meant to provide the reader with additional sources and examples.

Apple
http://www.apple.com/environment/complete-lifecycle/#
transportation
CSX (transportation)
http://www.csx.com/?fuseaction=about.environment
DESERTEC solar power effort
Red Paper: Summary of the project http://www.desertec.org/en/
concept/redpaper/
White Book: 65 pages of details on the projecthttp://www.desertec.org/
fileadmin/downloads/DESERTEC-WhiteBook_en_small.pdf
FedEx
http://www.environmentalleader.com/2008/02/20/ups-fedex-find-
ways-to-save-gas/
The Gap
http://www.gapinc.com/GapIncSubSites/csr/Goals/Environment/
En_Overview.shtm

General Electric

http://ge.ecomagination.com/

GreenTouch—consortium of IT and Telecom, with academic partners

http://www.greentouch.org

Home Depot

http://greeninc.blogs.nytimes.com/2009/02/02/wal-mart-announces-fuel-efficiency-gains/

Interface

http://www.interfaceglobal.com/Sustainability.aspx

Also see Interface's nonprofit sustainability community:

http://www.missionzero.org

Liberty Mutual Insurance Company

http://www.libertymutualgroup.com/omapps/ContentServer?pagename=LMGroup/Views/LMG&ft=4&fid=1138356784591&ln=en

L.L.Bean

http://www.llbean.com/customerService/aboutLLBean/background.html?nav=ln

Macy's

http://www.macysinc.com/AboutUs/sustainability/sustain.aspx

National Resource Defense Council's Smart Companies

http://www.nrdc.org/cities/living/paper/companies.asp

National Science Foundation

http://www.nsf.gov/index.jsp

Patagonia

http://www. Patagonia.com

Procter and Gamble (video)

http://www.pg.com/company/our_commitment/video/sustainability/index.html

Public Service of New Hampshire

http://www.psnh.com/Energy/PSNH_Environment/default.asp

Shaklee

http://www.shaklee.com/causes_achievements.shtml

Telecom/IT industry effort launched 2010 – GreenTouch

http://www.greentouch.org

University of Massachusetts–Amherst

http://www.umass.edu/green

For further reading about U. Mass's green effort: http://www.combinedcyclejournal.com/5Q-Pacesetter/Amherst.pdf

Walmart
http://greeninc.blogs.nytimes.com/2009/02/02/wal-mart-announces
-fuel-efficiency-gains/

WEB SITES WORTH A VISIT AND A STAY

Biodegradable Products and Packaging
http://www.bpiworld.org/
http://www.sustainablepackaging.org/
http://www.greenerpackage.com/
Children's Scrap Store—collects safe waste from businesses for reuse as
a low-cost, creative resource; also collect paper, card, foam, plastic
pots, tube, tubs, netting, fabric, books, and CDs
http://www.childrensscrapstore.co.uk/
Database for State Incentives for Renewables and Efficiency
http://www.dsireusa.org/
Eco-Friendly Products
http://www.eco-coffee.ca/corporate.html (organic coffee, biodegradable cups)
http://www.imusranchfoods.com/index3.aspx?categoryid=105
(green cleaning products)
http://www.steelcase.com/na/ (green office furniture)
Environmental Protection Agency (U.S.)
Purchasing
http://www.epa.gov/epp/pubs/guidance/finalguidance.htm
Green House Gas Emissions
http://epa.gov/climatechange/emissions/co2_human.html
Climate Change Partners
http://www.epa.gov/climateleaders/partners/index.html
European Environmental Agency (EEA)
http://www.eea.europa.eu/
(See especially their Multimedia section, and in particular a video,
"OneDegreeMatters,"locatedat:http://www.eea.europa.eu/cop15/
bend-the-trend/one-degree-matters-movie#downloadmovie.)
Statistical Data on the Effect of Their Global Public Procurement
http://ec.europa.eu/environment/gpp/pdf/statistical_data.pdf

248 • Green Project Management

Friends of the Earth
  http://www.foe.co.uk/
Global and Bailouts Focused on Green
  http://globaldashboard.org/wp-content/uploads/2009/HSBC_
    Green_New_Deal.pdf
Green Data Centers
  http://207.46.16.252/en-us/magazine/2009.gr.datacenter.aspx
GREENGUARD Environmental Institute
  http://www.greenguard.org/
Green Jobs
  http://www.whitehouse.gov/sites/default/files/rss_viewer/jobs_
    forum_report.pdf
International Organization for Standardization
  http://www.iso14000-iso14001-environmental-management.com/
Lean
  http://www.lean.org/WhatsLean/
  http://www.leanprimer.com/downloads/lean_primer.pdf
  http://www.poppendieck.com
LEED: Leadership in Energy and Environmental Design (LEED)
  certification is a recognized standard for measuring building sustainability. Achieving that certification is a way for a company to
  demonstrate that their building project is "green." The rating system is administered by a nonprofit organization, the U.S. Green
  Building Council, a Washington, DC–based coalition of building
  industry leaders. As with green project management, the purpose
  of LEED certification is to encourage the use of green building
  practices that will increase profits, by designing and building using
  energy-saving alternatives for example, while reducing the negative
  impacts on the environment, and improving the health and welfare
  of the employees.
  http://www.nrdc.org (National Resource Defense Council)
  http://www.usgbc.com (U.S. Green Business Council)
Life Cycle Assessment Software
  Multiple vendors provide software and consulting for conducting an
    LCA and generating the appropriate reports. The list that follows
    is not exhaustive; it is also not meant to be any sort of endorse-
    ment. However we do provide it for reference because these may
    each be the source of excellent information regarding life cycle
    thinking and LCAs.

CAMSAT (Carbon Management Self-Assessment Tool): CAMSAT provides a simple means of assessing the quality of a company's internal system for responding to climate change. The tool consists of a series of 23 multiple-choice questions, the result of which is one overall score and a synopsis of suggestions for ways in which carbon management can be improved in relation to the risks and opportunities identified. CAMSAT is applicable to all companies with an interest in maintaining or strengthening their environmental reputations and/or those whose business may be affected by policies intended to reduce human-induced climate change. The tool will be of direct relevance to companies within the following groups:

UN Global Compact

FTSE4Good

Dow Jones Sustainability Index

WBCSD Members

Equator Group

The free tool runs on MS Excel. http://www.unep.fr/energy/information/tools/camsat/xls/SelfAssessmentTool-v1.5.xls

Ecoinvent: The Swiss Ecoinvent-database (http://www.ecoinvent.ch) with more than 2,500 processes (also many on bioenergy systems) can also be imported. The Ecoinvent data contains international industrial life cycle inventory data on energy supply, resource extraction, material supply, chemicals, metals, agriculture, waste management services, and transport services.

ERGO: This model was developed for estimating energy and emissions budgets of bioenergy systems. ERGO was originally developed in the early 1990s with the primary aim of estimating energy and carbon budgets of bioenergy production from short rotation coppice tree systems. An important secondary objective was to provide a tool that could be used to compare different systems of bioenergy production directly, consistently and fairly. http://www.ieabioenergy-task38.org/softwaretools/ERGO.pdf

FAIR 2.0: Framework to Assess International Regimes for differentiation of future commitments (climate, emissions allocation, and costs model) It provides evaluation of the Kyoto Protocol in terms of environmental effectiveness and economic costs. The FAIR model consists of three linked models:

1. A climate model: to calculate the climate impacts of global emission profiles and to determine the global emission reduction objective, based on the difference between the global baseline emissions scenario and emission profile

2. An emissions allocation model: to calculate the regional emission targets for different climate regimes for future commitments within the context of this global reduction objective

3. A costs model: to calculate the abatement costs for each region using these emissions targets of the regimes and to distribute the global emission reduction objective over the different regions, gases and sectors following a least-cost approach, making use of the flexible Kyoto mechanisms

For further information, see http://www.pbl.nl/images/FAIR2.0_poster_tcm61-36353.pdf.

GaBi: a family of tools and databases for sustainability analysis from P. E. International

http://www.gabi-software.com/

GORCAM (Graz/Oak Ridge Carbon Accounting Model): This is an Excel spreadsheet model that has been developed to calculate the net fluxes of carbon to and from the atmosphere associated with land use, land use change, bioenergy, and forestry projects.

http://www.ieabioenergy-task38.org/softwaretools/gorcam.htm

IEA Bioenergy: an international collaboration of bioenergy

http://www.ieabioenergy-task38.org/softwaretools/software-tools.htm

KCL EcoData: developed in Finland, joint government and industry (KCL, Espoo), to evaluate environmental products and services. "KCL EcoData" is a continuously updated LCI database and is primarily intended for life cycle inventory calculations related to forest products. It contains nearly 300 data modules covering, e.g., energy production, pulp

and paper chemicals, wood growth, and harvesting operations for spruce, pine and birch, pulp, paper, and board mills.
See http://kcl.fi/eco/index.html for more details. This tool
includes an uncertainty analysis, but no cost parameters.

NREL (The National Renewable Energy Laboratory): NREL
and its partners created the U.S. Life-Cycle Inventory (LCI)
Database to help life cycle assessment (LCA) experts answer
their questions about environmental impact (http://www.nrel.
gov/lci/).This database provides a cradle-to-grave accounting
of the energy and material flows into and out of the environment that are associated with producing a material, component, or assembly. The LCI Database is a publicly available
database (http://www.nrel.gov/lci/database/default.asp) that
allows users to objectively review and compare analysis
results that are based on similar data collection and analysis
methods.

RETScreen (Renewable Energy Technology Project Analysis):
The government of Canada's RETScreen International
Clean Energy Project Analysis Software is a unique decision support tool developed with the contribution of numerous experts from government, industry, and academia.
The software, provided free of charge, can be used worldwide to evaluate the energy production, life cycle costs, and
greenhouse gas emissions reductions for various types of
energy-efficient and renewable-energy technologies (RETs).
To download the free software and other related tools, please
visit the RETScreen Web site at http://www.retscreen.net.

SimaPro: (currently sold in version 5.1 by PRé Consultants,
Amersfoort, NL, http://www.pre.nl/simapro/): It is a com-
puterized LCA tool used to collect, analyze, and monitor
environmental information for products and services, with
integrated databases and impact assessment procedures.[1]
Each step is clear, and the process tree can be used to display
results, showing a high degree of transparency since calculations are shown alongside each process box. It is possible to
view parts of the life cycle at different scales, and to display
their contributions to the total score. Definition of functional
units is incorporated, as is sensitivity analysis. SimaPro has no
function for calculations of costs. Transparency is somewhat

reduced in SimaPro as algorithms are not immediately obvious in inventory results compilation, and incorporation of allocation and reference system is not clear.

Sustainable Minds: (Software as a service, http://www.sustainableminds.com). Combines eco-design and LCA to provide on demand, a Web-based software service. Their mission is to bring environmental sustainability into mainstream product development and manufacturing in an accessible, empowering, and credible way.

Team: TEAM is Ecobilan's powerful and flexible life cycle assessment software (http://www.ecobalance.com/uk_team.php). It allows the user to build and use a large database and to model any system representing the operations associated with products, processes, and activities. This software enables the user to describe any industrial system and to calculate the associated life cycle inventories and potential environmental impacts according to the ISO 14040 series of standards.

Umberto: Developed in Germany (IFU Hamburg and IFEU Heidelberg), this software allows the user to evaluate material and energy flows for products. To facilitate this assessment, Umberto provides a module library that contains extensive data sets on numerous generic upstream and downstream processes (including ecoinvent data). These data consider all relevant flows and enable Umberto to provide visualization of the entire process—from raw-material extraction to waste disposal. This can be used to analyze various scenarios and identify the optimal and most ecologically sensible production process. See http://www.umberto.de/en for more information.

Mother Nature Network
  http://www.mnn.com/
The Natural Step
  http://www.thenaturalstep.org/
Recycled Waders (no part of our economy or our lifestyle is exempt from sustainability—for fishermen, products made from recycled wading boots)
  http://www.recycledwaders.com/

ADDITIONAL TOOLS AND RESOURCES FOR GREEN PROJECT MANAGERS

General Management Podcasts for PMs
   Manger Tools: http://www.manager-tools.com
   The Cranky Middle Manager: http://tpn.cmm.com
   The PM Podcast: http://www.project-management-podcast.com/
Green Social Networking
   facebook: http://www.facebook.com/
   Gantthead Interest Group: http://www.gantthead.com/GIGs/
   Linkedin: http://www.linkedin.com/
   missionzero: http://missionzero.org/
   Twitter: http://twitter.com/
Interview with the Authors of This Book
   http://www.arraspeople.co.uk/Newsletter/2009/Sep09/2009_sep09_
      projectmanagementnewsletter.html#LETTER.BLOCK13
Podcasts with the Authors of This Book
   http://projectshrink.com/potion/project-potion-episode-1-the-
      green-thing/
   http://cmm.thepodcastnetwork.com/2009/12/20/the-
      cranky-middle-manager-show-220-green-project-management-
      maltzman-and-shirley/
Structured Decision Making
   http://www.structureddecisionmaking.org/
      ToolsInfluenceDiagram.htm
   http://mindtools.com
Theory of Constraints
   http://www.dbrmfg.co.nz/Production%20DBR.htm
   http://www.tocc.com/
   http://www.ciras.iastate.edu/library/toc/fundamentals.asp

Note: The endnotes of every chapter also contain information to lead you to further reading.

ENDNOTE

1. M. Goedkoop and M. Oele, *Introduction into LCA methodology and practice with SimaPro 5*, PRé Consultants, Amersfoort, 2002.

Index

4L approach, 188
5S method, 183, 186–187
14-point business philosophy, 41

A

Abbott Laboratories, green initiatives, 227
Abington Shoe Company, 192
Acidification, as life cycle impact category, 165
Actual costs (AC), 128
Adventure, 71
Agricultural residues, 32
Air pollution, 8
Air Resources Board (ARB), 12
Al Gore effect, 151
Albom, Mitch, 1
Alternative products, environmental impacts, 150
Alyward, Bruce, 233
Ambient air pollutants, 215
Ambiguity, eliminating in progress reporting, 140–141
American Recovery and Reinvestment Act (ARRA), 216, 218
  funding overview chart, 217
Apple Computer
  case study, 224
  GHG emissions commitments, 47
  green efforts, xiii, 245
Apple iPad, xiii
Appraisal costs, 48
Aquatic toxicity, as life cycle impact category, 166
Aqueous phase processing, 33
  sugar sources, 34
Asynchronous tools, 235, 236
Attitude, NASA tips, 138

B

Balance, 19
Band-aid strategies, 139–141
Bank of America, case study, 224
Bar of soap
  flowchart, 162
  life cycle analysis, 161, 163
Baselining, 131
Behavioral change
  fostering in children, 57–58
  in project ideation stage, 76–77
  through issue reengineering, 76
Benchmarking, xxii
  need for, 132
Best practices, xxii
Big Dig Project, 61–62
Bio-based feed stocks, 150
Bioaccumulative pollutants, 215
Biodegradable, 25–26
Biodegradable diapers controversy, 25–26
Biodegradable products, 247
Biodegradable Products Institute, Inc., 26
Biodiesel
  Google shuttle service, 236
  recycling kitchen grease as, 203
Biodiversity, loss of, 8
Biomass, sustainable, 32–35
Biomass boiler system, 225
Blower door tests, 222, 223
Bottom-up demand, as green driver, 14–16
Brainstorming, 77–78
Braungart, Michael, 146
Brin, Sergey, 196
British Standards Institute (BSI), 154
Budget at completion (BAC), 141
Building Materials Exchange, 55
Business decisions, bottom line driven, 24
Business success, 53

C

Cake recipes, standard vs. green, 91–92, 93–94
California AB32, 12–13
CAMSAT, 249
Cape Wind, 51

Car-sharing programs, 236
Carbon dioxide, 14
    annual savings per Google server, 197
Carbon emissions
    as NPO, 130
    reductions by Office Depot, 201
Carbon exchange programs, 58
Carbon footprint, 17–20, 148
    biggest project impacts, 234–235
    direct and indirect components, 17–18
    improvements at Timberland, 193
    reducing through electronic
        communications, 120
    reducing with LED tube lights, 204
Carbon footprinting, LCA basis, 154–155
Carbon monoxide, reductions in Boston,
    62
Carbon neutrality, in GA Project, 58
Carbon offsets, 18, 58
    as Band-Aid strategy, 139
    JetBlue initiative, xxi
    purchasing, 18, 58
Carbon Trust, 154
Carbonfund, 18
Cartridge recycling, 238
Case studies, 189
    General Electric, 205–206
    Google, 196–199
    Interface, 194
    Microsoft, 202–204
    Office Depot, 199–201
    Patagonia, 190–191
    profit enhancements, 223–229
    Steward Advanced Materials, 206–207
    Sun Chips, 207–208
    Timberland, 192–194
Cell phone recycling, 238–239
Cellular manufacturing, 183
Centricity Electronic Medical Records
    (EMR), 205
Certified SmartWay, 201
Change agents, PMs as, xii
Change control process, 110, 135
    and greenality, 133–135
    NASA tips, 137–138
Chevrolet Volt, 73
Children, fostering behavioral change in,
    57–58
Children's Art Program, 55

Chu, Steven, 218
Citadel complex, 7
Cities, world population living in, 7
City Year, 24–25
Clean energy, DESERTEC concept, 59
Clean Water Act, 12
Climate change, 3–5
    and concern for life cycle perspective,
        151
    falsely connecting greenality to views
        on, 113
    vs. global warming terminology, 3–4,
        86
Cloud computing, 235
Coca-Cola Company
    can waste case study, 185–186
    and LCA origins, 152
Code of ethics, revisions to PMBOK
        guide, 46–47
Coffee pods, recycling issues, 63–65
Collaboration tools, 235, 244–245
Combined Standards Glossary, 19
Commensurate effort, 129
Commercial buildings, energy provider
        rebates, 221
Commitment, to greenality, 120, 126
Commitment statements
    by core project team, 112
    in project charters, 85
Communications
    greenality of, 85
    greening with social media, 118–120
    moving from paper to electronic form,
        102
    multiple media, 139
    NASA tips, 139
    percentage of time spent by PMs on, 120
    spirit of, 85–86
    trusting, 235
Commuter rail lines, 58
Completeness check, in LCIA, 169
Compostable materials, 203
    Google cafeterias example, 236
    Portsmouth Brewery example, 228
Computer industry, reuse in, 45
Conservation Alliance, 191
Consistency check, in LCIA methodology,
    169
Constancy of purpose, 41

Continuous improvement, 41
Controlling. *See* Project monitoring and
     controlling
Controversy, at kickoff meeting, 113, 114
Cool Roof project, 79–80
Cooling towers, Google use of, 197, 198
Corcoran, Bob, 205
Core project team, 112
Corn, use by Microsoft initiatives, 203
Corporate social responsibility, 23–25, 100
     case studies, 189–208
     Microsoft's commitment to, 202
     at Office Depot, 201
Corrective actions, 136
Cost-benefit analysis, 79–81
Cost performance index (CPI), 141
Cost savings. *See also* Profitability
     adoption of green technology due to,
          90
     and greenality score, 102
     misconceptions about, 134
     through greening, 102–103, 211
     through insulation, 81
Cost variance, 129, 141
Cradle to cradle (C2C) concept, 21–22
Cradle-to-gate boundaries, 160, 161
Cradle to grave concept, 158
     and life cycle assessment, 147
Cranky Middle Manager, The, 235
Creep. *See* Effort creep; Feature creep;
          Hope creep
Crop-based ethanol fuels, unintended
          consequences, 149
Crosby, Philip, 40, 41
Cumulative project investment, 112
Cunningham, Storm, 37
Customer demand, as project driver,
          72–73
Customers, bottom-up demand from,
          14–16
Cycle of sustainability, 20–21

D

Damage clauses, 102
Data
     advancing into information,
          knowledge, and wisdom, 128
     in DIKW pyramid, 125

Data accuracy, in LCA, 169
Data age, 169
Data centers
     consolidating, 225, 226
     hosting project data on servers, 235
     server efficiency, 237
Data collection and analysis, 127–130
Data gaps, in LCA, 159
Data source, in LCA, 169
Dead Zone, 150
Decision makers, LCA support for, 160
Decision-making tools, 77
     brainstorming, 77–78
     cost-benefit analysis, 79–81
     force field analysis, 79
     green component of, 75
     reverse brainstorming, 78
Decision validation, 81–82
Deforestation, 8
Degradation, consequences of, 49
Delivery trucks, optimizing empty, 240
Deming, W. Edwards, 40, 41, 103
Deming cycle, 136
Deming Prize, 103
Deming quality, 105
Dennison, Brackett III, 205
DESERTEC Concept, 24, 31, 58–60, 245
Detailed LCA, 147
Diagnostic tools, for energy audits,
          222–223
DIKW pyramid, 125–126, 128
Direct flights, 241
Direct impact, green by, 60–62
Disasters, natural *vs.* human-made, 8
Discovery channel, 241
Discovery of Heaven, The, 145
Disposable diapers, 25–26
Disposal
     considering in life-cycle thinking, 146
     in life cycle analysis, 163
     reducing costs of, 228
Document shredding, using as packing
          materials, 238
Drought
     links to sea surface temperatures, 15
     need for permanent/sustainable
          solutions, 99
     water projects to counteract, 87
DuPont case study, 228

E

E-Grid, 161
E-readers, 86
E-waste recycling, 56
Earned environmental value (EEV), 129
Earned environmental value management
	(EEVM), 46, 115, 128, 129
Earned value (EV), 128
	case for, 139–141
	using to eliminate reporting
		ambiguity, 140
Earned value management (EVM), 128
EarthPM, 40, 119, 194
	five assertions, 53, 54
Eastern States Standard, 13–14
Eco audit, 28–29
Eco-friendly products, 247
Ecoinvent, 249
Ecological impacts, 46
Ecological intelligence, 151
Ecomagination goals, 206
Economic incentive, in Green Allowance
		Project, 57–58
Efficiency, greenality and, 113
Efficient computing, 196
Effort creep, 121, 132
Electricity
	annual savings per Google server, 197
	generating in desert regions, 58–60
Electronic components
	burning, 37
	Google disposal of, 198
Electronic media, 120
Electronic recycling, 36–37, 238
	Apple iPad, xiii
Eltona, The, 56–57
Emissions, reductions by Timberland,
		193
Emotional issues, project derailment due
		to, 131, 132
Employee creativity, waste of, 180–182
End-of-life impacts, 160
Energy and Water Development
		and Related Agencies
		Appropriations Act of 2010, 216
Energy audits, 222–223
Energy costs
	for cloth vs. disposable diapers, 25

Cool Roof project, 79–81
	reductions at Microsoft, 202
Energy crops, 32
Energy Policy Act, 12
Energy providers, grants and rebates,
		221
Energy Star compliance, 215, 217, 222,
		225, 239
Environmental assessments, support for,
		159
Environmental damage, 108
Environmental degradation, 8
Environmental efficiency, links to quality,
		9
Environmental impacts, xxi, 157
	adding to project management tools,
		239
	of alternative products, 150
	comparing for EPP program, 214–215
	as criterion for decision making, 239
	cumulative, 149
	at different product life cycle stages,
		156
	establishing baseline of, 159
Environmental lens, xxii, xxiii, 20, 62,
		100, 212
Environmental management plan (EMP),
		46, 109–110
Environmental management systems
		(EMSs), 9
Environmental performance information,
		for EPA EPP program, 215–216
Environmental policies, establishing, 238
Environmental projects, 98–99
Environmental Protection Agency (EPA),
		11–12
Environmental responsibility, 36, 75, 108
	of projects, 74
Environmental risks, 50–51
Environmental scope, 50
Environmental sustainability, xi
Environmental Sustainability Dashboard,
		203
Environmentally preferable purchasing
		(EPP), 212. See also EPA
		Environmentally Preferable
		Purchasing (EPP) program
EPA Environmentally Preferable
		Purchasing (EPP) program, 212

environment, price, performance principles, 212–213
environmental impacts comparisons, 214–215
environmental performance information principle, 215–216
high-priority human health stressors, 215
life cycle perspective principle, 214
pollution prevention through, 213
EPA Toxics Release Inventory (TRI), 161
Equipment, turning off, 241
ERGO software, 249
Erin Brockovich, 11
Escalation processes, 86–87, 121
Estimate at completion (EAC), 141
European Commission Joint Research Centre, 154
European Environment Agency (EEA), 11, 247
European Platform on Life Cycle Assessment, 154
European Union Global Public Procurement guidelines, 211
Eutrophication, as life cycle impact category, 165
Execution phase. *See* Project execution
Expert judgment, 82
    avoiding supplier greenwashing by, 87
    enhancing with SMEs, 119
Extreme programming, addressing wastes via, 181

F

Face-to-face communication, 139
Failure costs, 48
FAIR 2.0, 249–250
Feature creep, 129
FedEx, green efforts, 245
Fertilizers, considering in LCA, 150
Flexible hours, 240
Flooring company, case study, 194
Fly Fisherman Magazine, 5
Focus, retaining, 114
Focus groups, 129, 130
Food wastes, 32, 34
Footwear, environmental footprint, 193
Force field analysis, 79

Forest reclamation, 58
Friends of the Earth, 248
Functional barriers, removing, 41

G

GaBi, 161, 171, 250
Gantthead.com, 119
Gasification, 33
General Electric
    Ecomagination goals, 206
    green efforts, 246
    greenality case study, 204–206
Genetically modified (GM) foods, 149
Geographical impacts, 214
Geographical representation, in LCA, 169
Geographical scale, 215
Geothermal energy, 31–32
GHG emissions cap, 12
Global agencies/mandates/guidelines, 9
    European Environment Agency (EEA), 11
    ISO 14000, 9–10
    Kyoto protocol, 10
Global Green Standards, 9
Global temperature record, 4
Global warming
    green efforts solutions, 44
    as life cycle impact category, 164
    rate of, 4
    sensitivity around conflicting information, 75, 86
    vs. climate change, 3–4
Global warming potential (GWP), 164
Goal definition, 168
    in LCA projects, 158–160
Goats, as grass trimmers, 237
Google
    annual savings per server, 197
    cooling towers, 197, 198
    electronic waste disposal, 198
    green initiatives, 236–237
    greenality case study, 196–199
    use of organic foods, 236
Google Ideas, 236
Google PowerMeter, 196
GoogleDocs, 236
GORCAM, 250
Gore, Al, 15

Government agencies/mandates/
guidelines, 8
global, 9–11
U.S.-related, 11–14
Government regulations, as project
drivers, 73
Grand Award in Green Technology, 206
Grants and rebates, 216
American Recovery and Reinvestment
Act (ARRA), 216, 218
energy audits, 222–223
from energy providers (utilities), 221
industry-specific, 223
international stimulus distribution,
219
State of Florida solar rebates, 220–221
U.S. Department of Energy, 218, 220
Great Pacific Garbage Patch, 21
Greed, 8
Green
gaining buy-in at kickoff meeting, 113
as good business, 90
Green advertising, 15
Green advocates, at project initiation
stage, 78
Green Allowance Project, 57–58
Green awareness, 58, 97
Green buildings, 151
at Google, 236
at Microsoft, 203
Office Depot commitment to, 200
Patagonia's commitment of, 191
Green business, as microcosm, xxi
Green Buyer's Guide, 199
Green by definition, 54–60
Green by intent, 98
Green charters, 82–83
Green Claims Code, 27
Green communications, social media as
tool for, 118–120
Green Communicators, 119
Green costing methods, 102
Green Data Centers, 248
Green efforts
corporate examples, 245–247
DESERTEC concept, 245
Federal Express, 245
The Gap, 245
General Electric, 246

GreenTouch, 246
Home Depot, 246
Interface, 246
issues or problems solved by, 44
Liberty Mutual Insurance, 236
L.L. Bean, 246
Macy's, 246
National Research Defense Council's
Smart Companies, 246
National Science Foundation, 246
Patagonia, 246
Procter & Gamble, 246
Public Service of New Hampshire,
246
Shaklee, 246
Telecom, 246
University of Massachusetts-Amherst,
246
Walmart, 247
Green-friendly decision-making
environment, 75–76
Green gasoline technologies, 32–33
Green government purchasing, 211
EPA Environmentally Preferable
Purchasing (EPP) program, 212
Green incentives, 240
Green Index card, 193, 194
Green innovation, 6
Green intent, xxiii, 79, 83, 113
Green IT, 237
Green jobs, 248
Green milestones, 133
Green Mountain Coffee, 63–65
Green PM, 119
Green PM toolbox, 233–241
Green process, 83
Green Project, The, 53, 54–56
Green project charters, 82–83
Green project fundamentals, 39
cost of greenality, 47–48
environmental risks, 50–51
environmental scope, 50
PMI and greenality, 45–47
project cycle of sustainability, 49–50
project life cycle thinking, 48–49
quality and greenality, 39–42
reducing nonproduct output, 43, 45
stakeholders, 51
Green project management, xi, xii

Green project managers, 23–25
Green project terminology, 17
    aqueous phase processing, 33
    biodegradable, 25–26
    carbon footprint, 17–20
    corporate social responsibility, 23–25
    cradle to cradle, 21–22
    cycle of sustainability, 20–21
    eco audit, 28–29
    environmental lens, 20
    gasification, 33
    green gasoline, 33
    green project manager, 23–25
    greenwashing, 26–27
    natural step, 22–23
    pyrolysis, 33
    reduce, redesign, reuse, recycle, 29
    renewable energy, 30–35
    smarter objectives, 35–37
    sustainability, 17–20
    triple bottom line, 28
    triple-P concept of sustainability, 29
Green projects, 53–54
    Big Dig project, 61–62
    green by definition, 54–60, 66
    green by product impact, 55, 62–65, 66
    green by project impact, 55, 60–62, 66
    green in general, 55, 65–66
    Keurig K-cups, 63–65
    rainbow of, 66
    UAE floating terminal, 60–61
Green purchasing guidelines, 100–102
Green quality, 105
Green Restaurant Certification, 203
Green risks, 107
Green savings, 102
Green schedule issues, 99
Green seal, 27
Green social networking, 253
Green spectrum, 55
Green technology, adoption due to cost
    savings, 90
Green tests, 27
Green thinking, xii, 21, 100, 239
    at concept stages of project, 213
Green to Gold, 194
Green Wave, xxi, xxii, 1, 4, 132
Green WBS, 91

Green Writers Ever Evolving Network
    (GWEEN), 119
Greenality, xxi, 20
    addition of risk through, 71
    adoption issues, 42
    in all projects, 71
    building into project, 136
    and change control process, 133–135
    contrasting quality masters with, 40
    corporate achievement of, 189
    cost of, 47–48
    data collection and analysis, 127–130
    designing in, 39
    driving to project management level,
        14
    falsely connecting with climate change
        views, 113
    as good business, 97
    human factors in, 134
    internal drivers, 47
    keeping projects focused on, 84–85
    lack of management commitment to,
        108
    manufacturing-based, 106
    misconceptions about costs, 134
    monetary commitments to, 85
    obtaining buy-in at kickoff meeting,
        114
    offsetting cost of, xxiii
    planning into project, 95
    as polarizing subject matter, 85–86
    product-based, 106
    of project communications, 85
    quality and, 39–42
    risk and, 107–109
    of suppliers, 87
    transcendent, 104, 105
    user-based, 106
    value-based, 107
Greenality action items, 114
Greenality assurance, 115–116
Greenality case studies. *See* Case studies
Greenality clauses, 102
Greenality control, 43
Greenality efforts
    additional costs due to, 123
    executing, 120–122
    role of project managers in, 42
    specific earned value, 115

Greenality improvement, 43
Greenality issues, actions for abating, 136–141
Greenality measurements, periodic review of, 133
Greenality outputs, 109–110
Greenality planning, 43
Greenality problems, human issues as key, 42
Greenality risks, 137
Greenality score, xxii, 16
  and cost savings, 102
GREENGUARD Environmental Institute, 248
Greenhouse effect (GHE), 15
Greenhouse gas (GHG) emissions, 12
  Apple Computer commitments, 47
  binding targets for reducing, 10
  climate change due to, 4
  reductions at GE, 204
  Schneider National reductions in, 224
Greenprint software, 238
GreenTouch, green efforts, 246
Greenwashing, 26–27, 215
  by suppliers, 87
Groundwater contamination, 11
Guide to the Project Management Book of Knowledge (PMBOK Guide), 45
Gulf of Mexico, zone of hypoxia, 150

H

Hazardous air pollutants, 215
Health Insurance Portability and Accountability Act of 1996 (HIPAA), 73
High-priority human health stressors, 215
High-voltage direct current (HVDC) transmission lines, 59–60
Hiking the project, 69, 72, 116
Hitch Hiker's Guide to LCA, 155
Home Depot, green efforts, 246
Home energy audits, 222–223
Hope creep, 121, 129, 132
Household garbage, 34
Human health
  as life cycle impact category, 166

  protecting, 215
Hurricane Katrina, 8
Hybrid vehicles, market demand for, 73

I

IEA Bioenergy, 250
Immediate reporting, 117
Impact assessment, 163–164, 167, 168
Implementation period
  and changes to project environment, 137
  NASA tips, 138
Inconvenient Truth, An, 15
Indirect impact, green by, 62–65
Individuals
  avoiding singling out, 131
  separating from issues, 132
Indoor air pollution, 215
Industrial wastes, 32, 34
Influence diagram, 79
Information, in DIKW pyramid, 125
Information technology
  energy reductions in, 225
  green, 237
Inputs, 147, 148
Institute of Medicine, 5
Interdependence, collaborating through, 138
Interface
  green efforts, 246
  greenality case study, 194–195
Intergovernmental Panel on Climate Change (IPCC), 3
  formation, 3
International Organization for Standardization (ISO), 153, 248
International stimulus distribution, 219
Interpretation phase, in LCA method, 167–170
Interviews, 129, 130
Inventory analysis, 168
  in LCA method, 160–161
Invitation to bid (IFB), 101
ISO 14000, 9–10
ISO 14040, 154, 158
ISO 14044, 154
Issues, separating from individuals, 131, 132

J

Japan, interest in Deming's ideas, 41, 103
Jeopardy processes, 86–87, 121
Jet Blue, carbon exchange programs, xxi, 58
Juran, Joseph, 40, 42, 103
Just-in-time equipment needs, 240
Just-in-time manufacturing, 183

K

Kaizen rapid improvement events, 183
Kanban, 183
KCL Ecodata, 250–251
Kenya, water projects, 98
Keurig Coffee, 63–64
   environmental statement, 64–65
Kickoff meeting, 113–115
Kinetic energy, 30
Knowledge, in DIKW pyramid, 125–126
Kohler Company case study, 228–229
Kudzu, unintended consequences, 149
Kyoto protocol, 10, 250

L

Labeling, greenwashing through, 27
Land use, as life cycle impact category, 166
Laptop computers, switching to, 237
LCA practitioner databases, 161
LCA software tools, 171–172
Lean
   defined, 178
   environmental benefits, 183–184
Lean development, 181
Lean enterprise supplier networks, 184
Lean methods, 177
   4L approach, 188
   5S, 186–187
   environmental benefits, 183–184
Lean thinking, 175
   case study, 178–179
   wastes and, 179–180
   and your project, 175–177
Learning-based planning mindset, 137
LED tube lights, 204–205
LEED standard, 151, 192, 200, 203, 225, 248

LeGuin, Ursula K., 143
Lessons learned, 124
Lewin, Kurt, 79
Liberty Mutual
   green efforts, 246
   green initiatives, 227
Life cycle assessment (LCA), 146, 147, 149–151
   bar chart/flowchart, 161, 162
   bar of soap example, 161, 163
   carbon footprinting based on, 154–155
   checklist categories and potential inconsistencies, 169
   completeness check, 169
   consistency check, 169
   as cornerstone of sustainability, 148
   framework, 168
   fundamentals, 157–158
   goal definition and scoping stage, 158–160
   history, 151–153
   impact assessment, 163–164, 167
   impact results subjectivity, 172
   interpretation phase, 167–170
   inventory analysis phase, 160–161
   limitations to conducting, 172
   maintaining transparency in, 172–173
   performing, 155
   as project, 158
   promoting use of, 155–156
   reference document components, 171
   reporting assumptions in, 172
   resource and time intensiveness, 172
   resources on, 243–244
   results reporting phase, 170–171
   sensitivity check, 169
   software tools, 171–173
   standards pertaining to, 153–154
Life cycle assessment framework, 168
Life cycle assessment software, 248–252
Life cycle-based approaches, 148
Life cycle greenhouse gas analysis, 148
Life cycle impact assessment (LCIA), 164
   characterization stage, 167
   classification stage, 164
   evaluation and reporting stage, 167
   grouping stage, 167
   impact category definition stage, 164
   models, 172

normalization stage, 167
steps, 164, 167
Life cycle impact categories, 165
  acidification, 165
  aquatic toxicity, 166
  eutrophication, 165
  global warming, 165
  human health, 166
  land use, 166
  photochemical smog, 166
  resource depletion, 166
  stratospheric ozone depletion, 165
  terrestrial toxicity, 166
  water use, 166
Life Cycle Initiative, 153
Life cycle inventory, 160
Life cycle management (LCM), 148
Life cycle thinking, 48, 72
  basics, 146–149
  detailed LCA, 147
  in EPA's EPP program, 214
  inputs and outputs, 147
  life cycle assessment, 147
  life cycle-based approaches, 147
  product improvement example, 151
  product life cycle, 156–171
  screening/streamlined LCA, 147
Life cycles, interrelating, 20
LinkedIn, 119
L.L. Bean, green efforts, 246
Local number portability (LNP), 73
Lockheed Martin case study, 225–226

M

Macy's, green efforts, 246
Malcolm Baldridge National Quality
  Award, 103
Maltzman, Rich, xvii
Man-made disasters, pollution due to, 8
Management, lack of commitment to
  greenality, 108
Manufacturing-based greenality, 106
Manufacturing sector wastes, 182
  reduction at Timberland, 193
Marginal lands, growing source plants
  on, 34
Market demand, 73
Material salvage, 56

Maui, wind farm project, 99
McDonough, William, 21, 22, 146
McLuhan, Marshall, 85
Meetings, virtual vs. travel-intensive, 234
Mercury-contaminated water, cleansing,
  206–207
Metrics, 128
Microsoft, greenality case study, 202–204
Microsoft Dynamics AX, 203
Mid-City Green Project, 54
Milestones. See Green milestones; Project
  milestones
Mini-wind farms, 56–57
Misleading claims, 26
Monitoring. See Project monitoring and
  controlling
Monster.com, 120
Mother Nature Network, 252
Muir, John, 69
Mulisch, Harry, 145
Multifunctional devices, 238
Multiple operating systems, running on
  single server, 202–203
Municipal wastes, 34
My K-Cup, 65

N

Nantucket Sound, 51
NASA, tips for dynamic environment,
  137–138
National Academies, 5
National Academy of Engineering, 5
National Academy of Sciences, 5
  climate change terminology, 3–4
National LCA databases, 161
National Renewable Energy Laboratory
  (NREL), 251
National Research Council, 5
National Research Defense Counsel,
  Smart Companies, 246
National Science Foundation (NSF), 33
  green efforts, 246
NativeEnergy, 18
Natural disasters, pollution due to, 8
Natural Step, 22–23, 190, 252
  conditions and principles, 23
  and green by definition projects, 54
Negative risks, 107, 108

Networked storage, 237
New Attack Submarine (NSSN) Program, 213
New-home construction, 45
New home construction, energy provider rebates, 221
New Orleans, The Green Project, 54–56
New Water project, 7
New York City, rooftop wind farms in, 56–57
New York Times, environmental impact, 102
NING, 236
Nissan Leaf, 73
Noncompliance, cost of, 41
Nonproduct output (NPO), 130
    corrective measures, 135
    reducing, 43, 45
Nonrecyclable materials, Keurig K-cups, 63–64
Normalization, 168
    in LCIA, 167

O

Observation, 127
    aim of, 128
Occupational exposure, 215
Office Depot
    being green, 200–201
    buying green, 199
    corporate social responsibility at, 201
    greenality case study, 199
    selling green, 201
Opportunities, 50
Organic products, 107
    Google use of, 236
Outputs, 147, 148
Ozone depletion, 8

P

Packaging, 247
    life cycle analysis, 163
    used shredded documents as, 238
Page, Larry, 196
Paint Exchange, 55
Palmer, Douglas H., 14
Paper cups, alternatives to, 241

Paper recycling, 238
    impact of, 108
    at Office Depot, 200
    repurposing unused printouts, 241
Paper weight, cost savings through reducing, 224
Pareto principle, 17, 42
PAS 2050, 154
Patagonia
    green efforts, 246
    greenality case study, 190–191
PDCA cycle. *See* Plan-do-check-act (PDCA) cycle
People, planet, profit connection, 28
People greening, 96–97
Perseverance, 138
Pesticides, considering in LCA, 150
Phantom power, 241
Pharmaceutical drugs, unintended consequences, 149
Pharmaceuticals in the environment (PIE), 149
Photochemical smog, as life cycle impact category, 166
Plan-do-check-act (PDCA) cycle, 9, 10
    corrective actions based on, 136
Planned value (PV), 129
Plastic utensils, alternatives to, 241
PMBOK Guide, 45, 90
    links to strategic plan, 74
PMI Certified PMPs, 119
Podcasts, for project managers, 253
Polar Bear story, 77–78
Pollution, 8
Pollution prevention, xiii
    through EPA's EPP program, 213
Pollution Prevention Act, xiii
Pollution Protection Act, 12
Popular Science magazine, 206
Population increase, 6–7
Portsmouth Brewery case study, 228
Positive risks, 107
Potatoes, use by Microsoft initiatives, 203
Preproduction planning (3P), 184
Preventative actions, 136–139
Prevention costs, 48
Preventive strategies, 136–139
Printouts, repurposing unused, 241

Problem drivers/indicators, 3
  biodiversity loss, 8
  bottom-up demand, 14–16
  climate change, 3–5
  environmental degradation, 8
  government agencies, mandates, and
    guidelines, 8–16
  population increase, 6–7
  rapidly developing nations, 7–8
  resource depletion, 7–8
Process baseline information, 159
Process development, LCA guidance for,
  160
Process redesign, to reduce NPO, 43
Process throughput, improving, 177
Procter & Gamble
  green efforts, 246
  life cycle perspective, 151
Procurement process greening, 100–102
Product-based greenality, 106
Product certification, LCA support for,
  160
Product development, LCA guidance in,
  160
Product improvement
  LCA example, 151
  use of LCA for, 152–153
Product life cycle, 156–157
  goal definition and scoping, 158–160
  and ISO 14040, 158
  LCA fundamentals, 157–158
Product redesign, to reduce NPO, 43
Product size reduction, 224
Profitability
  Abbot Laboratories initiatives, 227
  Apple Corporation case study, 224
  balancing with commitment to
    environment, 189
  Bank of America case study, 224
  case studies, 223–229
  correlating with environment, 192
  DuPont case study, 228
  grants and rebates for, 216–223
  green enablement of, 211
  green government purchasing,
    211–216
  of greenality, xxiii
  Kohler Company case study, 228–229
  Liberty Mutual initiatives, 227

  links to sustainability, 195
  Lockheed Martin case study,
    225–226
  Portsmouth Brewery case study, 228
  Raytheon case study, 226
  Schneider National case study,
    224–225
  Staples initiatives, 227
  University of Michigan case study,
    226–227
Progress reporting, 117–118
  ambiguity in, 140
  standardized method, 140–141
Project charters, 82–83
  commitment statements in, 85
  lack of greenality statement or funding
    in, 109
  linking corporate commitment to
    sustainability in, 89–90
Project completion, 72
Project control, 72
Project costs, greening, 102–103
Project cycle of sustainability, 49–50
Project development, 72, 89
  environmental management plan,
    109–110
  greenality outputs, 109–110
  people greening, 96–97
  procurement process greening,
    100–102
  project cost greening, 102–103
  project planning, 89–95
  project quality greening, 103–107
  project requirements, 96
  risk and greenality, 107–109
  schedule greening, 97–100
  solicitation documents, 101
  sustainability and the WBS, 95–96
Project drivers, 72–73
  customer demand, 72–73
  government regulations, 73
  market demand, 73
  technological advances, 73
Project environment, changes over time,
  137
Project execution, 111
  capturing greenality lessons learned,
    124
  executing greenality efforts, 120–122

greenality assurance in, 115–116
greening communications with social
    media, 118–120
kickoff meeting, 113–115
progress reporting, 117–118
project tracking, 116–118
status reporting, 117–118
supplier greenality, 123–124
team composition, 111–112
warning signs of greenality problems,
    122–123
Project ideation, 71
    acting on ideas, 84
    behavioral change aspects, 76–77
    decision-making tools, 75, 77–81
    decision validation, 81–82
    green charters, 82–83
    green-friendly decision-making
        environment for, 75–76
    and greenality of project
        communications, 85
    initial project kickoff meeting, 83–84
    jeopardy and escalation processes,
        86–87
    project drivers, 72–73
    project selection, 74–75
    spirit of communications, 85–86
    supplier greenality, 87
    tools and techniques, 84–85
Project implementation, 72
Project kickoff meeting, 83–84
Project life cycle thinking, 48–49
Project management
    as accidental profession, xxiii
    accomplishing greenality through, 14
    as breeding ground for corporate
        leadership, 189
    defined, 22–23
    as microcosm of business, 189
    social networking sites, 119
Project Management Institute (PMI), xix,
    19
    Code of Ethics and Professional
        Conduct, 46–47
    and greenality, 45–47
    membership growth, 42
Project Management Link, 119
Project managers
    additional tools and resources, 253

    as change agents, xii
    changing role as greenality focus
        changes, 66
    considering multiple attributes and
        impacts, 214
    grass roots level of, 5
    green tendencies, xxiii
    role in greenality efforts, 42
    as skeptics, 172
Project milestones, 127, 128
Project monitoring and controlling, 125,
    132–133
    abating greenality issues, 136–141
    band-aid strategies, 139–141
    change control and greenality,
        133–135
    corrective actions, 136
    DIKW pyramid, 125–126
    greenality data collection and analysis,
        127–130
    preventative strategies, 137–139
Project phases, six real, 127
Project planning, 89–95
Project processes, 132
Project product, 132
Project quality
    greening, 103–107
    Toyota Way, 104
Project requirements, 96
Project selection, 74–75
Project Shrink, 134
Project success
    commitment to greenality as criterion,
        126
    dependence on high greenality, 115
    kickoff meeting determinants, 113
Project team, 111–112
    introducing at kickoff meeting, 114
Project tracking, 116–117
    status and progress reporting,
        117–118
PSODA, 233–235
Public policy, LCA support for, 160
Public Service of New Hampshire, 246
Public transportation, unintended
    consequences, 149
Purchasing documents, 101
Purdue University library, 32
Pyrolysis, 33

Q

Quality
    five dimensions of, 103
    Green vs. Deming, 105
    and greenality, 39–42
    greening project, 103
    links to environmental efficiency, 9
Quality control, 43
Quality/greenality trilogy, 43
Quality improvement, 43
Quality management, father of, 40
Quality management plan (QMP), 109
Quality masters, and greenality, 40
Quality planning, 43

R

Radioactive wastes, cleaning up, 207
Rain forest. See also Deforestation
    destruction of, 8
Rapidly developing nations, 7–8
Raw materials
    acquisition, 147
    reducing waste-producing, 43
Raytheon case study, 226
Recognition, for achieving greenality
        objectives, 133
Recovery time, 215
Recruiting, NASA tips, 138
Recycled Waders, 252
Recycling, 147
    at Apple Computer, 47
    e-waste, 56
    kitchen grease, 203
    limitations of, 36–37
    savings from paper, 108
    through The Green Project, 56
    vs. reuse, 45
    of worn-out clothing, 191
Reduce, redesign, reuse, recycle (4Rs), 29
Redundancy, reducing uncertainty
        through, 138
Regional low fuel standards, 13
Renewable energy, 30
    geothermal, 31–32
    Patagonia's commitment to, 191
    solar, 30–31
    sustainable biomass, 32–35

    wave motion and tides, 35
    wind, 30
Request for proposal (RFP), 101
Request for quote (RFQ), 101
Resistance to change, 42
    Deming's ideas, 41
Resource and environmental profile
        analysis (REPA), 152
Resource constraints, green efforts
        solutions, 44
Resource depletion, 7–8
    as life cycle impact category, 166
Resource instability, 122
Resource planning, 96
Resources
    books, 243
    collaboration related, 244–245
    green corporate examples, 245–247
    life cycle assessment, 243–244
    web meetings, 245
    Web sites, 247–252
Results-oriented focus, 138
RETScreen, 251
Reuse, 45, 147
    waste reduction through, 195
Reverse brainstorming, 78
Reversibility, 214
Risk
    and greenality, 107–109
    reducing through social networking,
        120
    vs. reward, 122
Risk analysis, 81
Rooftop wind farms, 56–57
Rubber Manufacturers Association, 35

S

S-curve, 111, 112
SAMMS, 207
Save Our Sound, 51
Scarless impact, 61
Scenario-based thinking, 76
Schedule greening, 97–100
Schedule performance index (SPI), 141
Schedule variance, 129, 141
Schneider National, case study, 224–225
Scope definition, 89, 168
    in LCA method, 158–160

Sea surface temperatures (SSTs), drought links to, 14
Sensitivity analysis
    in LCIA, 169
    wind farm example, 80
Server virtualization, 225, 226, 227
    tradeoffs, 227
Service sector wastes, 182
Seven wastes, 179–180
    of software development, 181
Shaklee, green efforts, 246
Shared bicycles, at Google, 236
Shared files, 236
Shared rides, 241
Shewhart cycle, 136
Shirley, Dave, xviii
SimaPro, 161, 171, 251–252
Six Sigma, 184
Skype, 235
SMARTER objectives, 36, 75, 85, 90, 108, 114, 237
Smog, 8
Social auditing, 190
Social media, 121
    greening communications with, 118–120
Social needs, 46
Social networking, 253
Social niceties, 235
Society of Environmental Toxicology and Chemistry (SETAC), 153
    Code of Practice, 155
Software as a service (SAAS), 233–234, 235
Software development, seven wastes of, 181
Solar collector technology, at Sun Chips, 207–208
Solar energy, 30–31
    and DESERTEC concept, 58–60
    partnering with Google, 236
    at Patagonia, 191
    state rebates, 220–221
    use at General Electric, 204
    use at Sun Chips, 207, 208
Solar rebates, 220–221
Solicitation documents, 101
Solid waste, 152, 157
Sony PlayStation 3, 72

Sort, Straighten, Shine, Standardize, Sustain (5S), 187. *See also* 5S method
Southern California Gas Company (SCGC), industry-specific rebates, 223
Species extinction, green efforts solutions, 44
Spectacle Island, 62
Sponsors, bottom-up demand from, 14–16
Sprinter vans, 201
Staffing, using social media for, 120
Stakeholders, 51, 84
    bottom-up demand from, 14–16
    and cost of greenality, 47
    couriering/posting documents to all, 234
    as driver for user-based greenality, 106
    greening, 96
    in life cycle analysis, 170
Staples, green initiatives, 227
Starbucks, commitment to ethical coffee sourcing, 34
State and local governments, grants and rebates, 216–218
State of Florida, solar rebates, 220–221
Statistical methods, 42
Status meetings, 121
Status reporting, 117–118
Steady-state operation
    getting to, 146
    greenality in, 62–63
    traditional focus on, 145
Steward Advanced Materials, greenality case study, 206–207
Stilthouses, 7
Stonewall Kitchen, 72–73
Strategic direction, changes in, 122
Strategic goals, project selection to align for, 74
Stratospheric ozone depletion, as life cycle impact category, 165
Streamlined LCA, 147
Structured decision making, 253
Subcontractors, working from home, 240
Subject matter experts (SMEs)
    enhancing expert judgment with, 119
    opinion on climate change, 4

Sun Chips, greenality case study, 207–208
Suppliers. *See also* Procurement process greening
  green thinking about, 100
  greenality clauses, 102
  greenality of, 87, 123–124
Sustainability, 17–20
  building into project scope, 89, 95
  commitment through project charter, 89–90, 133
  corporate commitment to, 194
  cycle of, 20–21
  four conditions of, 22, 23
  LCA as cornerstone of, 148
  links to profit, 195
  PMI definition, 19
  project cycle of, 49–50
  project management definition, 19
  role of GPM in, xiii
  through server retirement, 196
  triple-P concept, 28–29
  work breakdown schedules and, 95–96
Sustainability index, Walmart development of, 151
Sustainable biomass, 32–35
Sustainable Minds, 252
Switchgrass, 34
Synchronous tools, 235
System boundaries, 146, 157
  in LCA, 169
System constraints
  elevating, 177
  exploiting, 176
  identifying, 176

T

Targeted groups, 119
Tassimo pods, 63
TEAM life cycle assessment software, 252
Team member attitudes, 122
Technical representation, in LCA, 169
Technological advances, as project drivers, 73
Ted Williams Tunnel, 61
Telecom, GreenTouch, 246
Teleconferencing technologies, 234
Temporal representation, in LCA, 169

Terminology. *See* Green project terminology
TerraPass, 18, 58
Terrestrial toxicity, as life cycle impact category, 166
Thalidomide, 149
The Green Life, 27
Theory of constraints, 253
Threats, 50
Timberland Corporation, 24
  Green Index card, 194
  greenality case study, 192–194
Timed reporting, 117
Tips and techniques, 233–241
Tire-derived fuel (TDF), 35
Total production maintenance (TPM), 184
Toxic chemicals, green efforts solutions, 44
Toxicity, removing, 206
Toxin Terminator, 206–207
Toyota Prius, 73
Toyota Way, 103, 104
Transcendent greenality, 104, 106
Transparency
  in data modeling, 171
  improving with virtual folders, 234
  in life cycle assessment, 170, 172–173
Transportation
  of equipment, 240
  life cycle analysis, 163
Travel
  greening, 241
  to meetings, 234
Tree huggers, 129
Treehugger.com, 30
Triple bottom line, 28
Trucking industry, 218, 220
  optimizing empty return routes, 224, 240
Trust, collaborating through, 138
Trust-based teamwork, 138
Turmel, Wayne, 235
Tweets, 119
Twitter, 119
Two-sided printing, 238

U

Umberto software, 252

U.N. Environment Program (UNEP), 153
Uncertainty management, in LCIA
    methodology, 168
Underdeveloped countries, population
    explosion in, 6
Underground homes, 32
Unintended consequences, 148–149
United Arab Emirates, floating terminal,
    60–61
United Nations Environment Programme,
    3
United Nations World Meteorological
    Organization, 3
University of Massachusetts-Amherst,
    green efforts, 246
University of Michigan, case study,
    226–227
Unsafe working conditions, Patagonia and
    elimination of, 190
U.S. agencies/mandates/guidelines, 11
    California AB32, 12–13
    Eastern States Standard, 13–14
    Environmental Protection Agency
      (EPA), 11–12
    U.S. Conference of Mayors, 14
    Western Climate Initiative (WCI), 13
U.S. Conference of Mayors, 14
U.S. Congress, failure to pass global
    warming legislation, 5
U.S. Department of Energy, trucking
    industry grants and rebates,
    218, 220
U.S. Environmental Protection Agency,
    xi, 247
    green purchasing guidelines, 100, 221
    P2 website, xii
U.S. Green Building Council, 200, 225
    LEED standard, 151
User-based greenality, 106
Utility companies, grants and rebates,
    221

V

Valuation, in LCIA methodology, 168
Value-based greenality, 107
Variance, calculating with EV, 140–141
Verizon Wireless, Hopeline program,
    238–239

Version control, 235
Video over IP, 234
Video sharing, 118
Virent Energy Systems, Inc., 33
Virgin wood, 32
Virtual project folders, 234
Voice over IP (VoIP) technologies, 234
Voluntary Interindustry Commerce
    Solutions Association, 224

W

Walmart
    green efforts, 247
    sustainability index development, 151
Warming, global rate of, 4
Washable utensils/mugs, 241
Washing machine, LCA example,
    156–157
Waste
    addressing via extreme programming,
      181
    Coca Cola cans case study, 185–186
    disposal of electronic, 198
    in manufacturing sector, 182
    reduction through reuse, 195
    in service sector, 182
    through underutilization of employee
      creativity, 180–182
    workload queues as sign of, 122
Waste management, 147
Wastes, 179–180
Wastewater, cleansing of, 207
Water, annual savings per Google server,
    197
Water pollution, 8
    from acid baths of electronic
      components, 37
Water projects, in Kenya, 98
Water recycling, at Google, 197
Water scarcity, green efforts solutions,
    44
Water use, as life cycle impact category,
    166
Waterless urinals, 228
Web meetings, 245
Web sites, 247–252
Webcams, 235
Western Climate Initiative (WCI), 13

Westerveld, Jay, 26
Wildlife preservers, 58
Will to win, 138
Wind energy, 30
    in Maui, 99
    NYC mini-wind farms, 56–57
    wind farm sensitivity analysis, 80
Windows 7, built-in power management, 203
Windows Vista, built-in power management, 203
Wisdom, in DIKW pyramid, 126
Witch hunts, avoiding, 131
Work breakdown schedule (WBS), 91

    building greenality into, 95
    and sustainability, 95–96
Working from home, 240
Workload queues, 122
World population, 6
Writing Mafia, 119

Y

YouTube, 118, 196

Z

Zone of hypoxia, 150

Printed in the United States
by Baker & Taylor Publisher Services

Printed in the United States
by Baker & Taylor Publisher Services